A Deep Well of Want

Reimagining Ireland

Volume 122

Edited by Dr Eamon Maher,
Technological University Dublin – Tallaght Campus

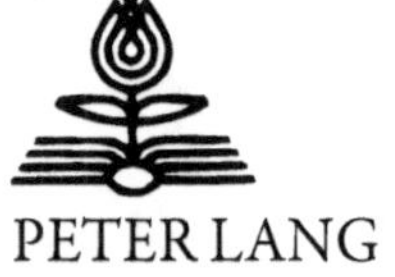

PETER LANG
Lausanne • Berlin • Bruxelles • Chennai • New York • Oxford

A Deep Well of Want

Visualising the World of John McGahern

Paul Butler

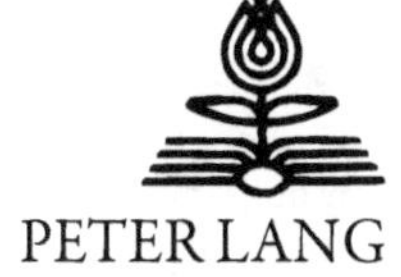

PETER LANG
Lausanne • Berlin • Bruxelles • Chennai • New York • Oxford

Bibliographic information published by The German National Library.
Die Deutsche Nationalbibliothek lists this publication in the German National Bibliography; detailed bibliographic data is available on the Internet at http://dnb.d-nb.de.

A catalogue record for this book is available from the British Library.

Library of Congress Cataloging-in-Publication Data

Names: Butler, Paul, (Photographer), author, photographer.
Title: A deep well of want : visualising the world of John McGahern / Paul Butler.
Description: Oxford ; New York : Peter Lang, 2023. | Series: Reimagining Ireland, 1662-9094 ; vol. 122 | Includes bibliographical references and index.
Identifiers: LCCN 2023002420 | ISBN 9781800798106 (paperback) | ISBN 9781800798113 (ebook) | ISBN 9781800798120 (epub)
Subjects: LCSH: McGahern, John, 1934-2006–Quotations. | McGahern, John, 1934-2006–Influence. | Ireland–In literature. | LCGFT: Photobooks. | Quotations. | Literature.
Classification: LCC PR6063.A2176 Z57 2023 | DDC 823/.914–dc23/eng/20230426
LC record available at https://lccn.loc.gov/2023002420

Cover image: The little gate is all that remains of what was once the McGahern homestead at Corramahon, Aughawillan, County Leitrim. Paul Butler, April 2018.
Cover design by Peter Lang Group AG

ISSN 1662-9094
ISBN 978-1-80079-810-6 (print)
ISBN 978-1-80079-811-3 (ePDF)
ISBN 978-1-80079-812-0 (ePub)
DOI 10.3726/b19557

Published by Peter Lang Ltd, Oxford, United Kingdom
info@peterlang.com - www.peterlang.com

This publication has been peer reviewed.

Contents

Preface by Eamonn Wall vii

Acknowledgements xi

List of Abbreviations xiii

CHAPTER 1
Introduction 1

CHAPTER 2
Landscape 39

CHAPTER 3
A sense of place 87

CHAPTER 4
Ritual 141

CHAPTER 5
Conclusion 191

Bibliography 201

Image Index 209

Index 213

Preface by Eamonn Wall

A few months ago at a Western Literature Association Conference in Montana, I attended a panel on the work of Wallace Stegner, an author like John McGahern whose work was primarily focused on the western region of his country. I was struck by the quality of the presentations that morning and deeply engaged by the approaches the speakers took to Stegner's work. Not only did they discuss his writings in the traditional manner – in every respect the scholarship was impeccable – but they also did something else. All spoke of the ways that Stegner's work had entered their own worlds and invaded their psyches, and they explored how his fiction and essays had helped them understand their own places on earth and pushed them toward enjoying more mature and meaningful lives. I loved these presentations for their combinations of insight and passion, vigour and fire. Also, their enthusiasm took me back to my own beginnings as a reader, student and scholar when I was reminded by my superiors of the need to depersonalize my responses to literature to become a better professional. In my own life as a scholar, this is a dictum that I have both heeded and resisted. On the one hand, I understand the need to establish some distance and reserve but, on the other, I have always found it hard to separate myself from the almost speechless emotion of first encounter with a book and an author. At that point where we meet it first, we might devour a novel or poem or essay or play with the whole fibre of our being. Vicariously and memorably, Paul Butler's work brings me to that overpowering place of first contact with a literary work.

A Deep Well of Want: Visualizing the World of John McGahern is such a welcome addition to the McGahern scholarship: in many respects, it is ground-breaking. Like the scholars I heard that morning in Montana, Butler brings a complex and nuanced vision to his study. His book is part traditional scholarship, underlined by the research and example of Susan Sontag, Jacques Derrida and others; part autobiography, in which Butler traces his engagement with John McGahern's work back to various alignments in his own life – the difficult and complex childhood that he shared with McGahern, and his move from Dublin to Leitrim as an adult – and it is in part a collection of original images that he has made that are set in McGahern country, that elucidate the writer's work, that reveal to us in images responses to the word pictures that McGahern painted on the page. Photography was Butler's first love, and it is an art that he has a unique talent for. He also possesses a deep empathy for McGahern's writing and the place that helped form and guide his writing.

A Deep Well of Want: Visualizing the World of John McGahern is a hybrid work or bricolage or collage or a multimedia work where all the parts run seamlessly together. Butler demands that we question what we mean when we use the term 'study'. It is not that he omits or devalues the traditional elements that belong in a literary study but that he adds to these by including two aspects of his own creative work – autobiography and images – and by taking this tack enlarges what literary criticism is. He pushes it in new directions. Butler's work can be compared to the work of other transgressive Irish writers such as Tim Robinson, Kevin Whelan and most recently Doireann Ní Ghríofa, whose *Ghost in the Throat,* her wonderful engagement with the life, writing and places of Eibhlín Dubh Ní Chonaill, is a companion text to Butler's. It is also a book that shares a vision and structure with John Berger's *Ways of Seeing*; however, to achieve similar ends Butler reverses Berger's process. Though genres are useful frames, they can constrict an artist's vision and may be set aside to allow a particular work to develop organically. When artists like Robinson, Whelan, Ní Ghriofa, Berger and Butler write literary criticism, or history, or geography, or folk-lore, or media studies, they engage with genres in new ways in producing work that is formally different, allowing them to ask new questions. The approaches that these writers take underline Environmental Literature, and Butler's settling in County Leitrim in 2001 is a mirror image of Cheryll Glotfelty's move from east to west, made two decades earlier:

> In 1990, I drove a Ryder van from Ithaca, New York, to Reno, Nevada, with a head full of ideas and a heart full of yearning. … In graduate school, I had periodically strayed from course work to become self-tutored in deep ecology and literary ecology, absorbing works such as Bill Devall and George Session's *Deep Ecology* and Joseph Meeker's *The Comedy of Survival.* The bioregional notion of reinhabitation

> struck a powerful chord, providing a theory to validate my deepest desires to have a lasting home. To those of us who cannot claim to be native to anywhere but the road, reinhabitation offers the hope that it is possible to become native to a place. The process of reinhabitating a place entails learning the natural history, indigenous lifeways, and cultural traditions of a place and, in turn, actively participating in the continuous making of the place. As the eloquent bioregionalist Gary Snyder suggests, 'find your place on the planet, dig in, and take responsibility from there'. That's exactly what I aimed to do.[1]

Glotfelty is a pioneer of ecocritical and bioregional literary studies: some might call her the founder of both. Reinhabitation can be applied to both McGahern's and Butler's decisions to settle in Leitrim. Paul Butler's specific focus is on *Memoir*. He engages with what is outside and inside, both the natural and built environments. Reading his text, we are privileged to see what he sees and to glimpse aspects of the area that McGahern portrayed so well and which played such an influential role in his formation. Butler, like all good scholars, guides us through an author's work and environment. When I first read McGahern, my sole focus was on his larger-than-life characters like Moran and Reegan, and I either ignored the environment or understood it in a very limited way. Like Glotfelty and Snyder, Butler puts the environment, in the largest sense, in the foreground – all writers paying homage to the non-human.

At the conclusion of *A Deep Well of Want: Visualizing the World of John McGahern*, Butler reveals how he has achieved a kind of mindfulness in his own life, in part the product of his engagement with the arts of photography, writing and McGahern's work. In his recent book, Derek Gladwin writes:

> In *The Truth About Stories: A native narrative*, the Cherokee author and professor Thomas King discusses the universality of stories in our social histories and in relationship to ourselves. He affirms that the 'truth about stories is that's all we are'. Stories simultaneously define, heal, and create our lives.[2]

1 Cheryll Glotfelty, 'Finding a Home in Nevada? Teaching the Literature of Place on Location', in Laird Christensen, Mark C. Long and Fred Waage (eds), *Teaching North American Environmental Literature* (New York: MLA, 2008), p. 5.

2 Derek Gladwin, *Rewriting Our Stories: Education, Empowerment, and Well-Being* (Cork: Atrium/Cork University Press, 2021), p. 9.

The arts he has learnt and practiced have helped Paul Butler to reframe raw material into an original work that is rich and life-affirming, while also being of high moral, intellectual, critical and artistic quality. Mindfulness is hardly the kind of term that John McGahern would have embraced; however, his work and the example of his life certainly pushed him, as well as his Irish readers, towards a deeper understanding of people, places and time on earth. Having read Paul Butler's work, and seen and reflected on his splendid photographic work, I certainly have gained a deeper understanding of John McGahern's work.

Eamonn Wall
University of Missouri-St. Louis

Acknowledgements

Much love to Rita and Luke, for their ongoing encouragement as I allowed myself to be consumed with this project.

A special thank you to my good friend Dr Eamon Maher, Head of the National Centre for Franco-Irish Studies at the Technological University of Dublin. Without his cajoling, guidance and encouragement, this idea would never have come to full fruition.

I am greatly indebted to Dr Dominic Dillane, Head of the School of Tourism and Hospitality Management at the Technological University of Dublin, who provided generous financial support for this project, without which it could never have come to pass.

Thanks to Eamonn Wall, Professor of Irish Studies and Professor of English at the University of Missouri–St. Louis for his contagious enthusiasm for this project and his wonderful preface.

Thanks to Dr Sarah Nolan, a lecturer of Urban, American, and Contemporary Anglophone and Irish Literature at the Institute of Art, Design and Technology (IADT), Dublin, for her editing advice and much-appreciated input.

Thanks to Madeline McGahern for finding favour with this project, and a special acknowledgement for her late husband, John McGahern. His literary treasure, hidden within this gem of a county that we know as Leitrim, is a gift to us all.

Acknowledgements

List of Abbreviations[1]

B *The Barracks* (London: Faber & Faber, 1963).

D *The Dark* (London: Faber & Faber, 1965).

L *The Leavetaking* (London: Faber & Faber, 2nd edition, 1984).

P *The Pornographer* (London: Faber & Faber, 1979).

AW *Amongst Women* (London: Faber & Faber, 1990).

CS *The Collected Stories* (London: Faber & Faber, 1992).

RS *That They May Face the Rising Sun* (London: Faber & Faber, 2002).

M *Memoir* (London: Faber & Faber, 2005).

LW *Love of the World: Essays*, edited by Stanley van der Ziel (London: Faber & Faber, 2009).

CE *Creatures of the Earth: New and Selected Stories* (London: Faber & Faber, 2009).

PW *John McGahern: A Private World* (Hummingbird Productions, Harvest Films/RTÉ, Bord Scannán na hÉireann, 2005).

1 List includes all the main works by John McGahern as they appear in the text.

CHAPTER 1

Introduction

'Do you want your images to make a statement, or do you want your images to tell a story?' This very insightful question was part of a review I had received from Lensculture in relation to a series of black and white images I had submitted for a competition. The remark struck a chord and really got me thinking. I like making visual statements, though I did wonder how deep those statements could go and how they might connect with an audience.

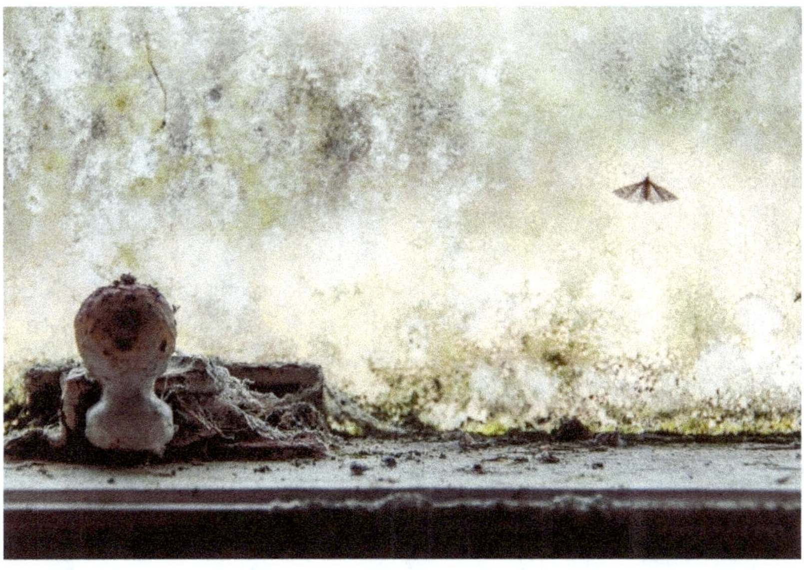

The Need to Fly and Create, Gortletteragh, County Leitrim – Image: Paul Butler, April 2011.

The scene captured in 'The Need to Fly and Create' of a small moth futilely seeking freedom through an old sash window resonates with my desire to let ideas float. And yet, the frustration that it can all be so near and so tangible, and yet so inaccessible, is constantly there. Did I really want my photographic statements to end with the simple and single viewing of an image, with no avenue or loose ends? Without a doubt, there is a place and a time for that, though, at this point in my life, that is not enough for me. I want to visualize a story, my own and that of the writer John McGahern, and show how the two interconnect and intersect.

This book centres on three main areas: 'Landscape', 'Place' and 'Ritual'. As it could be perceived that there are clear overlaps between 'Landscape' and 'Place', I should point out here that for me landscape is the physical place – the soil, the land, the seasons, the colours – whereas place is the built presence created by those who have gone before us, a feeling of belonging you get, a sense you might have, for example, that an abandoned old house was once alive and is replete with memories and untold stories, that discarded bicycles have their backstory also.

The aim of this book is to provide a visual representation of McGahern's fiction and how it intersects with the autobiographical account of his life, *Memoir*. The images act as a window out onto that world. Granted, text and image are two different mediums, but I have discovered that when you combine images with passages from his work, interviews and articles, they flow into each other. This book exhibits McGahern's country, the hidden and lovely Leitrim, a place close to the writer's heart and to mine. The project is, as far as I am aware, the first time that anyone has tried to visualize the writing of John McGahern in the manner that I propose to do. Hopefully, the book may alert people to the tourism potential of 'McGahern Country' and bring more visitors to the north-west midlands of Ireland where most of his work is situated.

In the introduction to the *Routledge Companion to Photographic Theory, Documentary Expansions*, Durden makes the following point: 'Abstract theories may lead us to reposition our relationship to photographs (Laurelle, Derrida, Deleuze) and lend nuances to what essentially underlies any photography theory – that is, the relationship of the image to the real world and how we conceive what that means.'[1]

1 Mark Durden and Jane Tormey, *The Routledge Companion to Photographic Theory* (London: Routledge, 2020), Introduction.

The bombardment of our world with imagery through social media has allowed everyone to document and lay bare their worlds. A lot of the imagery, I feel, says nothing, being bland, pointless and at times narcissistic: the creator[s] is [are] taking pictures, but not seeing the image. I find myself trawling through Instagram and other social media outlets and nothing registers until you come across the photography of the true documentarians, like the World Press organization, Magnum Agency and the like. These are the images that stop me in my tracks; images that tell a story. That is what documentary photography means to me, and this project has reinforced that view.

While I would not consider myself comparable in any way to the great documentary photographers, my style has always been to chronicle the beauty of the ordinary, and this work is a testament to the power and the beauty of the ordinary and the everyday. It contains all that you miss when you do not truly 'see'. For I am always looking. Likewise, John McGahern's words lifted the ordinary into the realm of the extraordinary; his observations on the universality of the everyday make his writing special.

I intend to bring his landscape to life and as such evoke for the viewer their own country lane or lost world, where they can lose themselves in their thoughts and memories, just as the writer did. I truly believe that John McGahern's words and the landscape of Leitrim deserve nothing less than the type of reimagining of both that I have in mind. I am an avid reader of McGahern's texts, but I do not claim to be an expert. Therefore, my 'reading' is one based on the hundreds of images I have collected of various scenes around where I live and the way in which they exemplify McGahern's evocation of landscape, ritual and place. The emphasis is strongly on the image, as is to be expected from someone of my visual background, and the ways I can, perhaps, illuminate elements of McGahern's aesthetic quest.

Why the book title: *A Deep Well of Want?*

I heard the phrase 'there is a want in them' so many times over the years. And it was never employed in a flattering sense; it was used to imply that there was something missing or something not quite right with the person at whom the comment was directed. Those words always jarred, well why wouldn't they? When those words are used, and especially when they are thrown in your direction, the relationship to that word, 'want', evolves as a form of hollowness, and it becomes a lonely badge of honour. 'Want' is therefore a word I would use to describe the feeling I get from the writing of McGahern. Following you throughout life, it is one of those phrases that is branded onto your subconscious.

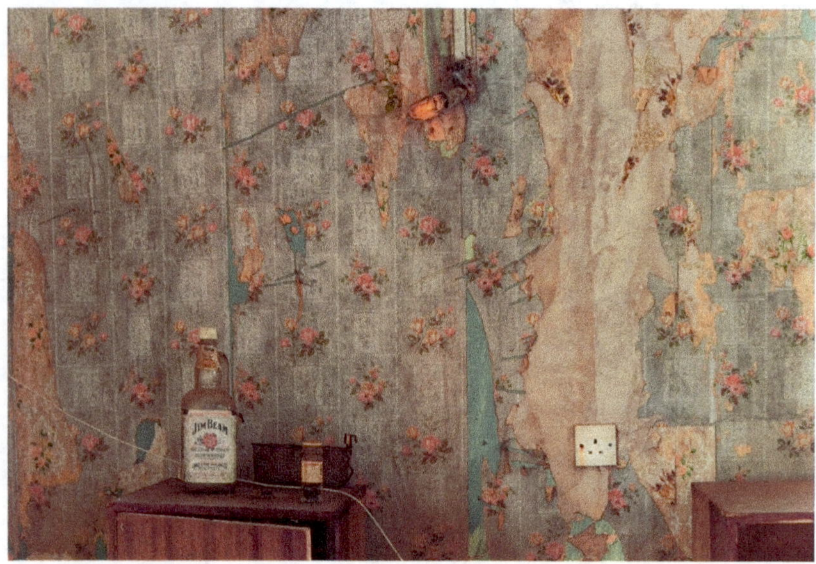

Sacred Heart Lamp and Bourbon, Aughnacliffe, County Longford – Image: Paul Butler, May 2017.

The words "A Deep Well of Want" slipped into my mind in the very early hours of an autumn night. I have always been a light sleeper, and I can become quite restless, especially when there is a new moon. However, I do not become agitated by being awake, and I never dwell on the time. And so I quietly made my way downstairs, where I could see a new milky moon hovering on the southern horizon. It bathed our house in a strong bluish-white glow. I stood at the hall window, studying the long shadows cast onto the stone floor. I followed this shadow trail across the floor as it made its way towards the garden. Outside, tall, dark and shadowy conifers that surround the perimeter fence silhouetted the now floodlit scene. The overall effect created a natural amphitheatre: it was spectacular. Viewing this scene, I realized the quiet rewards of sleeping light. These moments are magical. As I drank in the scene, the words A Deep Well of Want floated through my thoughts. Before the moment passed and I forgot the phrase – I am notorious for forgetting things – I gently opened the kitchen door, turned on the light and at the kitchen counter wrote down A Deep Well of Want on a notepad. I looked at the words for a moment. They really struck a chord. Our Jack Russell, Nama, was lying on his bed in the alcove, and he stuck his hind leg up in the air as I passed. He just wanted a quick belly rub or maybe a piece of chewy stick for the inconvenience of being disturbed. I gave his leg a rub and patted his head, turned off the light and went back to bed. And so, it is that phrase that helped to kickstart this book on my visualization of McGahern, a niggling phrase constantly chipping away at my psyche. A constant hunger or a need is what drove McGahern, the writer. A hunger or need drives me, the photographer. It too is A Deep Well of Want.

John McGahern: The writer

John McGahern was born in Knockanroe, County Leitrim, in 1934. He was the eldest child of seven and was extremely close to his mother, Susan, a primary school teacher. In his early life, the family moved between various homes as his tyrannical father, Frank, a former IRA leader during the War of Independence, was a member of the recently formed police force, An Garda Síochána. Susan was eventually offered a permanent teaching position in a two-teacher school on a hill in Aughawillan, less than three miles from Ballinamore, County Leitrim. Severe illness plagued her during this time, and with the sale of her husband's homestead at Gowna, County Cavan, a small farm and house was purchased less than a mile from the school in Aughawillan. The family had at last put down roots. The McGahern family looked after the home and small farm, while their father Frank, now a sergeant, was based in the barracks at Cootehall, County Roscommon, over forty kilometres away.

Life was tough in those early years; everyone had their chores and McGahern neatly sums up the everyday and harsh conditions that he and his siblings endured. McGahern's portrayal of winter in Leitrim is quite a rough canvas; one can sense the short breaths and freezing hands in this scene.

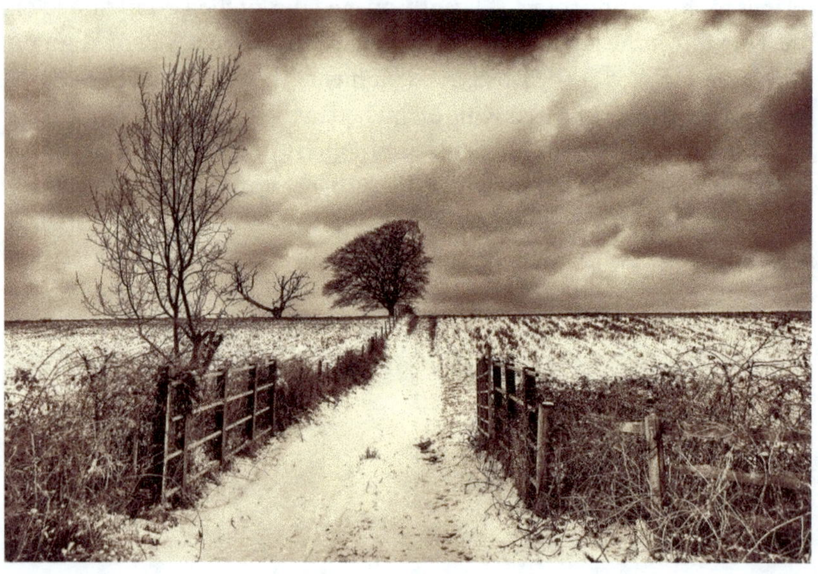

Snow on the High Field, Farnocht, County Leitrim – Image: Paul Butler, March 2018.

> That winter was hard but dry. We woke into white mornings. Ice had to be broken in buckets, in barrels, on ponds, even on the spring well. [*M*, p. 98]

Throughout *Memoir*, the close bond between John and his mother shines through. He had a very special, though short, relationship with her. Susan took John everywhere, and he loved to be by her side. He was like her shadow, carrying groceries and basking in the warmth and atmosphere of love and affection she created wherever she went, and when the shopping was complete, the two of them went to the church to pray. I offer the scene 'Dedication' to visualize John's feelings towards his mother.

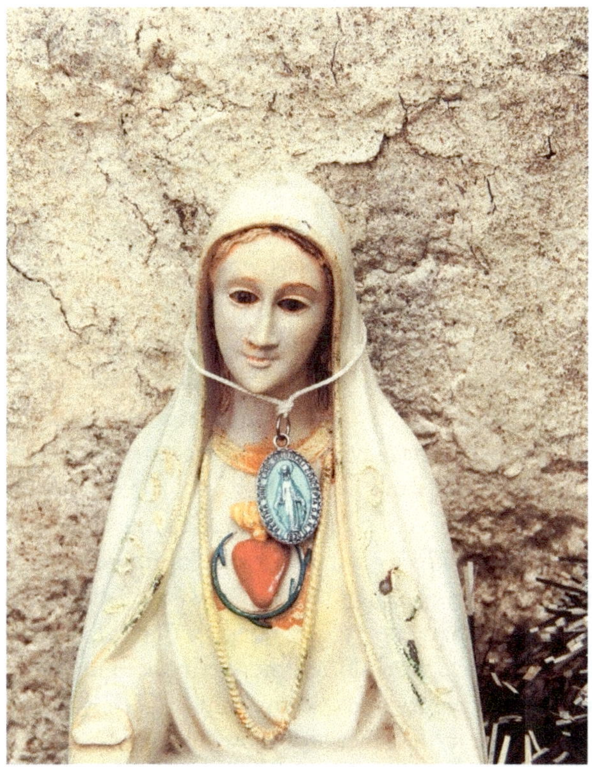

Dedication, Ogulla Shrine, County Roscommon – Image: Paul Butler, July 2016.

> Everywhere people stopped her, and she'd smile and listen and give words of sympathy or congratulation or encouragement, and people looked happier when they left us. [*M*, p. 74]

A seminal moment for John McGahern: The little gate at Corramahon, Aughawillan

The image 'Little Gate at Corramahon' on the cover of this book is all that remains of the McGahern home in the townland of Corramahon, near

Aughawillan, County Leitrim. I use that image to illustrate my reasoning towards McGahern and how his 'want' evolved. Locked behind this gate I believe that the writer's path was set. The young McGahern spent some happy years at this location with his siblings and especially with his mother, who had a permanent position in the nearby two-teacher national school. The fact that the father was based in the barracks at Cootehall in a neighbouring county gave them space and sanctuary. I feel that gates invite one to project, to consider their purpose. Is the function of a gate to hold back, to keep out, to welcome or to contain? The little gate at Corramahon symbolically traps powerful memories. In other countries and possibly in other parts of Ireland, this gate would have been properly preserved, respected and signposted in tribute to the writer. How many people have passed this gate, unaware of its past and significance? It is an absolute tragedy that the gate is not a protected structure, for behind this gate the seminal moment in the young writer's life occurs.

The premature death of Susan McGahern to cancer in June 1944 was to have a devastating effect on ten-year-old John. From this house the McGahern children and all their belongings were piled onto a truck and driven to the Garda barracks in Cootehall, County Roscommon. The father's decision to leave the children's mother to succumb to breast cancer and die alone in that empty house in the field at Corramahon was, I feel, so cruel and cold. John McGahern was now ripped from the safe cloak of his mother's love and cast into the cold and harsh world of his father. This deeply scarred him and from that day forth, the emotional path for the ten-year-old child to become a writer was set.

Life without his mother

Frank McGahern's regime was harsh and oppressive, in stark contrast to the loving blanket the children had known with their mother. Frank McGahern possessed a bitter and angry personality, mixed with resentment at his lot in life. I wonder if demons haunted him due to a violent past during the War of Independence. His brooding feelings of not receiving due recognition or respect for his role during the war festered.

Add to that his resentment of an unfulfilled life and the sense that little had changed within the new Irish Free State, and you have quite a potent mix. His belief that a kind of status quo continued in Ireland and that his sacrifice in the War of Independence changed little. This anger resulted in the imposition of an extremely violent regime on the McGahern children.

His father's violence left many deep emotional scars which continuously appear within John McGahern's writing. The warm and guarded memories for his departed mother, in conjunction with the pure and innocent love the young McGahern held for her, were a constant guidance and comfort. But the loss of his mother left an emptiness within or, as I call it, a 'want'. In Pat Collins's moving 2004 documentary, *John McGahern: A Private World*, there are moments when that deep silent loss is visible and overwhelming. There is such a sadness within McGahern's eyes, and the eternal pauses he takes when searching for the right words make this a memorable documentary. Within those pauses one can sense the sadness and potent memories. It stayed with John as he grew into adolescence and the seed of an idea to become a writer began to take hold. His initial desire to be a priest, which had been his mother's wish, fell away.

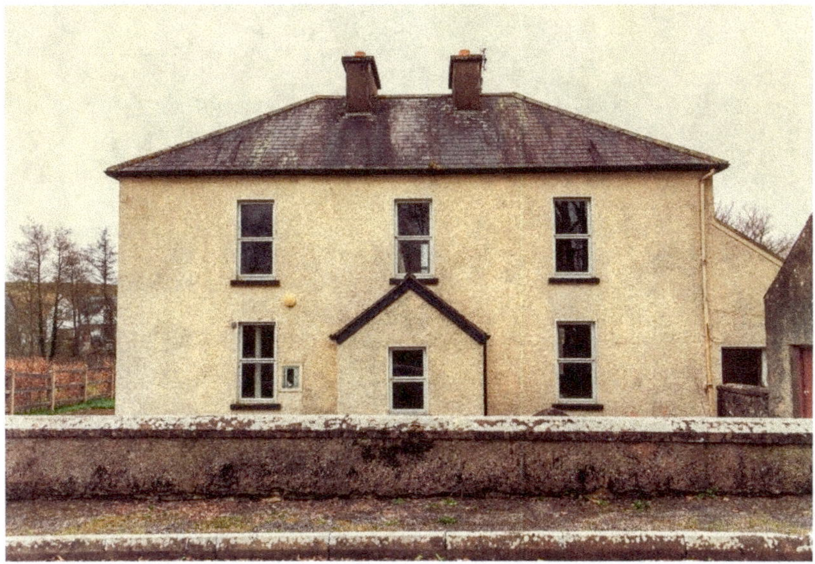

The Former Garda Barracks at Cootehall, County Roscommon – Image: Paul Butler, April 2018.

> As I grew older in the barracks I actually used to help the guards write their reports and they used to jocosely call them patrols of the imagination. And in a way they were the first fictions I took part in. [*PW*]

However, for a young McGahern, not everything was a struggle. The old barracks in Cootehall sit on the bank of the Boyle River, connecting the village with Lough Key to the west and the River Shannon to the east. The river became his escape and sanctuary.

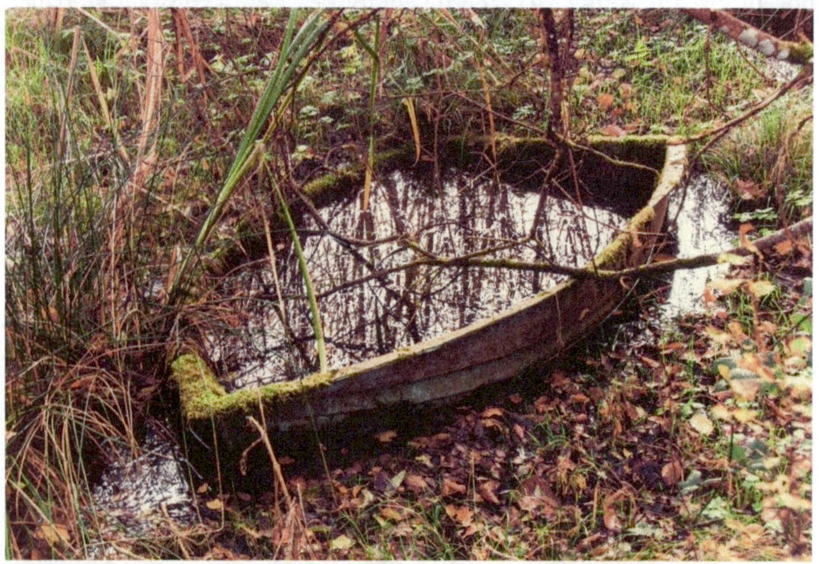

Abandoned Boat at the Former Estate Managers House, Lough Rinn, County Leitrim – Image: Paul Butler, October 2010.

> If I didn't want to fish, I rowed into an inlet, and among the reeds and drowning leaves I read. [*M*, p. 205]

John won a scholarship to the Presentation Brothers secondary school in Carrick-on-Shannon, and afterwards, he went to train as a primary school teacher at St Patrick's College, Drumcondra. He began his career as a primary schoolteacher at Scoil Eoin Báiste (Belgrove) in Clontarf before returning to third-level education at the UCD, where he graduated in 1957. McGahern published his first novel *The Barracks* in 1963 to critical acclaim. In 1965, he published his second novel, *The Dark*, which was banned by the Irish Censorship Board for its alleged pornographic content along with the implied sexual abuse by the protagonist's father. Due to the controversy, John was dismissed from his teaching post and forced to move to England where he worked in a variety of jobs before eventually returning to Ireland with his wife Madeline, to write and farm on a small holding near Fenagh in County Leitrim.

In *A Private World*, McGahern talks about his love of the land:

> I'm a writer that just happens to have a farm, like I was a writer that happened to be a teacher, and I grew up on a farm and it's actually much more enjoyable working around the land than it is writing. But it's not my main activity. [*PW*]

Throughout his life, raw emotion and a simmering resentment lingered towards his tyrannical father, and I use the image 'Discarded Grave Markers' to visualize McGahern's view on the death of his father.

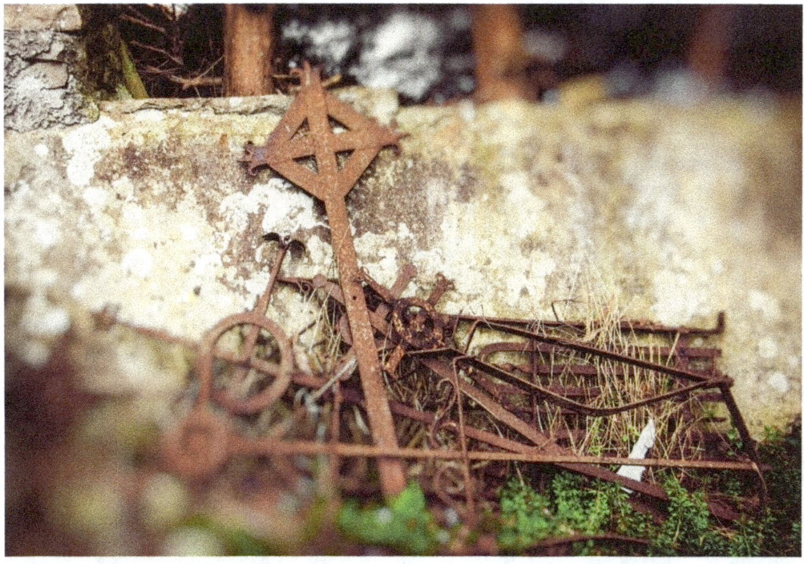

Discarded Grave Markers, St Patrick's Church, Ballinamuck, County Longford – Image: Paul Butler, April 2013.

> When word of my father's death reached me, the intensity of the conflicting emotions – grief, loss, relief – took me unawares. [*M*, p. 271]

Those words really connect with me and that is why I feel a strong connection with John McGahern's writing. My own loss and hurt stem from a dysfunctional and somewhat violent childhood: that too was a big loss, and it left me with a deep 'want'. Over time, I found it takes deep courage to face up to the cold reality that you are broken. All you ever want is not to feel empty and to try and lose that feeling of deep insatiable hunger. The child or children of [an] unfulfilled parent[s] will always suffer and carry that burden through life.

John McGahern died from cancer in the Mater Hospital in Dublin on 30 March 2006, aged seventy-one. He is buried in St Patrick's Church, Aughawillan, alongside his beloved mother, Susan. He is survived by his wife, Madeline. His resting place with his mother at Aughawillan, within the grounds of the church of his childhood, brings a type of closure to what was a long journey for John McGahern. His wandering through country lanes has ended, and he has come home. His memories and deep 'want' are now at rest. His wishing is now sated, and the soothing balm and golden moments have returned.

I offer the scene 'Little White Statue at Shankill Cemetery' as a visualization of his mother, Susan, waiting for him. Susan is represented by the small and bright figure of Mary Immaculate waiting to take her son's hand once again.

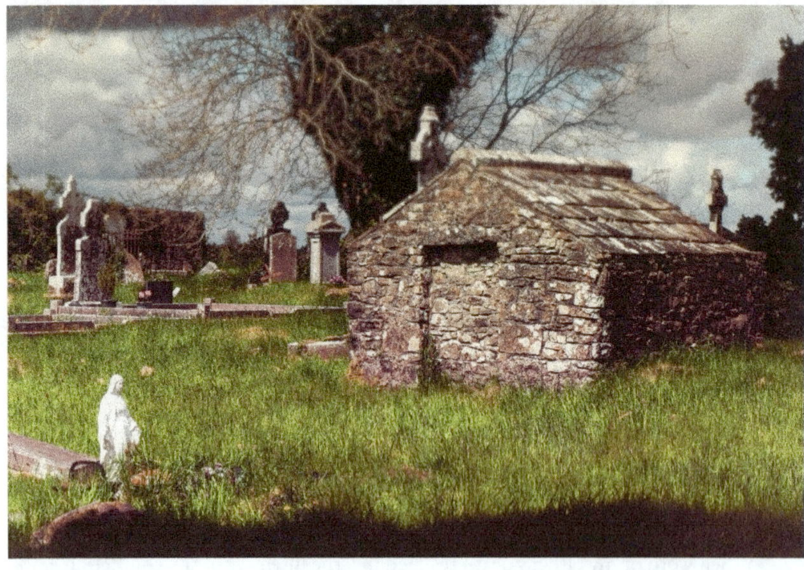

Little White Statue at Shankill Cemetery, Elphin, County Roscommon – Image: Paul Butler, May 2016.

Why a project on John McGahern?

My first introduction to John McGahern was on a sun holiday in Crete back in 1990. A friend passed me a copy of *Amongst Women*. While intrigued by the main threatening character, Moran, McGahern's strong descriptive language appealed to me. His minute description of the landscape ignited my imagination. I could visualize through his words the changing seasons, the wildlife, hedges, colours and weather. As his descriptions leaped from the page, they registered in my mind, reigniting times spent birdwatching and exploring the landscape. I described it in an *Irish Times* article:

> I was really drawn to his precise detail, especially the way he detailed the countryside, the customs of the people, the landscape and house interiors. His collected short stories became a well-thumbed book that followed me through college and stayed with me in a particular way. In the 90s being a penniless mature student, I could certainly relate to some of the settings.[2]

There is a very insightful moment in the documentary *A Private World*, when McGahern provides a glimpse into how he approaches the ordinary and the everyday within his writing: 'I always think that the writing I do is based on the image and the image not in any grand term but a wedding ring or an orange peel, an apple, a broken piece of glass' [*PW*].

2 Paul Butler, 'John McGahern and the Deep Well of Want: Portraits of the Artist's World': <https://www.irishtimes.com/culture/books/john-mcgahern-and-the-deep-well-of-want-portraits-of-the-artist-s-world-1.2592043> (30 March 2016).

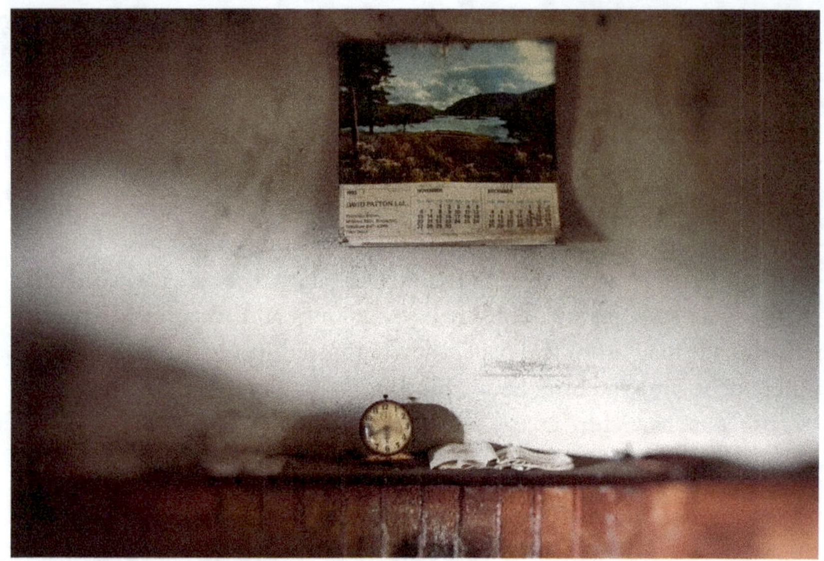

Clock & Calendar, Curraghroe, County Roscommon – Image: Paul Butler, April 2016.

I really like the symmetry and shadow within this scene – if you listen closely, you can hear the ticking of the small clock. Close your eyes and inhale the smell of turf on an open fire and the sweet smell of an unfiltered cigarette. Later in this wonderful documentary McGahern elaborates on his process: 'And when one is writing fiction one is trying to draw those images out of the darkness that will illuminate or animate what's happened' [*PW*].

I believe each short story by McGahern can easily evolve into a film script; the plot is malleable while at the same time, the use of words is quite minimalist. They guide you into a particular time and place with no beginning or end, always searching for a hook, portraying the ordinary and making it into something extraordinary. He had a rare ability to whittle down a story to its bare bones while still retaining a deeper vision and backstory. To portray so much with so few words takes astonishing skill. Eamon Maher elaborates on this process in *John McGahern: From the Local to the Universal*:

> McGahern is masterful at describing situations and people in an economical style that never wastes its time trying to show off. If he is easy to read, it is precisely because he puts so much care into his writing. He has thought long and hard about what he is seeking to achieve from his art. At the centre of all his endeavours is the image.[3]

McGahern the storyteller was an observant and technical writer. Through his craft you discover that many of his details came from memory. Within his mind, he meticulously built a scene before committing them to paper, as he related in the documentary *A Private World*: 'I've never written anything unless certain rhythms or images stay in my head and will not go away. Sometimes they are three or four years there, sometimes they're more than that' [*PW*].

The following paragraph by Eamon Maher, taken from a chapter that we co-authored for the *Canadian Journal of Irish Studies*, sums it up quite succinctly:

> John McGahern was a writer who always demonstrated a keen sense of place. He was acutely aware of how important it was to write from personal knowledge, from everyday experience, to capture the beauty that can be found in the ordinary experiences of people going about their daily lives in small rural communities, mostly located in the Leitrim/Roscommon area where McGahern spent the majority of his life.[4]

I can easily visualize the world about which he wrote. I have always been a visual person, in how I see, look and speak of things. I visualize scenes and colour; it is in every part of my fibre. While McGahern took pen to paper, I take a lens to the world. Not for me the deep critical textual analysis based on tenuous connections. The image I live by is my most effective form of communication. I use it to record the everyday, the scenes we pass by mostly unnoticed, to portray our ordinary world and to reveal its extraordinariness. This is such an important element of what this book seeks to achieve.

3 Eamon Maher, *John McGahern: From the Local to the Universal* (Dublin: Liffey Press, 2003), p. 3.

4 Paul Butler and Eamon Maher, 'John McGahern: His Time and His Places', *Canadian Journal of Irish Studies*, Vol. 39, No. 2 (2016), pp. 27–54, p. 27.

Kathleen Stewart, in *Ordinary Affects*, defines the ordinary as 'a drifting immersion that watches and waits for something to pop up'.[5] This is exactly what happens when I look through the lens. I observe the beautiful ordinary as it comes to life. John McGahern wrote about the everyday, and his universe was Leitrim. In a way, his world could be anywhere; while rooted in a specific place, his stories have a universal resonance: 'I think words are things, and I think that each word has a colour and a personality and that if you take out one or change one word you change the whole sentence.'[6] McGahern's memories and his continuous quest to hold onto those precious images became in turn his words. When I visualize these private worlds, they open a doorway and the emotional reaction from the viewer helps to personalize that moment. I wish for this book to act as that doorway.

For example, the scene 'Turf Drying on the Bog' in Gortletteragh can simply constitute quite a visually appealing landscape to the viewer. However, for the locals it is another important task during the good weather to cut and set the turf. The locally raised bogs are well used, with turf possibly being the most popular form of fuel. We do not use turf in our house as it creates a lot of ash waste; hard woods would be our preferred fuel source. At weekends during the summer, the bogland close to home is alive with cutting and setting. And now with legislation protecting most bogland within Ireland, this image visualizes a tradition that is now consigned to history.

5 Christopher Schaberg, 'Ordinary Affects (review).' *Western American Literature*, Vol. 44, No. 2 (2009), pp. 179–80.

6 Denis Sampson, 'A Conversation with John McGahern', *Canadian Journal of Irish Studies*, Vol. 17, No. 1 (July 1991), pp. 13–18, p. 13.

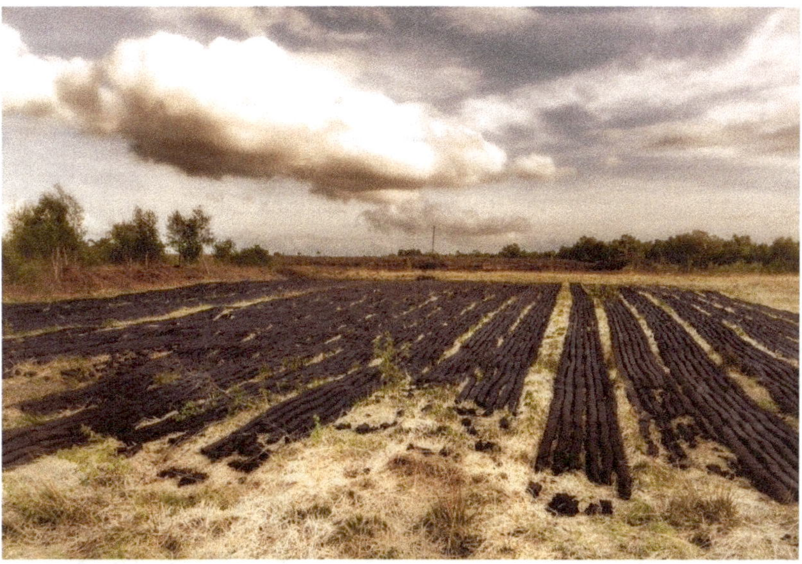

Turf Drying on the Bog, Breanross South, County Leitrim – Image: Paul Butler, May 2011.

McGahern relates the practice of footing and turning with the following passage from *That They May Face the Rising Sun*:

> One day I was watching them turning sods. There were two other men in the field with Jackie that I won't name. I was watching through the hedge. Bill's job was to trample the sods into place with big wellingtons. [*RS*, p. 13]

In 2010, a controversial law was introduced banning non-commercial turf cutting on thirty-two raised bogs, and similar restrictions came into effect on twenty-three other sites the following year. This legislation has not gone down well across rural communities in Ireland, but the preservation of most of the raised bogs is necessary. Interestingly, in 2016, cutting returned to three local bogs in County Leitrim.

Paul Butler: The photographer

'Dog Silhouette' was one of the first serious images I created many years ago. The original print still hangs on our bedroom wall. Initially, my intention was to capture the still pond at St Anne's Park, Raheny, through the pillars of the old folly.

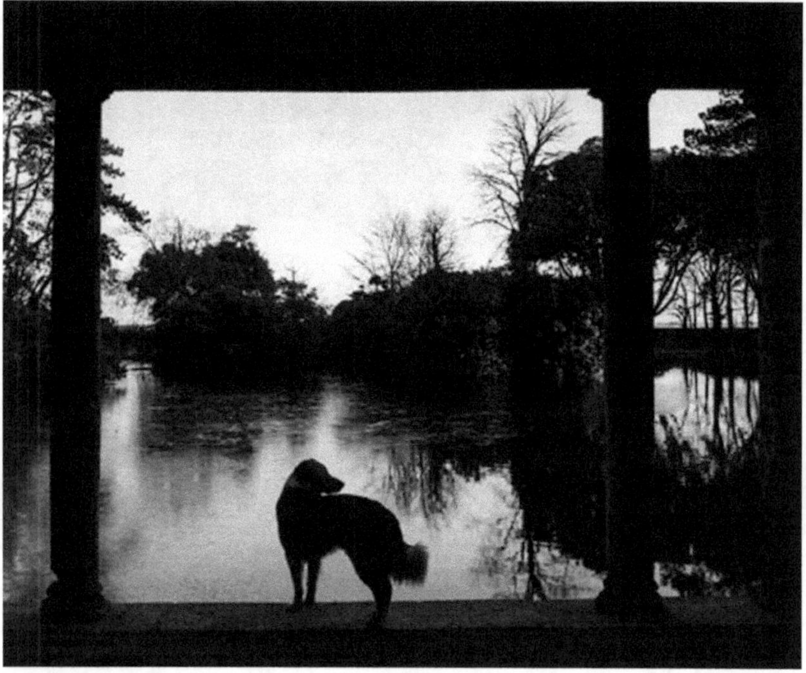

Dog Silhouette in St Anne's Park, Raheny, Dublin 1984. (35mm Negative) – Image: Paul Butler, 1984.

Photographic Note: This image was created with a deep red filter covering the lens; I wanted to get as deep a contrast as possible.

This beautiful park, a legacy left to the state by the Guinness family, is not far from where I grew up in Artane, in north Dublin. I set up the camera on a tripod and placed a deep red filter over the lens as I wanted to create a very high-contrast black and white image. As I was about to press the camera release cable button, a beautiful collie stepped into the scene. The dog waited and then turned his head, as if to set up his pose. I pressed the cable release and captured the moment. As quietly as he entered the scene, the collie left. Personally, I love this image as I can easily relate to its solitude and in some sense to its loneliness. Because of the deep contrast and the mood, I look at this picture and I see myself in it. To paraphrase writer Susan Sontag – 'All photographs are memento mori.'[7] My photos certainly comply with this definition. We will return to Sontag later.

When I look with raw honesty at my early relationship with my mother, it was at times quite awful. I constantly walked on eggshells, forever waiting for an explosion. And that feeling of 'keeping the peace' is always with you, in some form or other. It makes you nervous and wary of people, you always try to please and to fill the silent gaps. This is emotionally draining and isolating because people pick up on the vibe. So you withdraw into yourself. You feel different, maybe even inferior. You think you are a bad person, all because someone else's rage has been inflicted upon you.

This was such a contrast to John McGahern's relationship with his mother. But then again, he only had his mother up to the age of ten, so his memories of her love and affection are frozen in a specific time. I will come back to that point later. As I alluded to earlier, the direction of Frank McGahern's anger and resentment towards his children, including his jealousy of the bond that John shared with his mother, carved deep emotional wounds within the future writer. And what really got me interested in this project was that the violence against a young me, and the violence against a young John McGahern, left such an indelible mark. Did it drive McGahern to write? I know and I feel that it drives me to create, to try and satisfy that emptiness and 'want'.

7 'Susan Sontag on Photography': <https://expertphotography.com/susan-sontag-on-photography-quotes/> (2019).

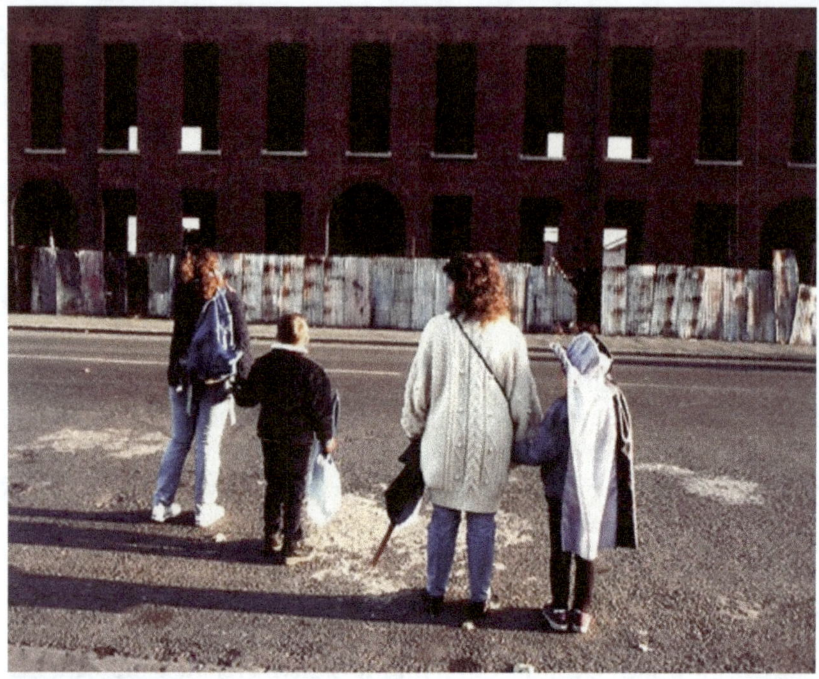

Dublin GAA Supporters Heading Home after the Game, Mountjoy Square, Dublin (Kodak Ektachrome) – Image: Paul Butler, 1993.

Photographic Note: Even back in my early photographic days, I was drawn to the juxtaposition of decay and everyday life. There is a jarring contradiction of decay, ordinariness and happiness within this image.

Now with maturity and hindsight, I can see that the anger poured onto me should have been directed at a father who somewhat neglected his family duties in an emotional and everyday sense. Why it was not, I do not know, but with the burden of everything on my mother's shoulders, the anger built. And so, through alcohol, that violence, bullying and frustration were vented towards us children. Every one of us got the volcano treatment, and I, being the runt of the litter, became a major outlet for a lot of that violent rage. Being young and not being able to push back, I was an easy target.

I did reconcile with my mother later in life, but the damage inflicted in those early years left its brutal mark. My father died when I was eighteen years old in 1982, and to be very honest, when I look back on my own life now, I would really have benefitted from good fatherly guidance, but alas that was not to be. My mother died in 2000, and it was sad to see her emotional pain affect her right to the end. It is sad to see someone so unfulfilled depart this mortal coil. There was without a doubt quite a lot of goodness within my mother and my father, and I carry a lot of good memories. I do hope that wherever they are now, they both have found peace. And so, just like John McGahern, I have certain scars courtesy of [an] unfulfilled parent[s]. And they are scars that will never heal.

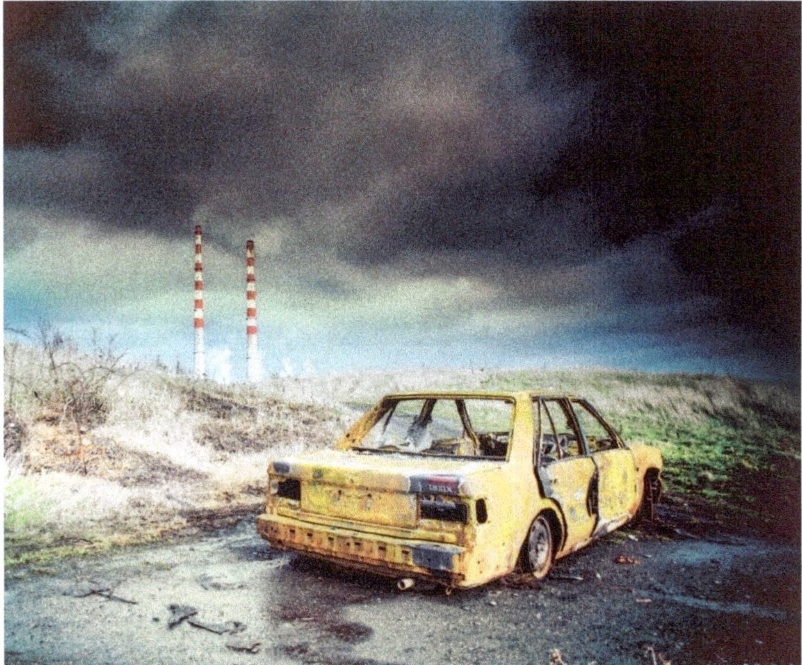

Burnt Out Car at Irishtown Nature Reserve (35mm Negative) – Image: Paul Butler, 1991.

Photographic Note: The use of a wide-angle lens adds drama to this scene. I really like the rusted car in total contrast with this wilderness area; it is as if an untamed world is always just below the surface. I am always drawn to discarded items; things left in a state of wanton destruction. This scene 'Burnt Out Car' is part of the Irishtown/South Wall Nature reserve. The reserve was developed on top of the original slag heaps from the old coal-fired power station.

Therefore, I strongly feel that McGahern's drive to put words to paper sated his 'want', and it connected with my drive to eventually explore his wonderful Leitrim landscape, a landscape that soothed his pain at times. It all comes down to my own 'Deep Well of Want'. Delving further into what I mean by 'want', this project is an auto-ethnographic exercise whereby I work out issues from my past by identifying with McGahern's experiences and communing with them through my own photographic imagery. It has taken a long time for my style of photography to evolve. I am neither a commercial photographer nor a portrait photographer. I wander and explore and, as such, the images within this specific project are a combination of storytelling, social commentary, the worked and working landscape, and the photography of the ordinary. The following words of wisdom, attributed to the photographer David Bailey, say a lot about my own approach and style: 'It takes a lot of imagination to be a good photographer. You need less imagination to be a painter because you can invent things. But in photography everything is so ordinary; it takes a lot of looking before you learn to see the extraordinary.' I include a link to David Bailey's inspirational work below.[8] And this is what I attempt to do with my photography: to transform the banal, the ordinary, the everyday, into something extraordinary. Within my soul, there is a nomad. I love to wander, and I get a great sense of pleasure from exploring the less-trodden path. I really enjoy my own company; for me wandering is an escape.

8 David Bailey, 'Landscapes & Travel': <https://www.davidbaileyphotography.com/landscapestravel>.

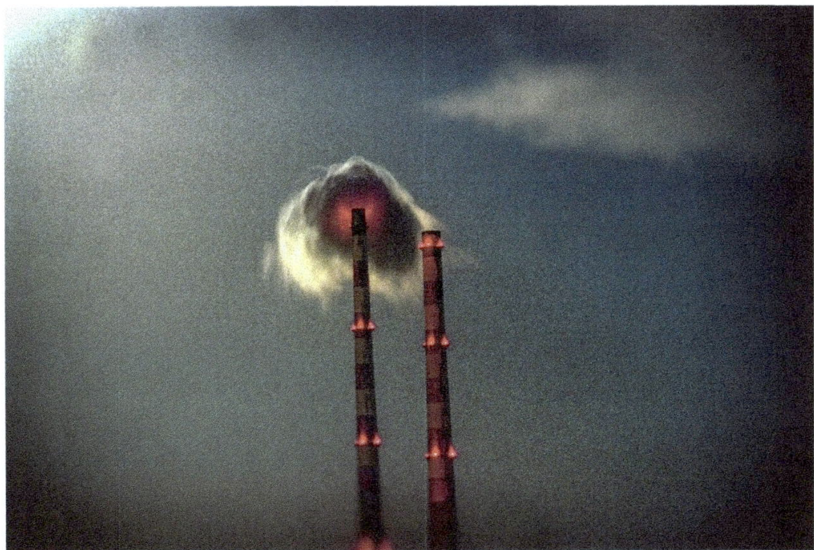

Pigeon House Towers at Poolbeg Power Station, Dublin (35mm Negative) – Image: Paul Butler, 1990.

Photographic Note: A long exposure gave the red glow at the top of the towers a volcanic appearance, a great way to visualize a high degree of unfulfillment.

One of my early images is 'Pigeon House Towers' which stand at just over 207 metres and are visible across Dublin, particularly from Sandymount Strand. They are a well-known landmark and one of the tallest structures in Ireland. For many years a thick black polluting smog continuously shrouded the city. At one stage, the smog permeated Dáil Éireann, and this forced the Minister for Health at the time, Mary Harney, to introduce a ban on smoky coal in the city in September 1990.

As a child, I spent a lot of time alone, not by choice I may add, but, as I pointed out earlier, I was denied an ordinary happy childhood and the need to continuously escape was essential. As I reached my early teens, I started to go hiking in the countryside. Early on a Sunday morning I would catch the first bus into Dublin City Centre from Artane and dash across the Liffey to catch the number 44 bus to Enniskerry, County Wicklow, outside Hawkins House. It was a matter of being at the mercy of the CIE buses (as they were then) being on time. This long journey on a rattling bus into County Wicklow was an adventure to a different world. Nowadays, suburbia has crept out to meet it. I would go walking and climbing alone, and at times I would go with friends, though I have never been afraid to go solo. Hence the connection I feel with my image of the collie sheepdog from St Anne's Park in Raheny. It was during my late teens that I started to develop a keen interest in photography. In 1984, I signed up with The National College of Art and Design (NCAD) in Dublin for an introduction to black and white photography. And so began my first steps to becoming immersed in my real passion.

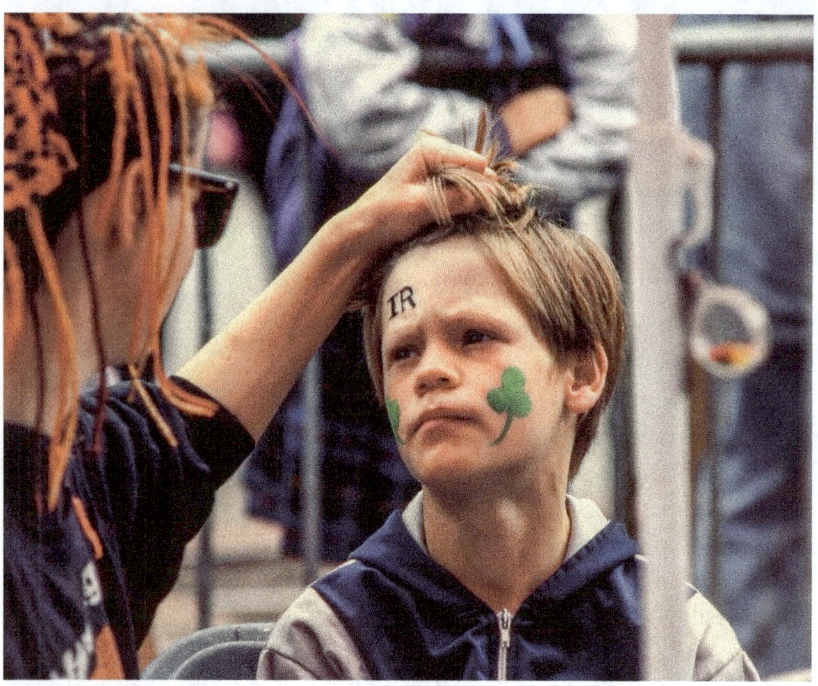

Face Painting at the Dublin Street Carnival (Kodak Ektachrome) – Image: Paul Butler, 1993. Photographic Note: What drew me to this scene was the look of total trust in the face of the boy. It is so full of emotion.

I love nature and the strong sense of the earth beneath my feet always gives me strength and confidence, though my head is inevitably in the clouds.

Back in the mid-1980s, ornithology became a wonderful release as I joined two good childhood friends and their passion for birdwatching. Travelling the length and breadth of the island, we searched the remotest headlands for migrant birds. These rare species turning up on our shore were as lost as ourselves, and our expeditions had become an escape route from the chaos at home. Those trips gave us a wonderful sense of freedom and created so many great memories. Ornithology led to photography, and bringing a camera on many of those trips evolved into the beginning of the journey to express myself visually. As life moved us in different directions, the days of dashing around our island came to an end. One friend took the road to Canada, never to return. He is now a professional part-time birdwatcher for the Canadian Wildlife Service. My other friend died in 1995. I miss him a lot.

In 1988, I headed on a one-year working visa to Australia. While there, I took the plunge into the technical side of photography. For over nine months I worked in a couple of photographic printing services. I then spent the last three months travelling by bus up the east coast of Australia and down the centre recording some incredible imagery using Kodachrome 64. Kodachrome 64 was an extremely fine grain film with a very high sharpness, possibly the best colour reversal film from Kodak Eastman which had been in use since 1935. Kodachrome was in effect a black and white film, with dye couplers in it that allowed it to become colour film at the time of processing. In contrast, another popular slide film, Ektachrome, has the colours in it (essentially) before you process it. The history and reputation of Kodachrome films are legendary. Kodachrome film stock possessed a 'look' that was difficult to reproduce in more contemporary films. It came 'process paid' with a yellow envelope in the box. When you used the slide film, you posted it off to a Kodak lab. Sadly, Kodachrome is no longer available. It was discontinued in 2010 after nearly seventy-five years due to a drop off in demand and the rise of digital cameras. There is also a movie dedicated to this titled *Kodachrome*: 'It is a 2017 American comedy-drama film, directed by Mark Raso, based upon a *New York Times* article written by A. G. Sulzberger. The movie stars Ed Harris, Jason Sudeikis and Elizabeth Olsen'.[9] I would highly recommend this movie as it does also

9 *Kodachrome* (The Film): <https://www.imdb.com/title/tt1880399/> (2017).

touch on the areas of place, belonging and the importance of memory and contains some beautiful imagery shot on Kodachrome.

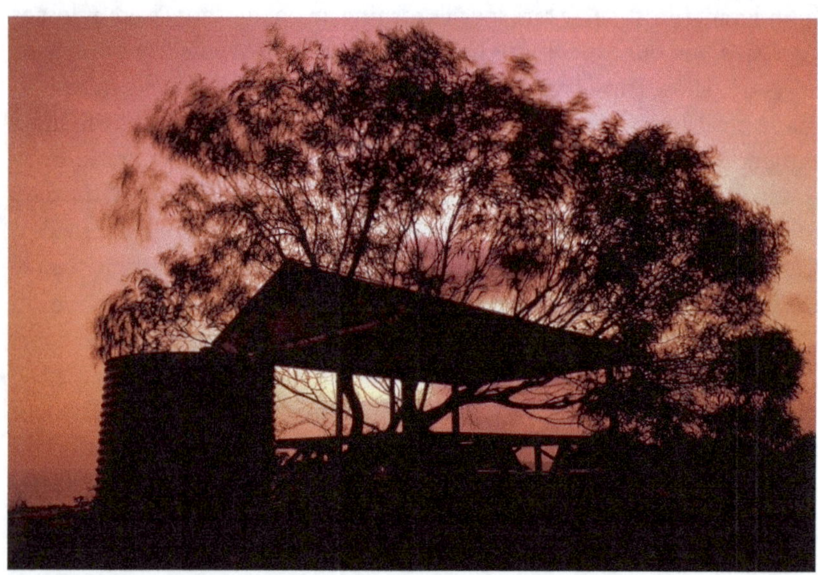

Sunset on Great Keppel Island, Southern Great Barrier Reef, Australia (Kodachrome 64) – Image: Paul Butler, 1989.

Photographic Note: This image was recorded on Kodachrome 64. I placed a magenta filter over the lens to dramatize the sky, and a tripod was used to keep the camera secure. This was necessary to keep the camera steady during such a long exposure. The beauty of this long exposure was to capture the sway of the trees in the scene.

I remember creating this image 'Young Boy in Shadow' as he stood close to a post box in the city of Darwin, Australia. We were waiting to join a small group heading for a few days' safari in Kakadu National Park in the Northern Territory. I noticed that a strong hard light was creating wonderful background shadows, and they gave a wonderful sense of depth to the scene. I asked the boy if he would like his picture taken, and he agreed. Instinctively he stepped into the hard light. I was very taken by his maturity; he exuded such worldly wisdom for a young boy.

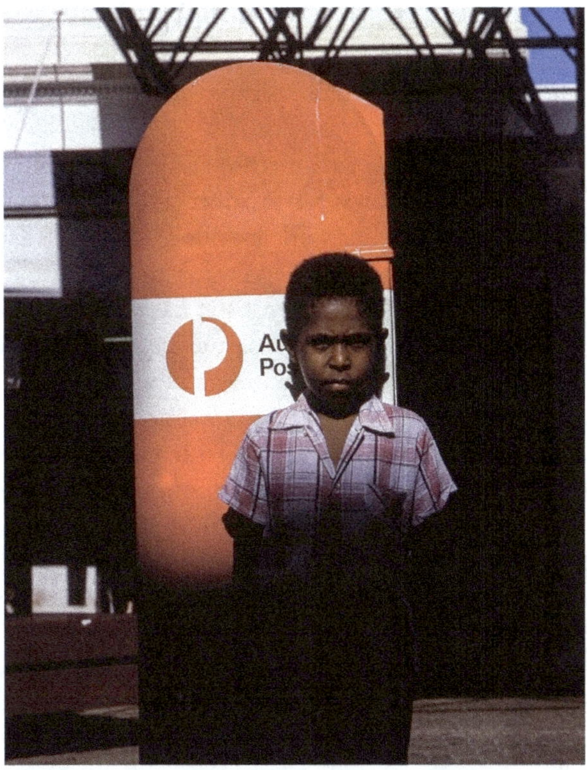

Young Boy in Shadow, Darwin, Northern Territory, Australia (Kodachrome 64) – Image: Paul Butler, 1989.

Photographic Note: This image was recorded on Kodachrome 64. The slight softness and rich depth of colour never fade. I really like the rectangular white strip that runs across the post box, it creates movement.

As I have mentioned previously, I like to wander and explore on my own, and I am very comfortable in my own skin. The American photographer Steve McCurry noted: 'My life is shaped by the urgent need to wander and observe, and my camera is my passport.'[10] I have included a

10 Steve McCurry, 'Behind the Scenes' (Blog): <https://stevemccurry.com/> (2022).

link to his work in the footnote. And for the record, I am not a total loner. I do have a few very close friends. Although someone once remarked to me: 'Paul, with you at times, it is like oil and water, they never mix.' I am a slow burner.

In 1990, I was accepted as a mature student into the Technical Photography Course in what was Kevin Street (DIT), part of the Dublin Institute of Technology. Juggling work in a photo laboratory and living in a series of dingy and damp bedsits, I put my life and soul into this course. This marrying of the technical and the artistic was right down my creative street. It was during these very lean times of studying that McGahern's short stories became a very important part of my cultural awakening. His short stories sparked a deep curiosity to explore and to observe the ordinary. In 1994, I qualified from Kevin Street (DIT) with a Diploma (Distinction) in Technical Photography. As the full-time course was three years long, I originally did the first year part-time but then went full-time, and that was tough. And with the change in Ireland of the awards qualifications in the early 2000s, today's equivalent of my award is an ordinary degree.

Quite recently and to my delight, I discovered Ektachrome transparency (slide) images I had recorded of an old and very run-down house in the Dublin Docklands area. I had recorded these scenes in the early 1990s on this colour reversal (slide) film using the available window light. As I reviewed the images, it struck me how they could easily work with and become part of the scenes I have been recording for many years in Leitrim for my project. In the scene 'Forgotten Bedroom', I really like that the diffuse light flooding through the net curtains acts as a gateway to an alternate and possibly happier world.

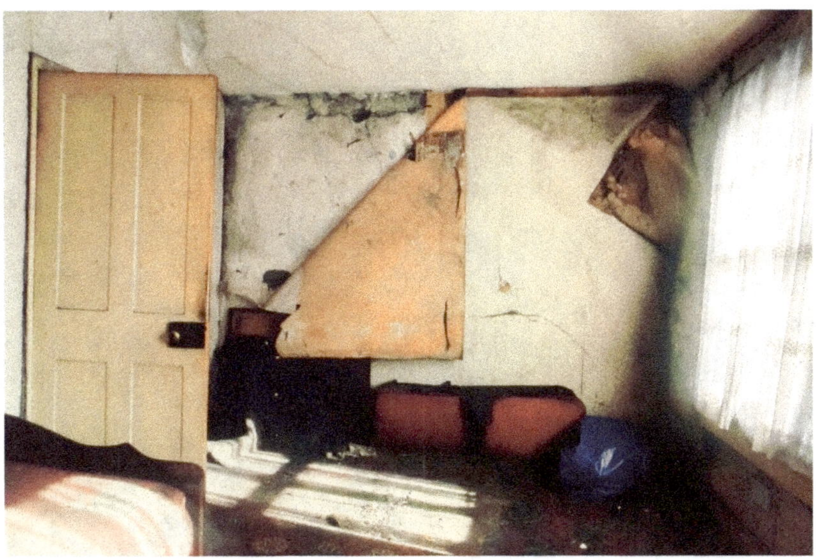

Forgotten Bedroom, Docklands, Dublin (Ektachrome) – Image: Paul Butler, 1993.

Photographic Note: Slide film is a lot trickier than colour negative film to use as your exposure must be spot on, particularly regarding shadow and highlights, whereas colour negative film is a bit more forgiving.

As I worked my way further down the landing, I noticed a door slightly ajar. In the empty bedroom, resting on a dusty dressing cabinet, lay two old photographs. My mind wandered. What was the relationship of the people in the photographs to this house? Were they former inhabitants? What was their previous life? What was their story? I found this scene very powerful, so I recorded 'Memories of a Home'. The slight colour cast from dull window light gives this scene a strong sense of nostalgia. Just like a lost soul, it creates a desire to know, a desire to delve further.

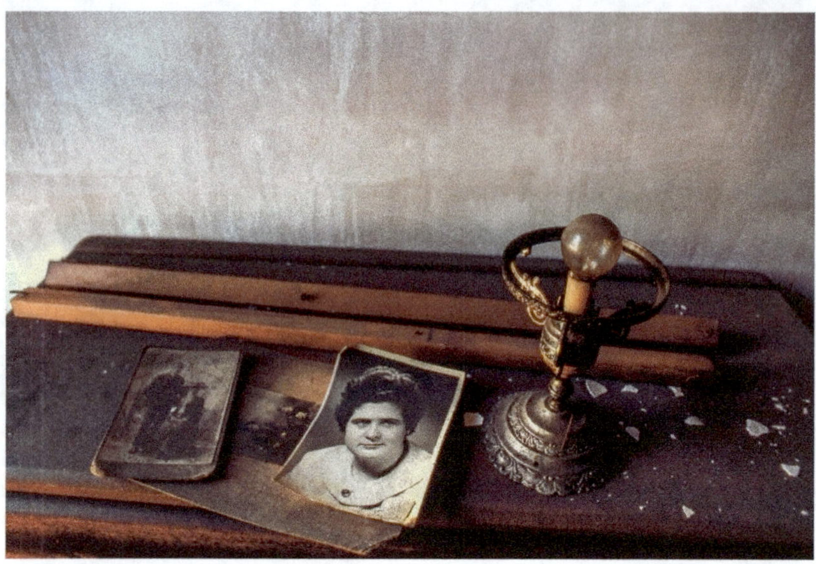

Memories of a Home, Docklands, Dublin (Ektachrome) – Image: Paul Butler, 1993.

The great British photojournalist Don McCullin argued, 'Photography for me is not looking, it's feeling. If you can't feel what you're looking at, then you're never going to get others to feel anything when they look at your pictures.'[11]

Moving with my family from Dublin to the townland of Farnocht near Mohill, County Leitrim in 2001, suddenly placed me right at the heart of McGahern country. Little did I realize that over ten years after photographing my first abandoned home in Dublin, I would start to explore abandoned homes in the north-west of Ireland and in greater detail. Unknowingly, I would start to meld my interest in the words of McGahern and my passion for imagery. It really took no time at all for scenes captured in abandoned old houses to quickly unfold into this fading setting – this place which seemed untouched by time. It was as if John McGahern and his characters had simply got up from a kitchen table, grabbed their coats and walked away.

11 Don McCullin, 'Irreconcilable Truths': <https://donmccullin.com/don-mccullin/> (2022).

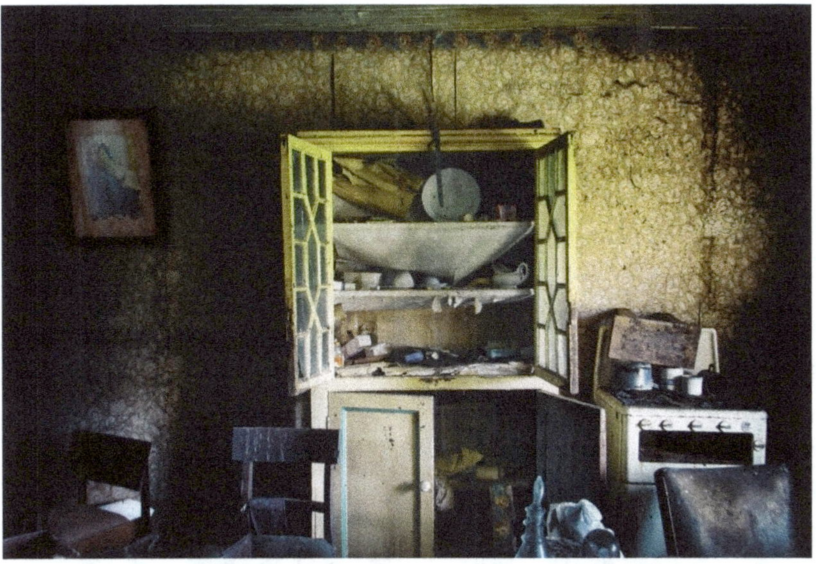

Derelict Kitchen at Curraghroe, County Roscommon – Image: Paul Butler, April 2016. Photographic Note: The open doors of the dresser just draw you right into the scene. In post-production I gave this image a vintage camera style, to extenuate colours and to introduce some grime and scratches.

Anne Goarzin is a Professor of Irish Literature and Culture at the Université of Rennes and an acknowledged McGahern expert with a strong interest in visual culture. She notes that my photography frames

> ordinariness through windows, a mirror there, elsewhere a gate, or the edge of a mantelpiece, the decrepit walls of a room. But it also pays inordinate attention to details. So, if we are to determine what counts as an event here, in the midst of the apparent ordinariness, one might say that it is not a 'thing' in particular, but rather the way in which we relate to the image: it is how we 'enter the middle, the between' in a creative way that makes the event. [12]

12 Anne Goarzin, '"The Sky Above Us": John McGahern, "The Image" and Paul Butler's Photographs of County Leitrim', in Derek Hand and Eamon Maher (eds), *Essays on John McGahern: Assessing a Literary Legacy* (Cork: Cork University Press, 2019), pp. 123–34, p. 132.

Goarzin's comments relate to my aesthetic quest – what I have tried to achieve in various articles and exhibitions.

As a documentary photographer, I have recorded so many scenes and visual statements. And since moving to Leitrim, I have photographed in situ many abandoned homesteads within this beautifully wild and untamed landscape of the north-west of Ireland. I look on my photography at times as a form of modern photographic archaeology. What I suggest by this is that I record an interior or exterior scene exactly as I find it, and that no re-positioning of items is carried out to make for a more aesthetically pleasing image. Everyday items come into view, just like 'Disused Commode', all helping the story evolve. This scene asks many questions. How mobile or immobile were they? Or was this commode just a collectible object? The questions are endless regarding the previous occupants' situation.

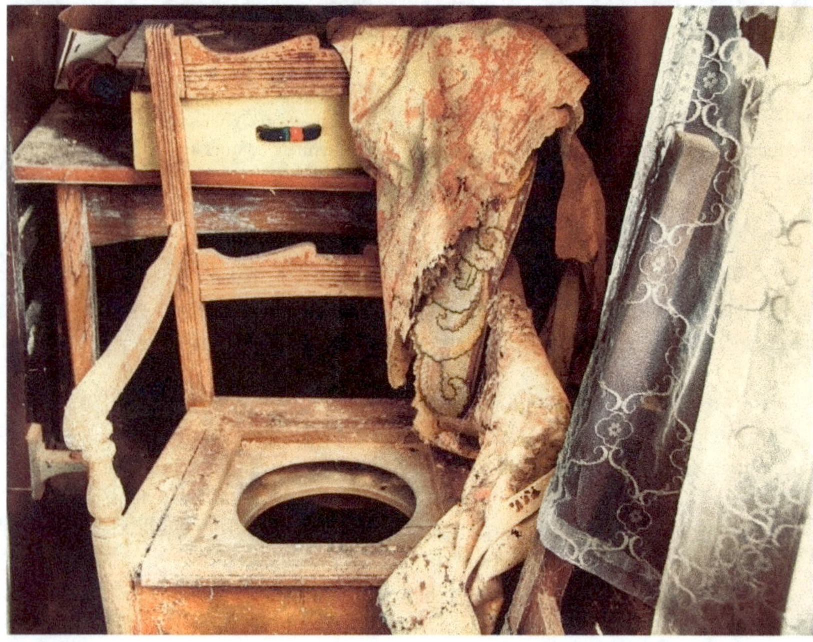

Disused Commode, Curraghroe, County Roscommon – Image: Paul Butler, April 2016.

Photographic Note: The word commode comes from the French word for 'convenient' or 'suitable', which in turn comes from the Latin adjective *Commodus*.

Leitrim is painted on a very rich canvas, and I am really drawn to recording this beauty of the daily and the ordinary; that is my passion. I need to explore the abundance of back roads and laneways that are so commonplace in Leitrim. There is also a large part of my being that needs to share, to give back. I need to share this place known as Leitrim with those who are unaware of its magical qualities, and at the same time offer an introduction to the writing of John McGahern. My first photographic exhibition related to this topic, *Still*, combined passages from McGahern's short stories with landscapes and abandoned homestead interiors. Why did I title my first exhibition, *Still?* I feel that this single word sums up Leitrim and where I live. So little changes, the seasons move slowly, and you live within that slow rhythm. The word '*Still*' fits perfectly.

During *Still*, I expected the audience's reaction to be non-committal because of its rural emphasis. The first exhibition was held in Ballyroan, County Dublin, which is not what you would call rural. However, comments left by visitors to the exhibition surprised me and gave me the confidence to move forward. Most of the comments were from people who had left rural Ireland many years previous to pursue a career and a life in the city. This exhibition really touched an emotional chord within them. It seemed to stoke a lot of memories, to open forgotten doorways. As part of the exhibition, I had left a series of McGahern quotes printed on coloured landscape scenes strewn around the exhibition space. The quotes were all taken home as little mementos. I was really delighted by this, and the many comments left by the visitors. I had achieved what I set out to do with this exhibition, and that was to give people a moment to step off the roundabout of their current life and to be 'Still'.

My next exhibition, *The Deep Well of Want*, centred on the rich vein of religious iconography I have captured in old homesteads and my observations on ritual within McGahern's work. This exhibition was hosted during a symposium held at St Patrick's College, which is part of Dublin City University. The occasion was to mark the tenth anniversary of John McGahern's death in April 2016. Following that event, an expanded exhibition combining both *Still* and *The Deep Well of Want* was hosted by the Atrium Gallery in Longford in June 2016. A review of this exhibition by Eamon Maher appeared on the *Irish Times* website on 8 June 2016, titled 'Tracing John McGahern's Steps through Memoir's Pages and Paul Butler's

Images.'[13] During March/April 2017, the exhibition took up residence at the Jury Room, the Dock Arts Centre in Carrick-on-Shannon, County Leitrim. In a roundabout way, that exhibition was a kind of coming home. The hosting of this exhibition at the Dock Art Centre was extended for a further two weeks as it was well received by the patrons and visitors. During the hosting of the exhibitions in Longford and Leitrim, the reaction of the viewer was more engaging: after all, it is their landscape, their home place and their ritual. I liked that the simplicity of everyday forgotten items really resonated with the audience.

In relation to *The Deep Well of Want* and *Still*, Anne Goarzin writes thus:

> [T]hese are images that literally operate a movement between the text and the photographs, as well as having a capacity to affect and to be affected by the appended text. This experiential method also seems to be more apposite to the visual dimension of McGahern's texts in a way that is faithful to the author's crucial statement: 'I write because I need to write. I write to see. Through words I see.' Paul Butler's photographs thus point to the essence of McGahern's writing and invite us to reflect on it. [14]

Such an analysis describes my ambition as a photographer quite accurately. I must take photographs – I literally 'have' to, not for the sake of taking an image but, as I explained earlier, in order to sate a deep desire. As John McGahern said, 'I've never written anything unless certain rhythms or images stay in my head and will not go away.' I have recorded many images, revisiting places I need to revisit. I also travel back through my catalogue, mixing and matching and refining the fit. If I see an image or place while driving or walking and it sparks something, I will return to record it for posterity and quench that current desire. The scene 'A Lick of Paint' brings back so many memories of being a child and how every summer the smell of gloss paint would permeate the house, as doors, windowsills and skirtings were given a fresh lick of paint. One can visualize the tin being opened, and a long and very thin piece of wood being used to slowly stir the paint. There was no rush; this was a job that would be completed in its own time.

13 Eamon Maher, 'Tracing John McGahern's Steps through *Memoir's* Pages and Paul Butler's Images': <https://www.irishtimes.com/culture/books/tracing-john-mcgahern-s-steps-through-memoir-s-pages-and-paul-butler-s-images-1.2676952> (8 June 2016).

14 Goarzin, 'The Sky Above Us', p. 127.

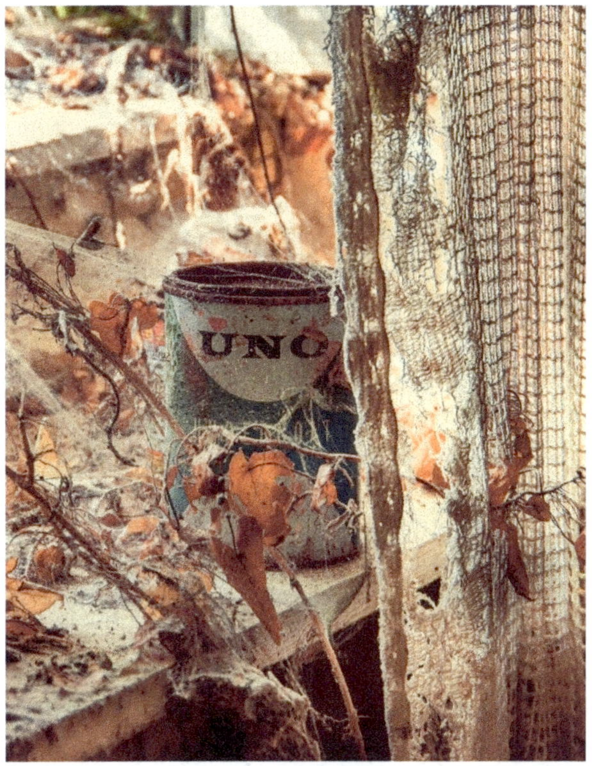

A Lick of Paint, Curraghroe, County Roscommon – Image: Paul Butler, April 2016. Photographic Note: I really like the warm light and the textures of the old curtains and the rusty can of UNO paint in this scene. UNO paints have been available for over eighty years in Ireland. There is a wonderful advertisement extolling the virtues of UNO paint available on the Irish Film Institute's archive.[15]

Photography is my way of expressing emotion, and as such it connects seamlessly with the words of John McGahern. What I have sought to achieve with my exhibitions is to open a door to a world that is slowly fading before our eyes. One definition of nostalgia describes it as 'a wistful desire to return in thought or in fact to a former time in one's life, to one's

15 Wilson Hartnell, 'Uno Paint Advertisement': <https://ifiarchiveplayer.ie/uno-paint/>.

home or homeland, or to one's family and friends; a sentimental yearning for the happiness of a former place or time'.[16] And this is the reaction I noted from many viewers of my exhibitions. As I have previously mentioned, the photographic and text exhibitions in their earlier forms touched many people, and they still have the capacity to evoke quite an emotional response. An emotional response is of the utmost importance to me because if there is no emotional connection, then what I have produced is nothing more than a series of images. Sontag's argument reinforces my intent: 'All photographs are memento mori. To take a photograph is to participate in another person's (or thing's) mortality, vulnerability, mutability. Precisely by slicing out this moment and freezing it, all photographs testify to time's relentless melt.'[17] The personal interpretation of McGahern's words that I choose to visualize and embellish is what I feel causes the viewer to reflect on the overall scene. And as I mentioned earlier, leaving passages of McGahern's words lying around the venue allows for the viewer to choose their own passages and compare them to the scenes. It gives them the space to create a doorway for themselves. And so, just like me, at times there are contradictions.

Anne Goarzin gives a further assessment of my work: 'Paul Butler's photographs do more than adhere to a registered literary trademark and they open up a window into the real "McGahern Country" of the imagination, which is first and foremost located in the texts of his novels, short stories, and essays as well as in the readers' minds.'[18]

In response to this assessment, let me say that what I am attempting within this project is to bring to life not just a fictional visual landscape but, in conjunction with specific passages, to reveal the past and living world of McGahern country. That this world still exists is only reinforced by this combination of imagery and McGahern's detailed descriptions of landscape, colour and light.

16 *Literary Devices*, 'Definition of Nostalgia': <https://literarydevices.net/nostalgia/> (2022).

17 'Sontag on Photography': <https://expertphotography.com/susan-sontag-on-photography-quotes/>.

18 Goarzin, 'The Sky above Us', p. 124.

The beautiful and moody scene 'October Sunrise at Cloone River' is perhaps a good example of my approach, as in it I offer my 'image' – my 'vision' of what it is exactly that the writer is seeking to achieve. There are hundreds of quotes from McGahern's work that could be used in conjunction with the image, whether it be the nostalgic realization of the beauty that surrounds Elizabeth Reegan in *The Barracks*, the sadness of Moran in *Amongst Women* when he truly 'sees' the meadow behind his house for the first time when he is on the threshold of death, or the numerous reflections on the landscape in McGahern's final novel, *That They May Face the Ri*sing *Sun*.

With McGahern, beauty nearly always has a bittersweet dimension, as though one needs to be shocked into an appreciation of the wonderful that is contained in the ordinary, everyday scenes that go largely unnoticed:

> It was so beautiful when she let up the blinds first thing that 'Jesus Christ', softly was all she was able to articulate as she looked out and up the river to the woods across the lake, black with the leaves fallen except the red rust of the beech trees, the withered reeds standing pale and sharp as bamboo rods at the edges of the water. [*B*, p. 170]

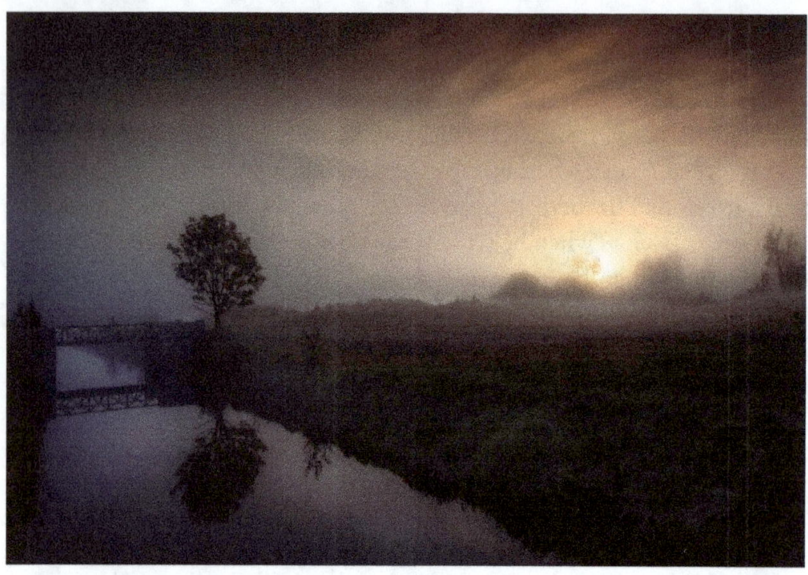

October Sunrise at Cloone River, between Lough Errew & Lough Rinn, County Leitrim – Image: Paul Butler, October 2012.

Photographic Note: The image 'October Sunrise at Cloone River' was created just before 8 am on a cold October Sunday morning. I was driving up the access road to collect our son from a party and I noticed a low mist sitting clinging to the fields. I stopped at a small red metal bridge that crosses the Cloone River near Lough Rinn House. The Cloone River was very still, and a gentle transparent mist sat atop the river. I could sense that in the far distance a slow glowing sun would break through. At that moment, I decided to capture the scene as I would miss it on the way back. Setting up the tripod I took a couple of long exposures and waited. The wide angle of the lens allowed me to create a nice panorama. After a couple of minutes, the sunrise intensified, and I repositioned the tripod to get the tree silhouette that would give some definition to the sun. As I usually shoot in RAW file, in post-production that allows me to bring out detail in the shadow area and reduce bright areas to obtain a more balanced tonal range. Areas of shadow can cause a blue cast on the image, so I added a Wratten (25) warm filter to reduce the coldness of the scene. I really like the muted colours and the quiet intimacy of this scene. Because less than half an hour later it was gone.

I end this introductory section by referring to the opening line of this book: 'Do you want your images to make a statement, or do you want your images to tell a story?' I definitely want my images to tell my story. My visual story of Leitrim, just as John McGahern has told his.

CHAPTER 2

Landscape

Leitrim: A very brief history

During the thirteenth century, the western side of the kingdom of Brefine was ruled by the O'Rourke family of Dromhair and Manorhamilton. On the eastern side of the kingdom, the O'Reilly clan ruled. During this time a split occurred and the kingdoms of west Brefine (Leitrim) and east Brefine (Cavan) were created. Invasion by the Normans followed, and the south of Brefine remained until 1620 when much of West Brefine was taken over and given to Villeirs and Hamilton with the intention of planting the county with English settlers. However, this was unsuccessful. In 1565, Deputy Sir John Perrot legally created County Leitrim and marked out the county borders.[1]

Five great forests are said to have stood in Leitrim, with a nineteenth-century county survey stating that 'a hundred years ago almost the whole County was one continued, undivided forest, so that from Drumshanbo to Drumkeeran, a distance of nine or ten miles, one could travel the whole way from tree to tree by branches'.[2]

1 Leitrim Tourism Network, 'History of Leitrim': <https://www.leitrimireland.com/the-history-of-leitrim/> (2016).

2 Gerard Boate, *Ireland's Natural History* (London: John Wright at the Kings Head, Old Bayley 1652).

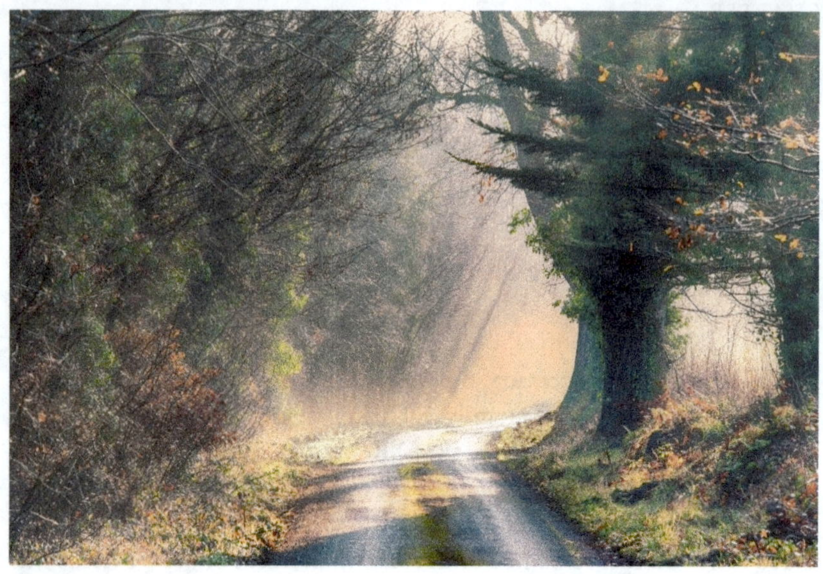

Nature's Diffuser, Farnocht, County Leitrim – Image: Paul Butler, November 2018.

In the fifteenth century, working of the county's rich deposits of iron ore started and this continued until the mid-eighteenth century. In the nineteenth century, coal mining became dominant in the east of Lough Allen near Slieve Anierin and in the west at Arigna, on the Roscommon border. The last coal mine closed in July 1990, and it now houses a successful visitor centre.

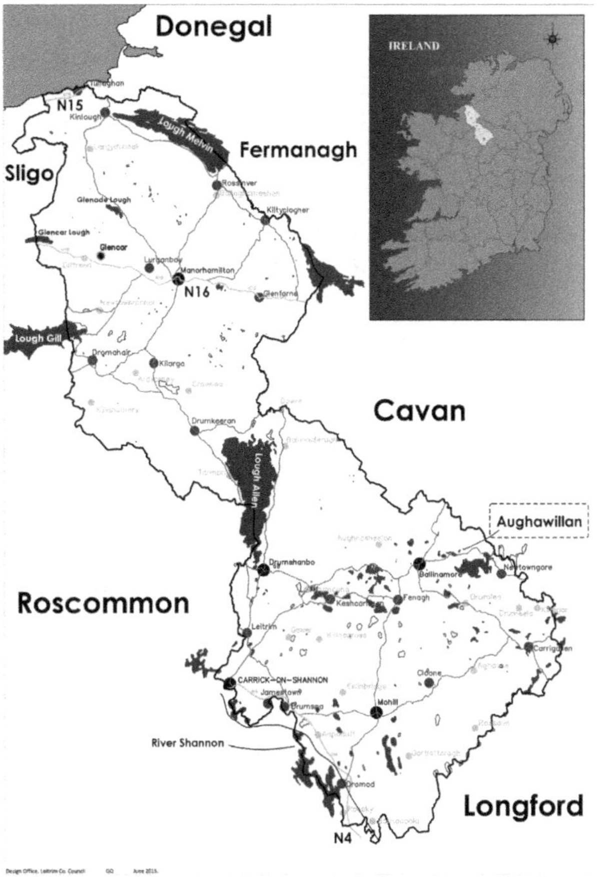

Map of Leitrim. Courtesy of the Planning Department, Leitrim County Council.

County Leitrim in Irish is 'Liath Druim', which means the grey ridge, and it is a popular misconception that the county is all trees, bogland and constant rain. The county takes its name from the village, Leitrim, which nestles beside the Shannon. Carrick-on-Shannon is the main county town of Leitrim. There are several large and beautiful lakes, the best known are Lough Gill, Lough Allen, Lough Rinn and Lough Melvin, the western shores of which are in County Leitrim. It is small and beautiful, and in its physical shape it looks quite feminine, as it is a county with a waistline. Forgotten and tucked into the north-west of Ireland, Leitrim is part of the province of Connacht and is bordered by two of its provincial cousins: Sligo to the west, and Roscommon to the south-west. Leitrim is also bordered by the Ulster counties of Cavan on the east, Fermanagh to the north-east and Donegal on the north. And to the south it shares a boundary with Longford, which is in the province of Leinster. And interestingly, due to Brexit, the County of Fermanagh currently resides in the United Kingdom, and this means that Leitrim now shares an international border with a non-EU country! And from *The Socio-Economic Impact of Forestry in Co. Leitrim*, we get this good geographical description; 'Leitrim County is situated in the north-west of Ireland. The northern half of the County is characterised by mesa (table-like) mountains, lakes, and deep glacial valleys while the southern half of the County is characterised by a drumlin belt interspersed with small lakes and rolling hillocks. Co. Leitrim has a number of large lakes including Lough Allen in the centre, Lough Melvin to the north-east of the County and Lough Gill to the west. The total area of the County is 1,558 km^2 (158,885 ha; 614 square miles)'.[3]

3 Áine Ní Dhubháin, Evelyn Stoettner, Julie Ballweg and Serge Garcia, 'The Socio-Economic Impact of Forestry in Co. Leitrim': <https://www.leitrimppn.ie/wp-content/uploads/2019/09/The-Socio-Economic-Impact-of-Forestry-in-Co.-Leitrim-Final-Report_compressed.pdf> (2019).

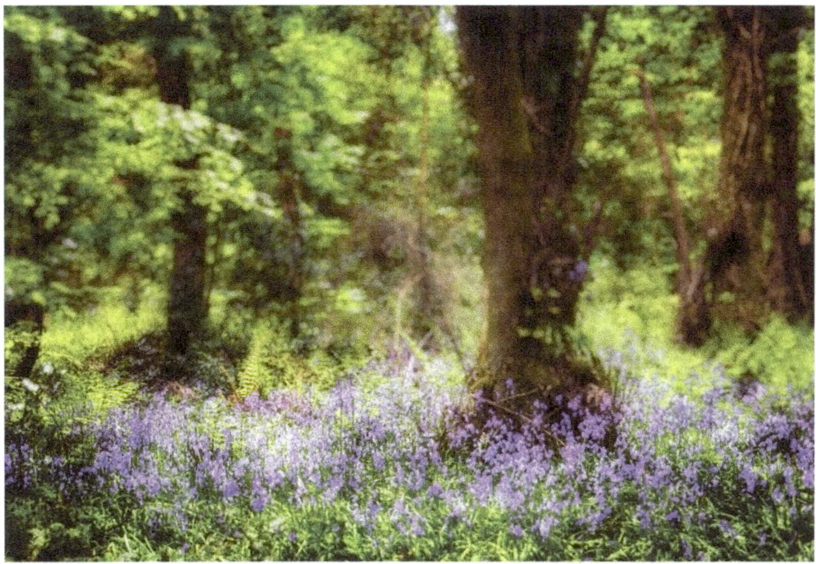

The Bluebells of May in the Old Native Wood on the Shores of Lough Rinn, County Leitrim – Image: Paul Butler, May 2018.
Photographic Note: Every April into May, the natural woodland bordering Lough Rinn comes to life with Bluebells. There is this stretch of old wood not far from our house. It is situated just off a right of way for those that like to fish on the lake. In this image, I used a slight Bokeh effect (it comes from the Japanese word *Boke,*[4] which means blur or haze) to draw the eye towards the middle of the scene allowing you to become immersed and gain a sense of the tranquillity that does prevail.

The south-west tail of Leitrim, as I call it, is clipped by the N4 (National Primary Route). The N4 crosses into the County of Leitrim just beyond the Tomisky Roundabout which is in County Longford. Approximately twenty-one kilometres later, as you cross the stone bridge at Carrick-on-Shannon, the N4 guides you through the village of Cortober, on the opposite side of the Shannon into the County of

4 Gabor Holtzer, 'How to Create Beautiful Bokeh Effect in Photos': <https://expertphotography.com/beautiful-bokeh-effect-photography/>.

Roscommon. At the northern tip of the county, the N15 from Sligo to Lifford crosses into County Leitrim at the River Duff. This primary route through County Leitrim bypasses the small coastal village of Tullaghan; originally the primary route went through the village. After close to four kilometres at the River Drowes, the N15 departs into the County of Donegal. And what makes these four kilometres special? They represent "Leitrim's Atlantic Coastline," and are a part of the Wild Atlantic Way, which I will talk about later.

Also, in the northern part of the county, the N16 from Sligo crosses east across Leitrim, through the large county town of Manorhamilton on its route towards Blacklion in County Cavan. This primary route then crosses the international frontier to join the A4 towards Enniskillen in the County of Fermanagh. So, there you have it, none of the primary routes cut through middle of the county. There are twenty-four regional roads within Leitrim. Add to that the vast number of old laneways, tracks and famine roads and without a doubt you have a vast treasure trove which is ripe for exploration.

The magnetic landscape of Leitrim

Leitrim is infectious; it seeps into your bones. I write somewhat impartially as I am not originally from these parts and yet the longer I live here, the more I realize that this is home, this is where I belong. It feels so right to be here with my feet in the soil and my head in the clouds wandering through laneways and rejoicing in the sweet clean air. John McGahern came back to these parts after his years of wandering, the call of home drawing him close to his roots. I can understand why.

I have an emotional connection with the camera and the unique landscape of Leitrim, and the north-west always draws me in, that deep feeling of clay and water and tall trees and the lonely misty bog. This is the subconscious force that drives me, and McGahern's writing is the meta tag for my imagery. And so, my photographic journey through McGahern country begins with this most unique landscape. The scene 'Misty Birch' was taken on a quiet and foggy Sunday morning in February 2011, not far from home. This patch of bog is just off the Drumlish to Mohill road, close to Fox's Pub of Tooman. It always takes a few hours for the fog to burn off, though some days it just lingers. Birch trees are abundant here, being really at home in the damp boggy soil. Within this scene, I particularly like the hidden horizon as it amplifies that solitary moodiness.

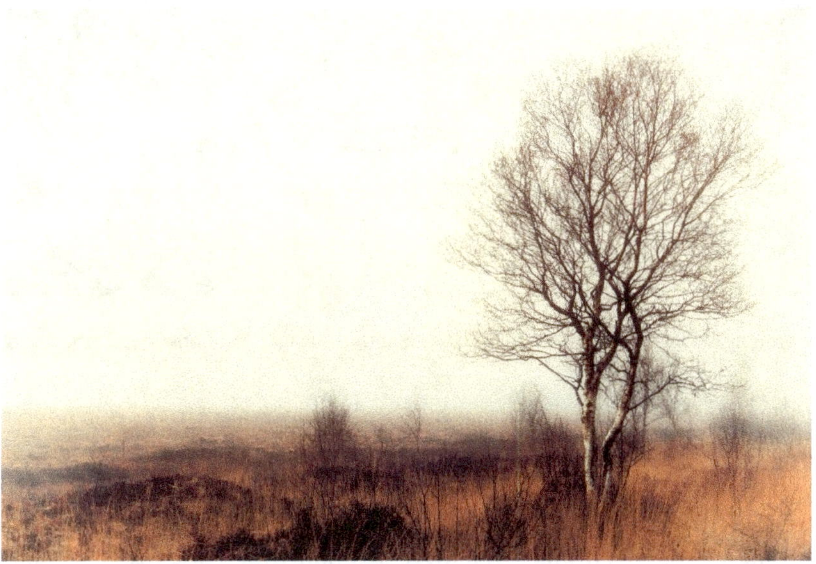

Misty Birch on the Bogland, Breanross South, County Leitrim – Image: Paul Butler, February 2011.

The county also has an unusual anomaly due to its geographical structure, with Lough Allen practically cutting through the middle of the county – hence the waistline. When you drive between the county towns of Carrick-on-Shannon and Manorhamilton on the (R280), the road leaves County Leitrim approximately two kilometres after the village of Drumshanbo at a small bridge over the River Shannon and passes through County Roscommon for a short distance, after which the road re-enters County Leitrim, near Cartonbeg.

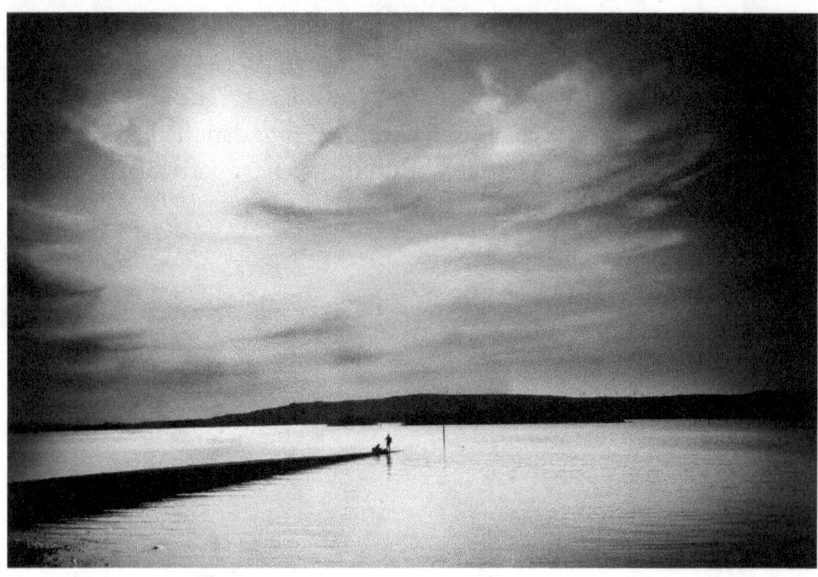

Cormongan Pier, Lough Allen, County Roscommon – Image: Paul Butler, September 2020.

As for the terrain, Leitrim is hilly and mountainous in the north-west and in the south-east, it is quite flat. And as I already mentioned, Leitrim possesses four kilometres of coastline, the shortest of any county in Ireland, wedged between Sligo and Donegal. Found within this small coastline is the surfing area near Tullaghan. The River Shannon, the longest river in Ireland and the United Kingdom, flows through Leitrim and is linked to Lough Erne by the Shannon-Erne Waterway, which is a cross-border initiative.

Here we have another simple description of the topography of the county from Patrick J. Flanagan in his book *The Cavan & Leitrim Railway*:

> Leitrim stretches from the River Shannon at Rooskey to the Atlantic Ocean at Tullaghan on the borders of Donegal. Lough Allen, the northern-most lake on the Shannon, effectively halves the County, and North Leitrim is both physically and psychologically different from South Leitrim. While barren tracts of mountain are the predominant features north of the lake, the land to the south is marshy and dotted with small lakes. Above all, Leitrim is known as the County of 'little lakes and little hills'.[5]

5 Patrick Joseph Flanagan, *The Cavan & Leitrim Railway* (London: Pan Books, 1972).

Leitrim is also known as 'The Wild Rose County', and that is a far more fitting description. It is the least populated county in all of Ireland; we will talk about that more in the chapter on place. When out and about, you stumble upon scenes like 'Buttercup Riot'...No wonder McGahern's memories evoked a childhood in Leitrim rich with colour, drama and landscape.

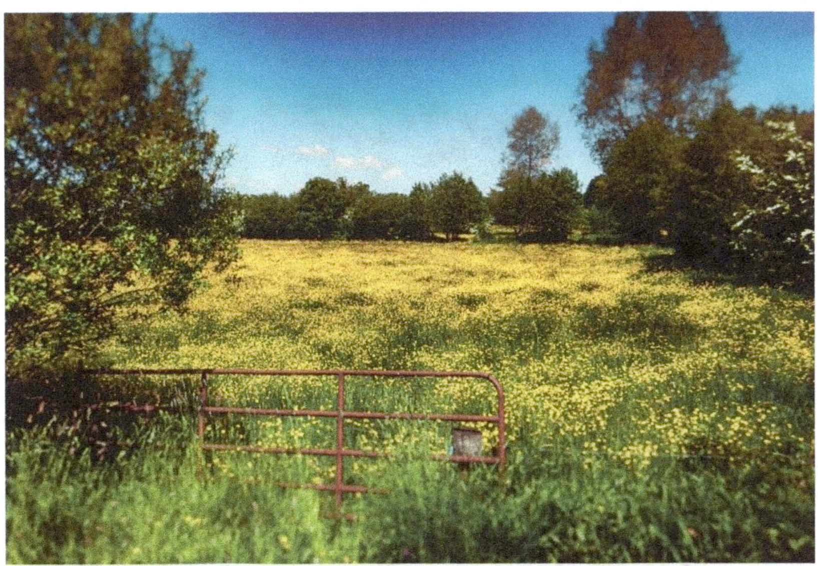

Buttercup Riot, near Keeldra Lake, County Leitrim – Image: Paul Butler, June 2013.
Photographic Note: From a photographic perspective, it can be hard for the camera metring system to register such a dominant yellow. It can overexpose dramatically and wash out detail quite easily.

During the month of June in 2013, the many small fields in this part of Leitrim were a sea of yellow. However, this buttercup invasion was not welcomed by the farming community. Because of their long invasive root sitting close to the surface, the buttercup binds and mats the field. But most importantly, buttercups are poisonous to livestock. The least known-about county in Ireland is Leitrim. That is why it has a particular draw for me. The great poet W. B. Yeats was quite taken with the landscape of Leitrim. Staying at Lissadell House near Drumcliffe in County Sligo would have allowed him easy access to the Glens of Leitrim. His poem 'The Rose of Inishfree' refers to the isle of Inishfree on Lough Gill, part of which is in

Leitrim. Here you will also find the Parkes Castle, a sixteenth-century restored tower house and plantation fort. Yeats also captured in his poem 'The Stolen Child'. the romantic Glencar Waterfall, which is not far from Manorhamilton. This scene, entitled 'Glencar Waterfall', was recorded during the first Covid lockdown. As Leitrim is a sparsely populated county, it was even more deserted, which is hard to describe because it felt like the world was empty. It really seemed like you had the place to yourself.

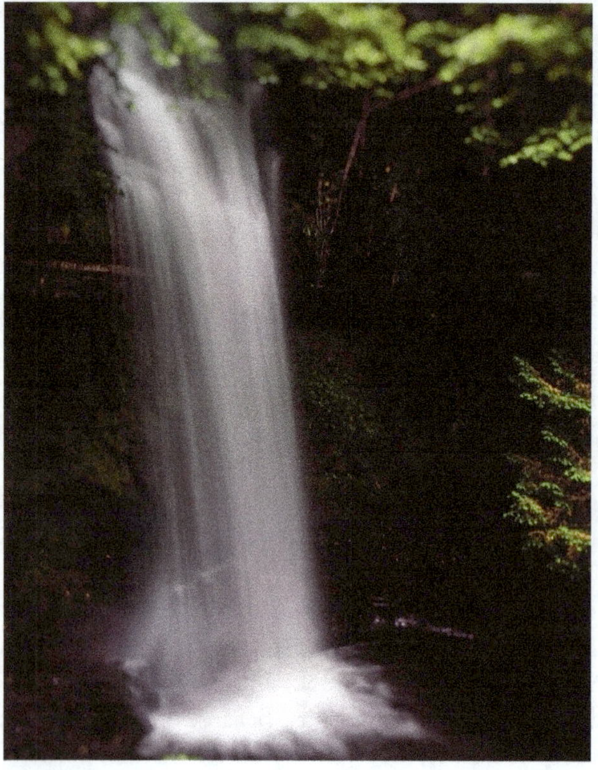

Glencar Waterfall, County Leitrim – Image: Paul Butler, June 2020.
Photographic Note: To get the soft milky motion on the cascading water a long exposure was necessary.

I have lived in Farnocht, south Leitrim, for over twenty-one years, and while McGahern transports us back to a disappearing way of life, the land and how it is worked still very much dictates the nature of people in this part of the country. The seasons determine the rhythm of life. When McGahern and his wife, Madeline, returned to live in Foxfield, in a house overlooking the lake, he had the distinct impression of coming home. The wonderful documentary *A Private World* shows the writer in his home and on his land. It portrays him interacting with the locals at marts and in the town of Mohill. He is indistinguishable from the other natives – a Leitrim man among other Leitrim men and women. In a sense, the seasons define the people, and it is to his beloved county that John McGahern returned as he mentions in *A Private World*:

> Now there was a lot of life here, but that it was local life. And that often the quality and spirit of the people varied enormously even over the course of a few miles. One of the pleasant things about here is that they take you for what you are, you know, rather than who you think you are. And sometimes they'd ask me: 'Is there much money in this writing business, John?'
>
> And when I assured them that there wasn't, they seemed quite satisfied and to accept it like most trades. [*PW*]

It is clear the peacefulness and tranquillity of the landscape appealed to him and that he viewed the inhabitants as being his people. He felt comfortable in this environment: it allowed him to write and to do a bit of farming on the side. And my experience is quite different. I am originally a native of the north side of Dublin who, as mentioned previously, moved to this part of South Leitrim in 2001 with my family. We were literally like fish out of water, nomads or what is more commonly known as blow-ins.

When I combine images with text, the process happens in various ways. There are times when I am out capturing images and a certain scene causes a particular passage from McGahern's work to invade my thoughts. The scene 'Approaching Hailstorm' was recorded quite close to home. While out walking with the dogs, the skies darkened, and a very low hail and rain cloud made swift progress towards me. As I stood at the edge of this waterlogged field, I found myself quoting the following line from the opening of *Memoir*: 'The soil in Leitrim is poor, in places no more than an inch deep. Underneath is daub, a blue grey modelling clay, or channel, a compacted gravel' [*M*, p. 1].

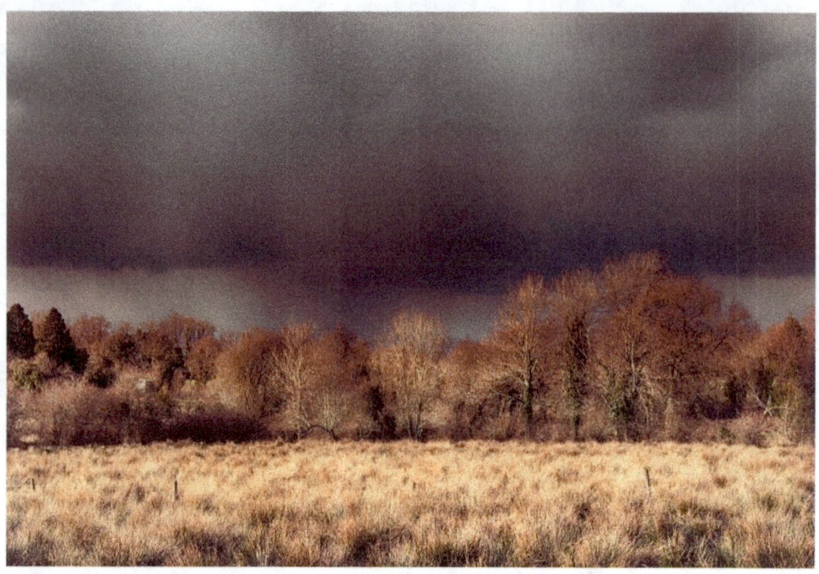

Approaching Hailstorm over Farnocht, County Leitrim – Image: Paul Butler, February 2018.

That simple description in *Memoir* is spot on. The soil of the county is extremely water-retentive and along with its many lakes provides the basis for the standard joke that land in the county is sold by the gallon rather than by the acre. According to the Irish Soil Information System, Leitrim has following types of soil: clayey drift with siliceous stones, peat, fine loamy drift with siliceous stones and fine loamy drift with limestone and in places river alluvium. And because of the poor nature of the soil, the less intensively worked small fields are enclosed within hedgerows rich in wildflower and fauna leading to a landscape that is relatively unspoilt. My personal experience of this soil on our own patch of land is that it is very heavy, incredibly sticky and full of large boulders. Trying to dig even the smallest hole becomes a major undertaking. The soil is not much use for growing anything without bringing in a lot of extra topsoil and manure. It took me a long time and a lot of money to realize that the only things that grow well here are the plants and trees that are already resident. Now, finally after many unsuccessful efforts, I had found sense. Many trees will not grow deep; instead, their roots finger out across the top of the heavy soil and are prone to collapse in heavy winds. However, there are plenty of the majestic oaks those that manage to get their roots to go deep, and they grow tall and majestic. When our son was born in 1996, we were given an oak seedling. Oaks are a slow growing tree, and when we were moving to Leitrim, I dug up the young tree and replanted it in Leitrim. It stands proud in the garden and thankfully after twenty-five years it is tall and thriving. It would probably have been cut down in Dublin or severely pruned as the garden was far too small for such a big tree.

During late spring and early summer, the hedgerows come alive, and wildflower takes hold. Great big skies roll by, and a large palette of greens dominates the landscape. Autumn brings golden yellow and rusty reds that filter through the dull grey light. Landscapes of Leitrim flow from the pages of McGahern, and I find it quite natural to visualize these scenes. The first lines of *Memoir* emphasizes the unique nature of the Leitrim landscape: 'The hedges are the glory of these small fields, especially when the hawthorn foams into streams of blossom each May and June' [*M*, p. 1].

It is the movement within the scene 'Cattle in May' that really appeals to me. The line of cattle take your eye across the canvas on a glorious journey. The beautiful hedges coming into bloom, the vibrant greens though full of rushes and the moody sky really gives this scene a timeless painterly quality.

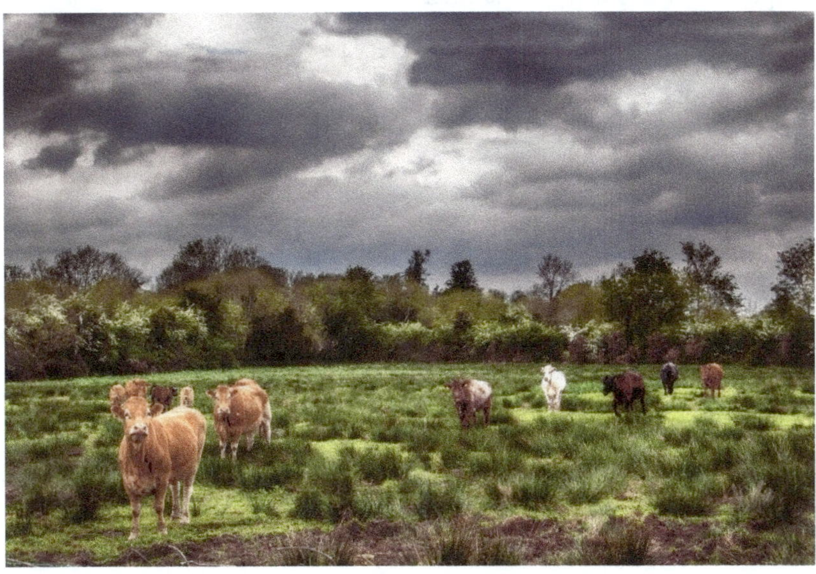

Cattle in May, Farnocht, County Leitrim – Image: Paul Butler, May 2011.

In his monograph on McGahern's work, Eamon Maher observes:

> When we read his books and short stories, we are transported back in time to a rural Ireland that is very close to extinction, an Ireland where people worked the land in a way that moulded their character.[6]

Maher's observation is astute, because after living in Leitrim for over twenty-one years, I have been quite immersed in McGahern's world. I believe that the people of Leitrim are still very much connected to the land and its traditions. While many have had to migrate for work, the people of Leitrim are worldly, deep and resilient. They have had to be. The landscape of Leitrim, either worked or barren, defines its people. It is a constant battle for the farming community to make a living on this poor soil, apart from forestry. Ruined houses, emigration and abandoned fields allude to a different era, but times have changed. According to the Central Statistics Office, Leitrim was the county in Connacht which grew most between 2016 and 2022; I will discuss this further in the section on place. The county also has quite a vibrant, musical and artistic vibe. However, tradition, ritual and the importance of land are as relevant today to its people as it was then. You can take the person out of Leitrim, but you cannot take Leitrim out of the person.

A landscape that speaks

Leitrim and the north-west are very distinctive. Hidden, forgotten and full of ancient mystery, I love where I live and over time and through what I record I have come to a realization of why John McGahern wrote so fondly of this place. Meadowsweet is a tall native perennial of damp waysides, meadows, marshes and woods flowers throughout Ireland from June to September.

6 Eamon Maher, *John McGahern: From the Local to the Universal* (Dublin: Liffey Press, 2002), p. 2.

Meadowsweet's herbal uses had a base in scientific fact, in common with many other folk and herbal remedies. In the 19th century, chemists isolated salicylic acid from Meadowsweet. The acid was a disinfectant, so it not only made rooms smell better but helped the fight against bacteria. It was a painkiller and anti-inflammatory but hard on the stomach. Only after it was synthesised did it become an acceptable candidate for mass production and sold in tablet form as 'aspirin' – 'a' for acetyl and '-spirin' for Spirea, the original botanical name for Meadowsweet.[7]

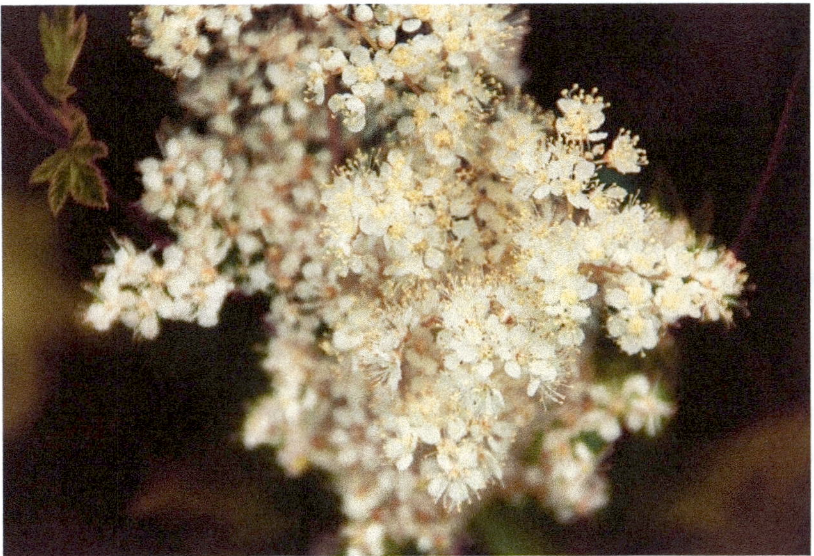

Meadowsweet, Farnocht, County Leitrim – Image: Paul Butler, July 2017.

Photographic Note: Only focusing on a specific part of the wildflower creates a slight disconnect with the present. If this was a completely sharp image it would create a 'Here and Now' statement. It would just be a recording of a plant. With this selective focus I wanted to create a sensation of pondering.

I really like it when, during late spring and early summer, the hedgerows come alive, and wildflower takes hold. Great large skies roll by, and a large palette of greens dominates the landscape. Autumn brings golden yellow and rusty reds that filter through the dull grey light. The landscape

7 Zoë Devlin, 'Wildflowers of Ireland – Meadowsweet': <http://www.wildflowersofireland.net/plant_detail.php?id_flower=166> (2022).

of Leitrim flows from the pages of McGahern, and I found it quite natural to visualize the scenes so close to the writer's heart. The landscape of Leitrim never fails to impress, just like the scene 'An Evening in late June', and as McGahern himself observed:

> In a novel or a short story you are always faced with material that is time and space and landscape. The problem for the writer is to actually dramatise that inert mass so that it comes to life and conforms to an idea or a vision. [*PW*]

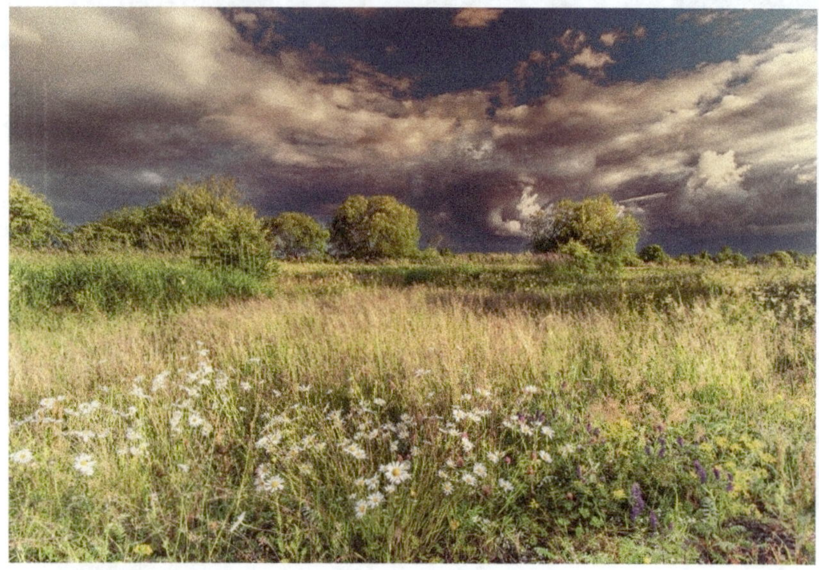

An Evening in Late June, beside the Rinn River at Tooman Bridge, County Leitrim – Image: Paul Butler, June 2022.

In the image 'Big April Sky', I really wanted to portray the big skies that roll across the landscape during the months of April and May, while at the same time, I wanted to keep the simplicity of the scene. What I find quite poignant about this scene is the little dog standing on the road. His name was Oscar, and he was a real character. Belonging to a neighbour, Oscar, a Jack Russell, was always in trouble. But every morning he came over to our house for a rich tea biscuit and a walk. And so Oscar adds to the natural framing of this painterly scene.

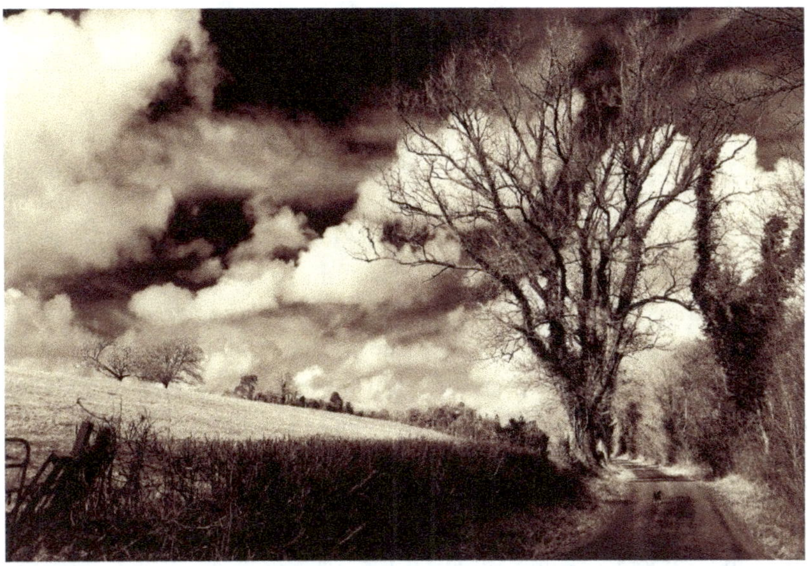

Big April Sky at the High Field, Farnocht, County Leitrim – Image: Paul Butler, February 2011.

Photographic Note: The lens setting for this scene was 22mm (digital), which is 33mm in the old analogue format. This setting gives a relatively wide and dramatic format. During conversion of the image into black and white in post-production, the percentage of red filtration was increased dramatically to darken the sky and isolate the cloud structure. The road positioning at the bottom right was a natural selection; it leads your eye towards the fantastically majestic oak, which is also home to a couple of red squirrels.

McGahern appreciated the importance of place better than most and his work, by concentrating on the small details of the everyday as lived out in the local, managed to create a universal experience that speaks in a special way to readers across the globe. My initial impression of Leitrim, before we relocated there, was of an empty, rainy place – green, damp and full of trees. No doubt this was related to the advertisements that appeared regularly back in the 1980s informing people of many acres for sale for tree planting in Leitrim. However, I must admit that my assumption was way off track. While the land is poor and marshy, it nevertheless displays a stunning beauty in all seasons.

Through the seasons: Spring to summer

There can be nothing more fulfilling than walking the local lanes close to home on a summer evening and observing a golden light filter through strands of old wood that run alongside a small stream. The land around is well grazed, and these last remnants of old native wood hark back to a time when natural woodland had the majority stake on the landscape. What you really notice on these golden evenings is the quality of light; it is clean, gold, warm and with vibrant green moss inhabiting many tree trunks, is testament to the air quality of Leitrim. There are beautiful old oak trees to be found hidden behind the stands of plantation forest, but they only account for a measly 0.7 per cent of forested land in Leitrim. And in *Memoir*, McGahern paints a vivid golden picture: 'and in the full leaf of summer it is like walking through a green tunnel pierced by vivid pinpoints of light' [*M*, p. 2]. Capturing light filtering through sycamore, oak and ash leaf is very rewarding, allowing you to observe the intricate structure and life pulsing within the green canopy. A final flourish is to throw the backlight out of focus to create a beautiful *Bokeh*.

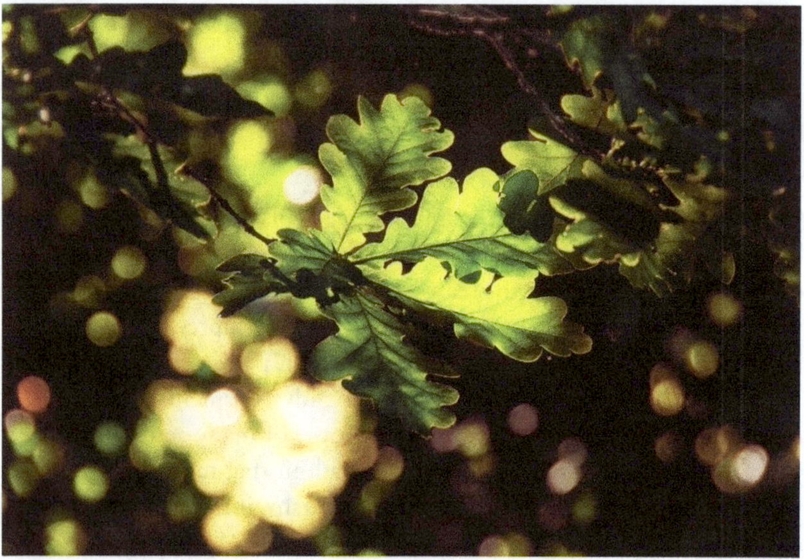

Summer Light Filtering through Oak Leaves, Farnocht, County Leitrim – Image: Paul Butler, June 2017.

Photographic Note: As previously explained, *Bokeh* comes from a Japanese word *Boke*, meaning blur or haze.

McGahern captured this aspect of life very well in an interview with Eamon Maher:

> When you're in danger of losing a thing it becomes precious and when it's around us, it's in tedious abundance and we take it for granted as if we're going to live forever, which we're not. [8]

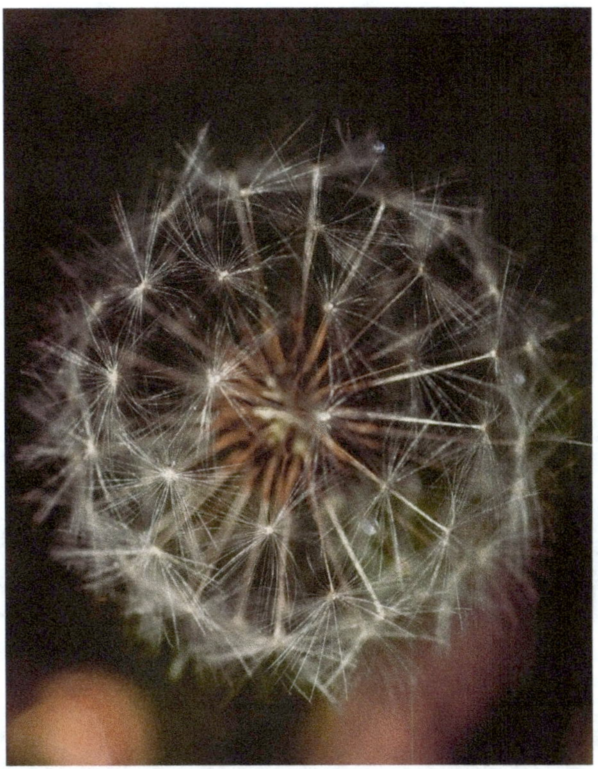

Dandelion Seed Head, Farnocht, County Leitrim – Image: Paul Butler, May 2016.

8 'Catholicism and National Identity in the Works of John McGahern'. Interview between Eamon Maher and John McGahern, *Studies: An Irish Quarterly*, Vol. 90, No. 357 (Spring 2001), pp. 72–83, p. 75.

Here is a beautiful and simple description from Nature.com about dandelion seed heads, also known by some as dandelion puffs: 'Each seed is suspended from a parachute-like stalk – easily released by a puff of breath.' The parachute is a bunch of bristles called a pappus. Each pappus carries around 100 filaments, each attached to a central point, rather like the head of a chimney sweep's brush.

The following image taken on Sliabh Bawn, County Roscommon, helps relive a memory of freedom and a light summer breeze that Elizabeth Reegan must have felt as she freewheeled down the hill in *The Barracks*:

> She could see the village as she came downhill, the light staring her in the face, the woods across the lake, the mountains beyond with the sheds and gashes of the coal pits on the slopes, the river flowing through into the Shannon lowlands. [*B*, p. 97]

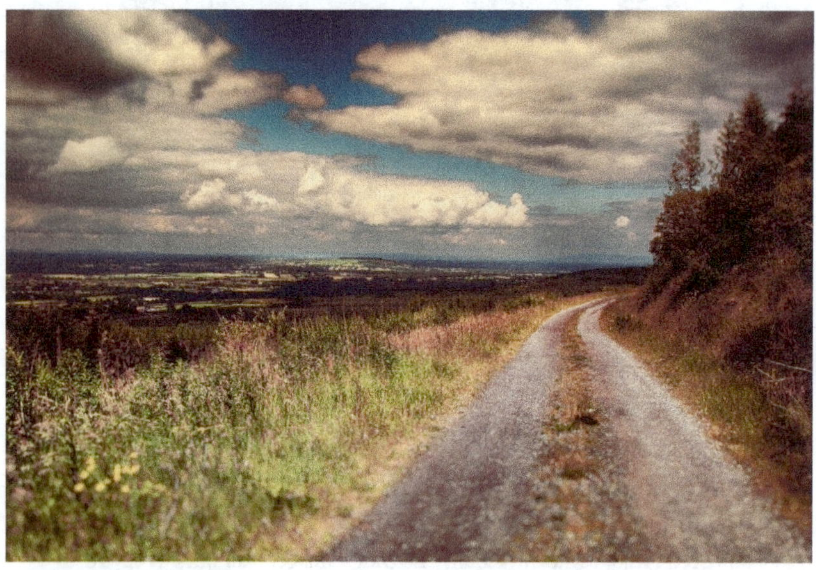

The view from Sliabh Bawn towards Strokestown, County Roscommon – Image: Paul Butler, June 2014.

Sliabh Bawn Wind Farm is located approximately five kilometres south-east of Strokestown, County Roscommon. The development is located at Doughill forest on Sliabh Bawn mountain and is now a fully operational windfarm and a wonderfully developed amenity area.

With Leitrim being that little further inland, you can be treated to a slightly later summer evening and usually a couple of extra degrees of warmth compared to at the coast. This passage from the short story 'The Country Funeral' recreates that atmosphere of golden warmth: 'On evenings like this I used to think it was on fire. Other times the sedge looked like gold. I remember it well' [*CS*, 'The Country Funeral' pp. 386–7].

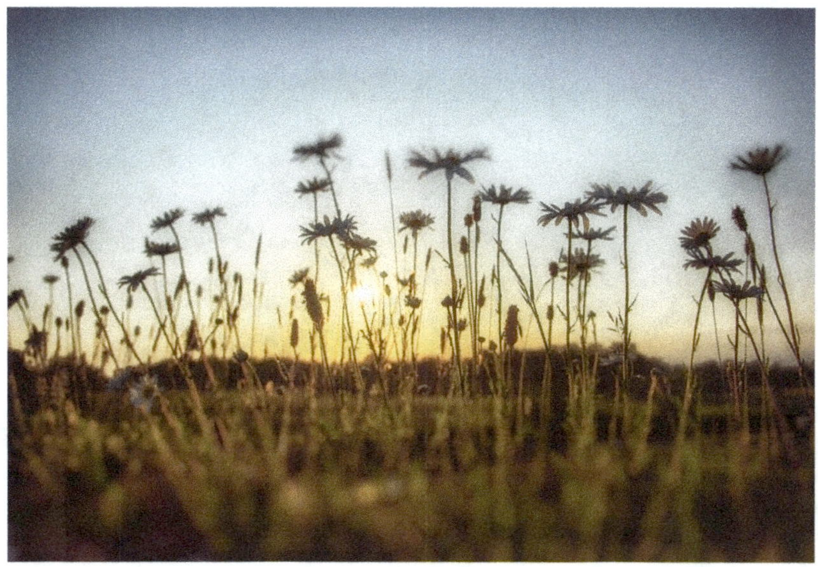

Golden Light on Wild Daisies at Tooman Bridge, County Leitrim – Image: Paul Butler, June 2018.

Photographic Note: These wildflowers grew happily among the crevices on Tooman Bridge.

During the summer month of June, wildflower start to sprout from within the crevices of the local bridges, which is a beautiful sight. In 2020, maintenance works were completed on Tooman Bridge, including repointing of the masonry. I do not think that wildflower will sprout from these crevices anytime soon. The fine weather signals a spring into action for the first or second cut, with local lads giving a strong salute as they hurtle past our gate on John Deere tractors pulling bouncing trailers full of silage. The cutting goes on through the night with the high fields floodlit and trailers in constant procession. Through the open bedroom window, the sound and heat carries through the night; there is no hiding from this essential part of country life. And if there has been a hot and dry spell, nothing matches the pleasure of those long and sweet-scented evenings that meander in rhythm with a distant and hypnotic engine hum. This is the second silage cut in motion.

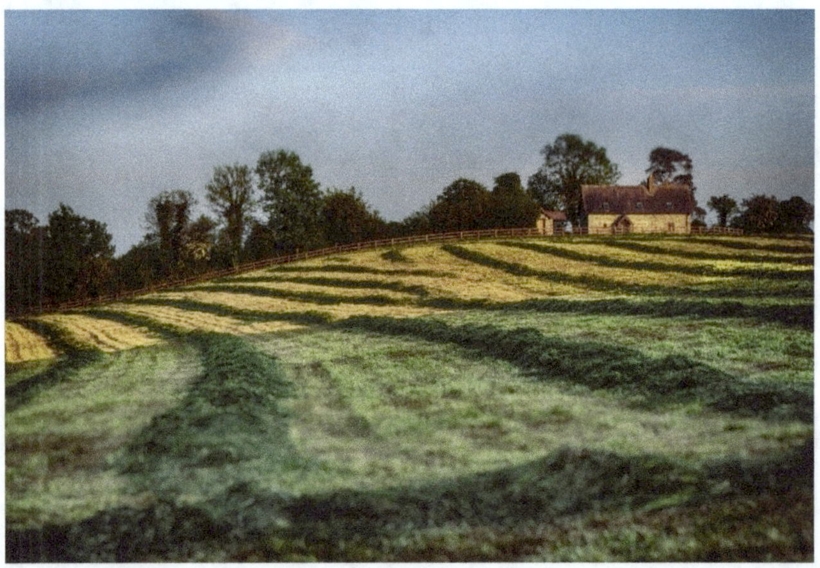

Drying the First Cut of Silage at the Pheasantry, Lough Rinn, County Leitrim – Image: Paul Butler, May 2012.

From a young age, the power of sunlight on this land had a profound effect on McGahern. His writing becomes powerfully spiritual as he details its emotional effect: 'If I could climb the hill while it rested in the whitethorns, I could walk through the sun to the gate of heaven' [*M*, p. 11].

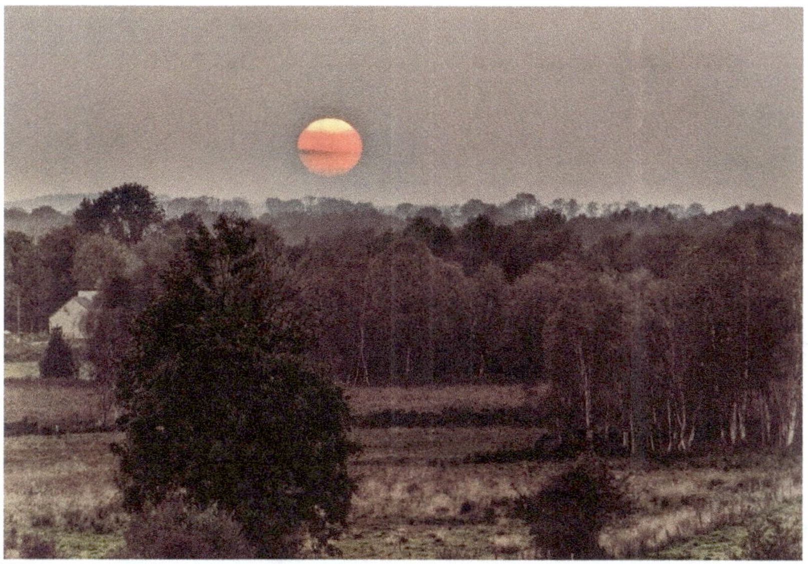

An Orange Globe Floats over Tooman, County Leitrim – Image: Paul Butler, October 2012.

And if you listen closely you can hear the soft whisper of a breeze gently rustling the lake shore.

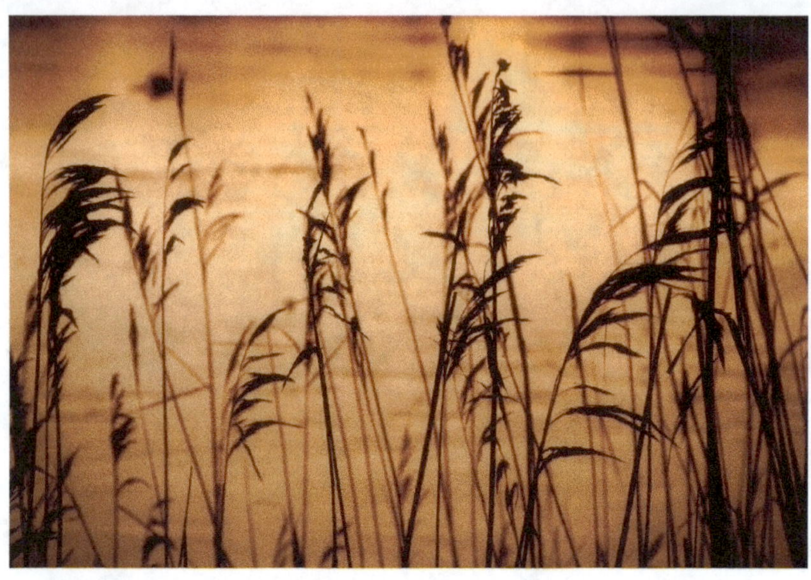

Golden Sunset at Lough Rinn, County Leitrim – Image: Paul Butler, January 2011.

> It was only the slow growing distance from the ring of reeds round the shore that told that the boat moved at all on the lake. [*CE*, 'High Ground', p. 190]

Walks under magical moonlight with his mother also left a profound mark on a young McGahern as he fondly remembers the safety and comfort he felt in her presence:

> The happiness of that walk and night under the pale moon was so intense that it brought on a light-headedness. [*M*, p. 64]

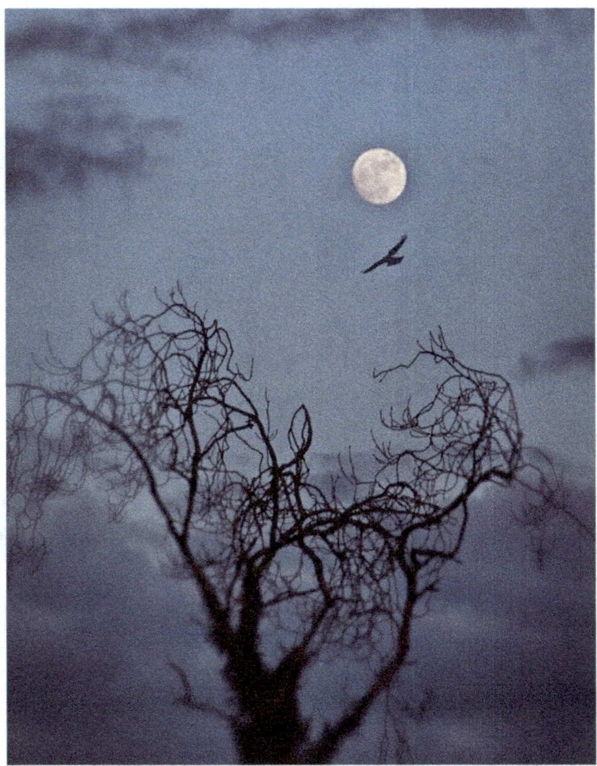

Bright Moon over Mel Grey's Farm, Farnocht, County Leitrim – Image: Paul Butler, February 2012.

Moonlit memories from childhood were stored, only to reappear later in his work.

> One night as I emerged from the tube, I was surprised by a round, orange moon above Whitechapel. For a moment, it seemed as if the moons of Gloria, of Oakport and Ollarton's had joined me in London. [*M*, p. 211]

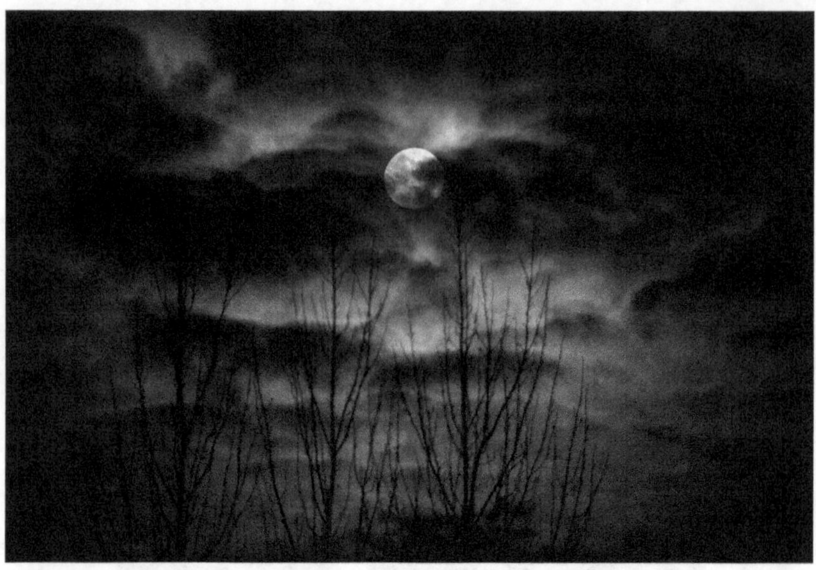

Winter Moon at Morning, Farnocht, County Leitrim Image: Paul Butler, November 2010.

Photographic Note: Photographing at night can be tricky because it is very easy to end up with a milky blob instead of a detailed moon. The idea is usually to expose for the moon to hold onto the detail: however, the foreground will end up dark and featureless as the exposure time will be relatively fast, which is fine if you just want silhouettes. If you expose for the foreground you will end up with a washed-out moon as the exposure will be too long. The image, 'Winter Moon', was a lucky shot. It was a cold November morning, and I was heading out into the car to drive to work in Dublin. The cloud cover broke, and a bright moon appeared through the boundary trees. The bruised black clouds were moving swiftly over the moon, and I just decided to take a snap. The lens was close to maximum, which is 300mm in 35mm terms. The aperture was set to f5.7 which is quite wide, and you would not have any foreground detail, the film speed (ISO in old terms) was set to auto. I was quite surprised by the result. It is not a great image technically: in fact, it is quite poor. Because it was so dark there is a lot of noise in the image (grain in the old analogue terms) due to the high speed needed to capture the scene. But the graininess of this image really creates a mood; it makes the image look more like a painting.

Lakes and rivers of Leitrim

As mentioned previously, Leitrim is home to many lakes and the River Shannon meanders through the south-west of the county. In recent years, the Leitrim County Council has been busy raising roads in certain areas that are prone to seasonal flooding. On either side of Tooman Bridge, heavy rainfall during the winter months causes Rinn River to fan out onto the surrounding callows (Irish: *caladh*). Callows are a type of wetland found in Ireland and are a seasonally flooded grassland ecosystem found on low-lying river floodplains. This can lend itself to help create a very moody landscape.

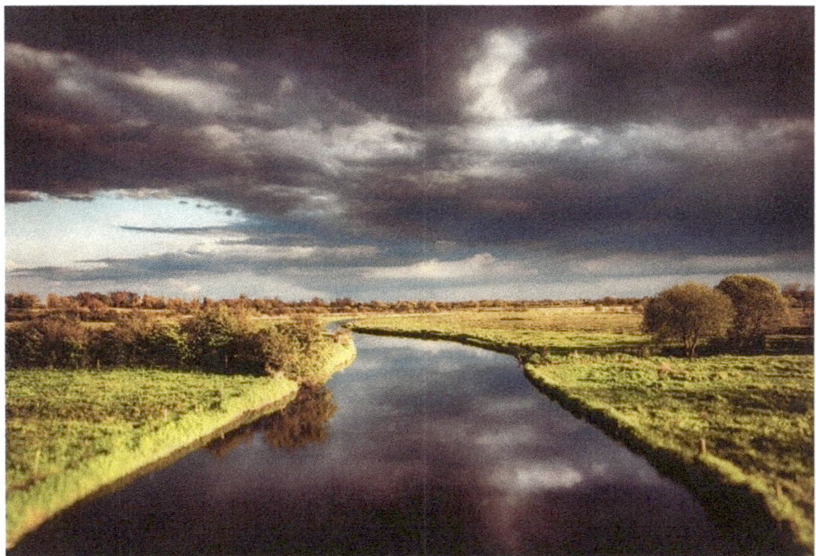

The Lazy Rinn River at Tooman Bridge, County Leitrim – Image: Paul Butler, May 2013.

The Rinn River is very slow moving and calm. In the winter months, it floods discreetly onto the surrounding callows and to such an extent that Leitrim County Council has had to raise the local road by quite a considerable height so that traffic can continue to use it. I like within the scene 'The Lazy Rinn' that the steel blue sky frames and reflects within the dark water, slowly meandering like a large snake. The stone capping in the foreground creates a nice perspective. On this May evening, a relaxed and setting sun threw a warm blanket across the sky. And within McGahern's work you will find many references to time spent on the water. The following passages really add drama to this moody black and white image of Lough Rinn on a cold and foggy October morning:

> The morning was clear. There was no wind on the lake. There was also a great stillness. [*RS*, p. 1]

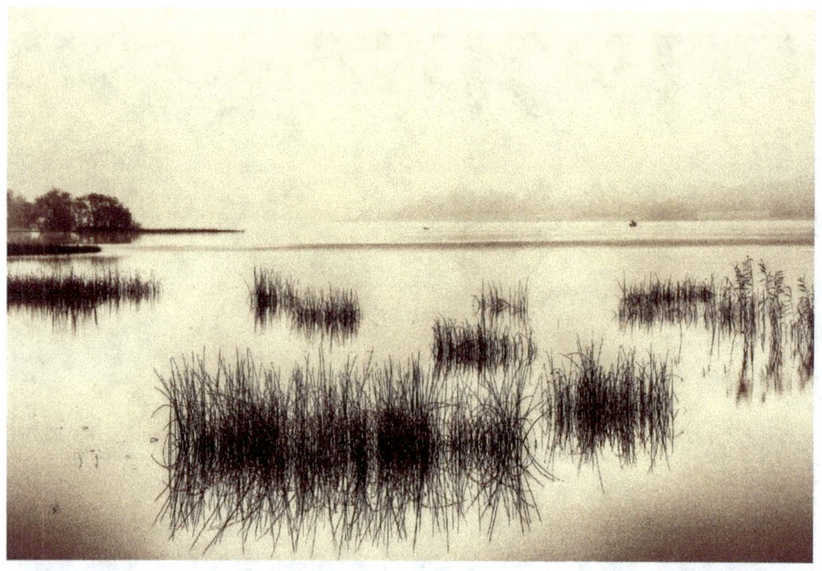

Autumn Morning Fog on Lough Rinn, County Leitrim – Image: Paul Butler, October 2010.

And just as the lakes and rivers of Leitrim entwine with the fabric of life, McGahern's memory of fishing with his father entwines with this dark passage from the short story 'Korea'.

> As the boat moved through the calm water and the line slipped through his fingers over the side I'd never felt so close to him before, not even when he'd carried me on his shoulders above the laughing crowd to the Final. Each move he made I watched as closely as if I too had to prepare myself to murder. [*CE*, 'Korea', p. 50]

'Korea' was adapted for the screen by Joe O'Byrne in 1995 and directed by Cathal Black. A powerful story of the relationship between father and son, John and Eamon Doyle, it is set in rural Ireland during the 1950s, a period of mass emigration and social change.[9]

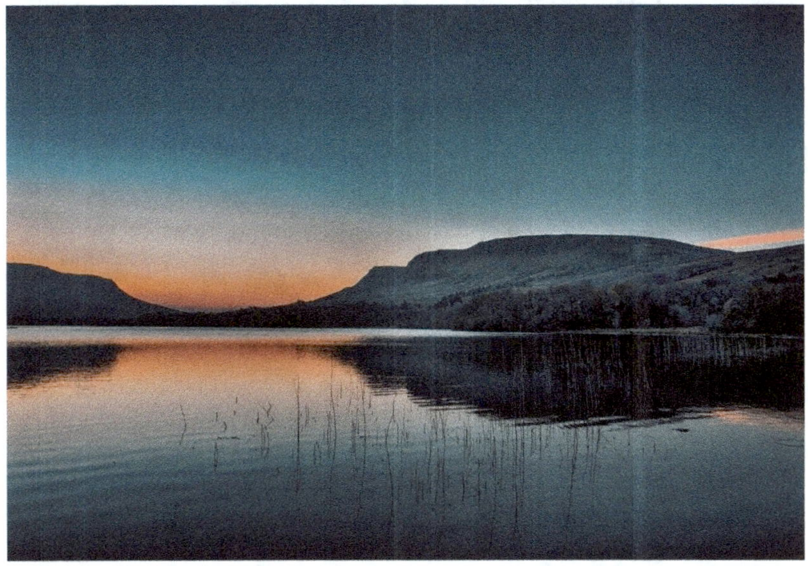

Sunset at Glenade Lough, County Leitrim – Image: Paul Butler, April 2021.

These beautiful and eloquent words quoted below, which are reproduced almost exactly from the story 'Love of the World', in McGahern's collection *Creatures of the Earth*, are inscribed upon a memorial dedicated to the writer close to the old Garda Barracks at Cootehall, County Roscommon, the setting for his first novel, *The Barracks*.

9 Cathal Black, *Korea*: <https://www.imdb.com/title/tt0113573/>.

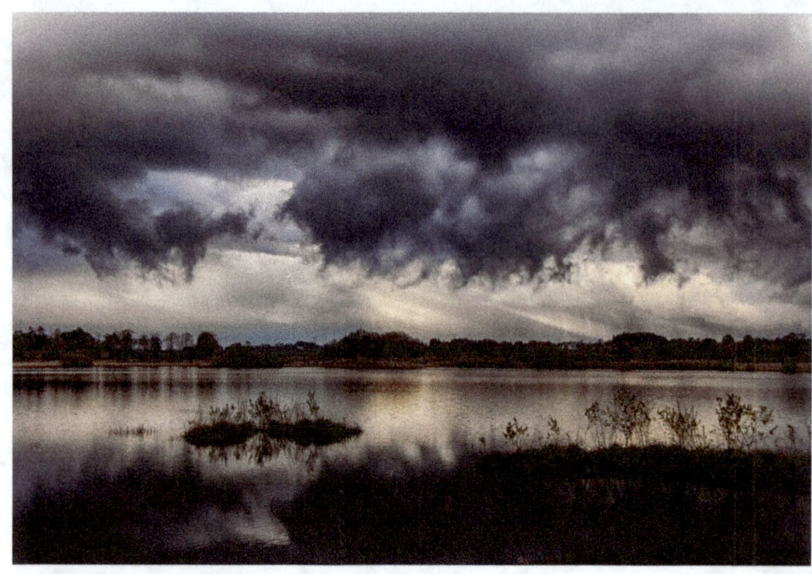

After the Rain, a Copper Sunset Washes over Lough Errew, County Leitrim – Image: Paul Butler, May 2013.

> A white moon rested on the water
> There was no wind
> The stars in their places were clear and fixed
> Who would want change since change will come without wanting?
> Who this night would not want to live?

This impressive stone bridge at Roosky rising over the Shannon was photographed from the Roscommon side. The bridge marks the county boundary between Leitrim and Roscommon. This five-arch masonry road bridge was built in 1845 by the Commissioners for the Improvement of the Navigation of the River Shannon. In 1970, an automatic lift bridge replaced the original swing bridge to allow cruise vessels to pass under.

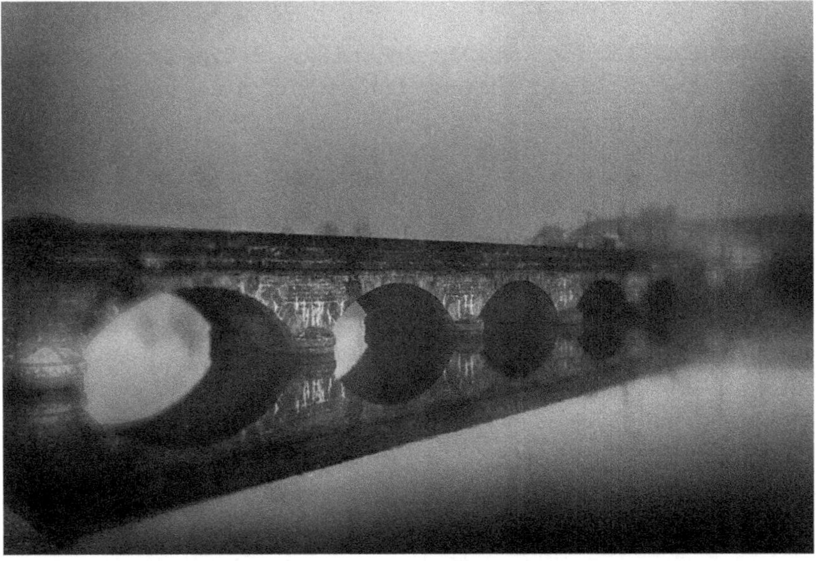

Early Morning Fog at Roosky Bridge, from the Roscommon side – Image: Paul Butler, February 2017.

Photographic Note: There was a slight fog that morning and the muted colours were helped by a heavily diffuse light as the sun fought to burn through the fog. I added some *Bokeh* to enhance the mood and atmosphere of this scene.

Roosky is approximately eight kilometres from our home in Farnocht. Roosky is an important stop for cruising vessels on the Shannon waterways. This village was once on the N4 primary route to Sligo and had a very good passing trade. Unfortunately, a devastating fire at the local Glanbia factory in 2002, which was a big provider of local employment, and the opening of the Roosky/Dromod bypass in 2007 caused the village to somewhat wither. Hard work by the community association helps keep the village tidy and vibrant. On the far right in the image 'Early Morning' is the Shannon Key West Hotel, which is situated on the Leitrim side of Roosky. This hotel has been closed since the economic downturn of 2011 and came to national prominence in 2018–19 when the government hoped to use it to provide accommodation for eighty asylum seekers. The objective to turn the former hotel into a direct provision centre for refugees from Syria ran into opposition. Divided local opinion about the location and suitability included demonstrations and two arson attacks that led to the project being abandoned. To date, the hotel remains shuttered.

The Glens of Leitrim

The northern part of the county is stunning: a treasure of mountains and lakes. If you take the Manorhamilton to Bundoran Road (R280) you will pass through the Glens of Leitrim, with the magnificent Dartry Mountains guiding you on your way towards the coast. The Dartry Mountains, Sléibhte Dhartraí, range across north Leitrim and Sligo. The mountains lie between Lough Melvin, Lough Gill and Lough MacNean. The highest section is at Truskmore which is 647 metres, and to the south in County Sligo, you will find the dramatic peak of Benbulben.

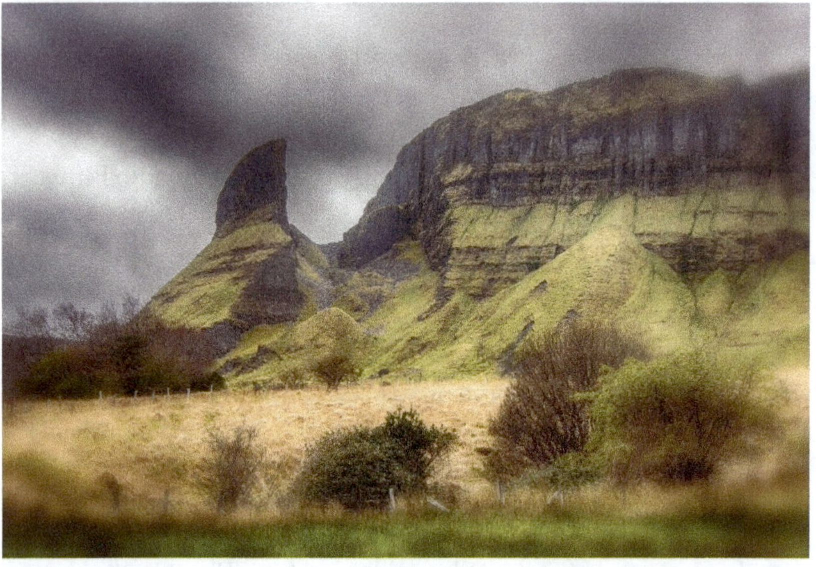

Eagle's Rock, Glenade, County Leitrim – Image: Paul Butler, March 2019.

Located in the beautiful Dartry Mountains is a cliff face that is officially named Eagle's Rock. It is in Glenade, County Leitrim, and is Ireland's highest free-standing tower; its peak is 330 metres above sea level and can be viewed for many miles in all directions. Many people are unaware that this type of dramatic scenery is a part of the landscape of Leitrim. Eagle's Rock looks more akin to the landscape of Death Valley in Nevada than this quiet valley in the north-west of the county. This dramatic scenery from a geological perspective is described here by Samuel Lewis in *A Topographical Dictionary of Ireland* (1837):

> The geology of the County presents many remarkable features. The lowest strata are those of the primary mountain range entering from the County of Sligo and extending from south-west to north-east: this range is mostly composed of mica slate; a green steatite, thickly studded with valuable garnets, has been found at the foot of a mountain near Lurganboy. On the western base of Benbo a clay of a blueish white hue has been found and used for fullers earth: the western side of the same mountain is traversed by a metallic vein containing copper pyrites, which was formerly wrought.[10]

I genuinely believe that the stunning scenery of north Leitrim is as good, if not better than that in the south of the country, particularly in Cork and Kerry. The difference and benefit to the southern counties is the presence of a large airport at Shannon which allows for the easy transportation of tourists, particularly Americans, to these counties. It is hard to understand why Leitrim and the north-west are really losing out in terms of tourism when north Leitrim is just over seventy minutes from Knock International Airport in County Mayo.

10 Samuel Lewis, 'Leitrim Geology': <https://www.libraryireland.com/topog/L/Leitrim-Geology.php> (1837).

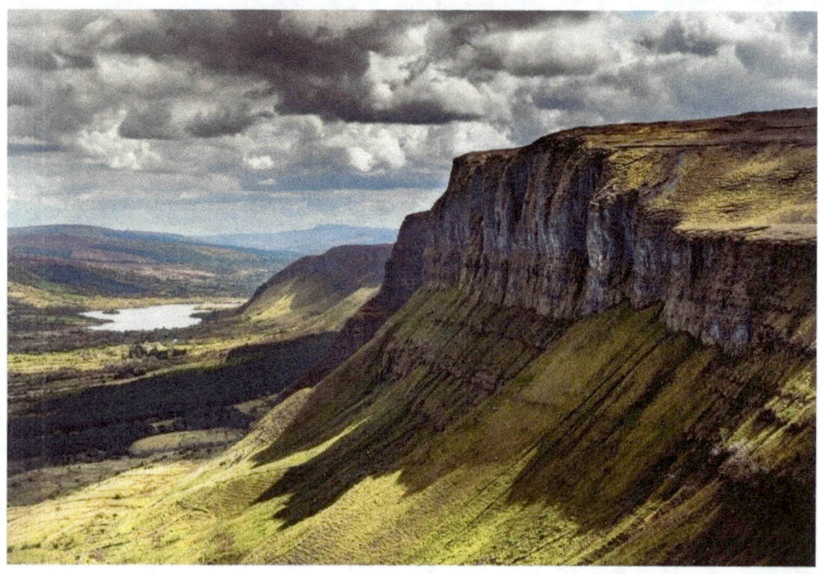

The View towards Glenade Lough, County Leitrim – Image: Paul Butler, May 2021.

Leitrim has a coastline

As discussed previously, people are very surprised when you mention that Leitrim has a coastline. The Leitrim coastline overlooked by the Arroo Mountain offers breathtaking views of the Atlantic Ocean towards County Donegal. It is a spectacular piece of coastline.

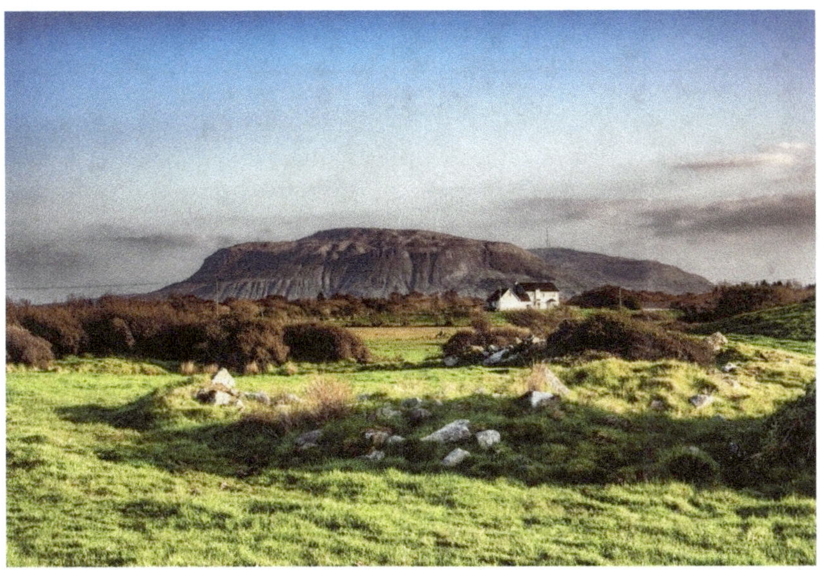

Looking towards Arroo Mountain from the Leitrim Coast Road – Image: Paul Butler, April 2021.

Tullaghan is the most northerly village in Leitrim and is located on Leitrim's four-kilometre coastline which happens to be the shortest coastline of any county in Ireland. As Tullaghan is bypassed you could easily miss the turn off for the village and be in Donegal before you realize it. The village is also the site of an ancient High Cross discovered on the shore after a storm and erected in 1778 by the local landlord. It is thought to have originated from a long-vanished monastery near the seashore. This strip of Leitrim coast wedged between Sligo and Donegal is a popular surfing spot. And now this piece of coast is part of the Wild Atlantic Way and as Fáilte Ireland states: 'Ireland's first long-distance touring route launched in 2014; the route stretches from the Inishowen Peninsula in Donegal to Kinsale in County Cork and is garnering significant interest overseas'. And on the official Wild Atlantic Way website, one reads: 'Lovely Leitrim might not be as well-known as some of its Wild Atlantic Way counterparts but underestimate it at your own peril.'[11]

11 Discover Ireland, 'Wild Atlantic Way': <https://www.wildatlanticway.com/highlights/your-wild-atlantic-way-in-pictures-2018>.

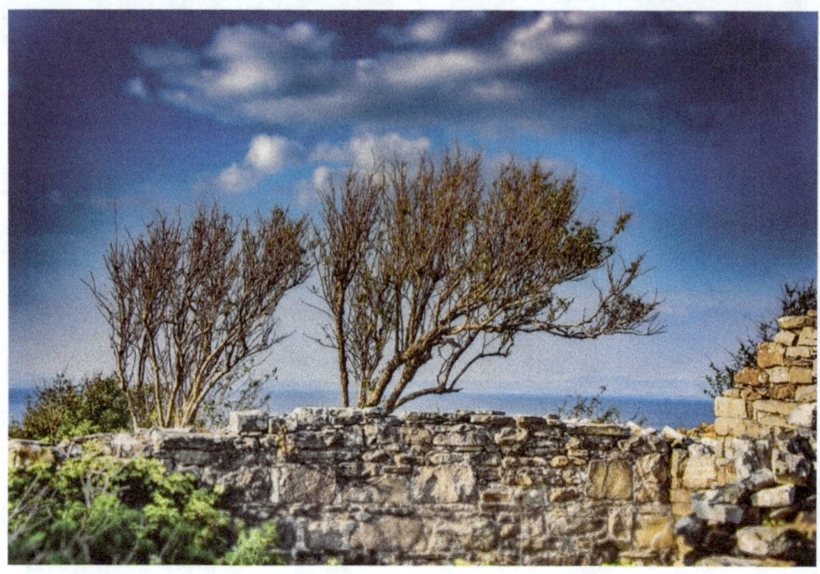

Leitrim Coast Road near Tullaghan, Looking towards St Johns Point in County Donegal – Image: Paul Butler, April 2021.

There is no actual beach on this stretch of Leitrim coastline; you will find only large stones and boulders. Public access to the sea on this stretch of coast is limited as it is private agricultural land. On either side of the Leitrim coastline, you have the wonderful strand of Mullaghmore to the south in County Sligo and Bundoran Strand to the north in County Donegal. The River Drowes enters the sea at Tullaghan and is well renowned for wild salmon fishing. McGahern, to my knowledge, does not mention the coastline of Leitrim, but I feel that it should not be overlooked.

Strandhill

Strandhill in County Sligo is evoked in McGahern's short story of the same name. It is possibly more accessible if travelling from south and mid-Leitrim. It also has a fantastic beach which, unfortunately, the Leitrim coastline does not. Strandhill is a place that is close to my heart, and I have spent a lot of time over the years photographing its shifting landscape and ever-changing horizon. Strandhill and Aughris Head, further along the Sligo coast, are my special places. I now allow McGahern's words and my images to evoke the mood.

> Even the strand, reached in good weather, the mile downhill accomplished, the mile home uphill yet out of mind, and in possession of strand of Strandhill, long and level for miles. [*CE*, 'Strandhill, The Sea', p. 39]

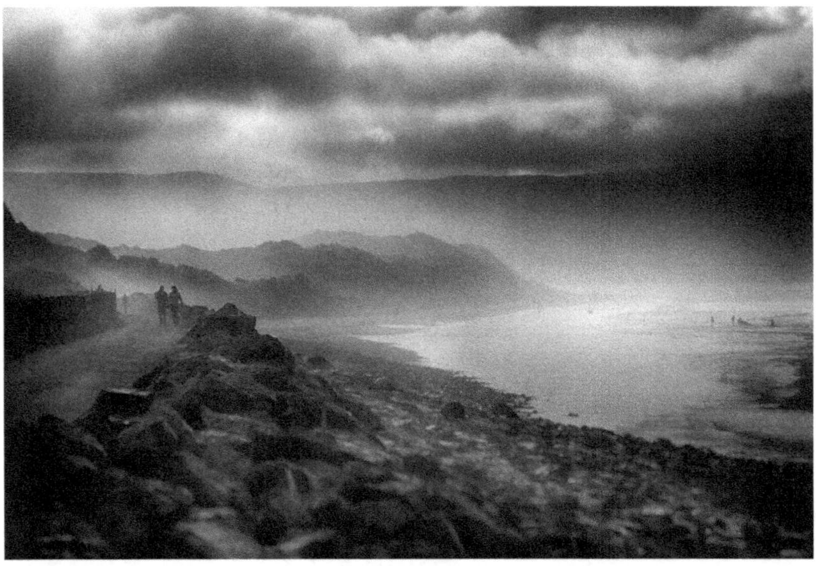

December Sea Mist and Rolling Cloud at Strandhill, County Sligo – Image: Paul Butler, December 2013.

Photographic Note: This is one of my favourite images from Strandhill; it was recorded on a cold December Day, the first day of December several years ago. The rolling sea mist and dark boulders give it a mythical, almost post-battle feel. The two people walking towards the camera draw your eye to the path while the far distant surfers add to the openness of the scene. I have a large 30 inch by 20 inch print of this scene hanging in my office.

The preferred time for visiting Strandhill is from October to April. There is a range of photographic opportunities owing to the quality of light and cloud formations, and these can alter within a few minutes as weather systems roll in from the North Atlantic. Usually, it is a case of running for cover as low rain clouds sweep ominously inwards, across the inlet, rushing up the strand and dousing everyone in its path. This is swiftly followed by a burst of sunlight tracing rays across the dunes. And within a short while, the whole weather process repeats itself, a phenomenon that is both refreshing and rewarding.

The late American landscape photographer and environmentalist Ansel Easton Adams was known for his black and white images of the American West.[12] He is possibly the greatest landscape photographer, and I admire his work immensely. His black and white images, shot on very large format cameras with incredibly long exposures and printed skilfully on platinum paper, are a sight to behold. In this section, with some of my black and white images of Strandhill, I pay homage to his work. McGahern mentions the annual trips to the sea in *Memoir*: 'Every year my father took a bungalow for two weeks beside the ocean in Strandhill' [*M*, p. 180].

12 Ansel Adams, 'Ansel Adams Gallery': <http://anseladams.com/>.

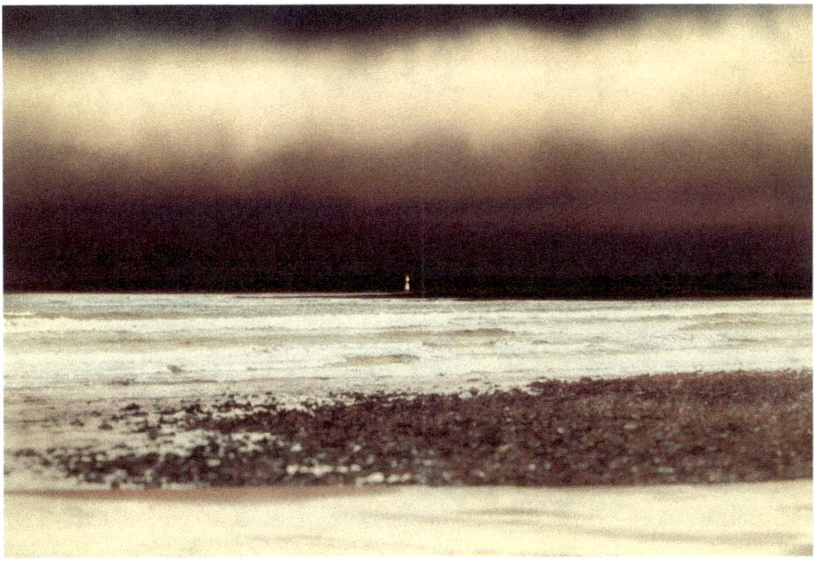

Forbidding Sky over Blackrock Lighthouse in Sligo bay, County Sligo – Image: Paul Butler, December 2017.

Photographic Note: The sky was darkening the day I recorded this image, and I noticed the Blackrock Lighthouse dwarfed and illuminated by the threatening sky. In post-production, I darkened the sky further (in the old hand printing days, this would be referred to as 'burning'). To make the lighthouse stand out, I painstakingly lightened it (in the old hand printing, days this would be referred to as 'dodging'). Your eye is drawn to the tiny bright beacon.

With Knocknarea and Queen Maedbh's Cairn dominating the skyline over Strandhill, it is one of the most striking landmarks in the entire country. The giant rocky cairn of 'Queen Maeve's Grave' atop the mountain is the largest unopened cairn in Ireland that is thought to conceal a Neolithic passage tomb. On a clear day, you can witness a panoramic view from the summit that is hard to rival. Due to its excellent surfing conditions, Strandhill has also been selected as the location for the National Centre of Excellence for Surfing which was due to open in 2020.

> Mist halfway down the slopes of Knocknarea, rain and mist blurring the sea.
> [*CE*, 'Strandhill, The Sea', p. 41]

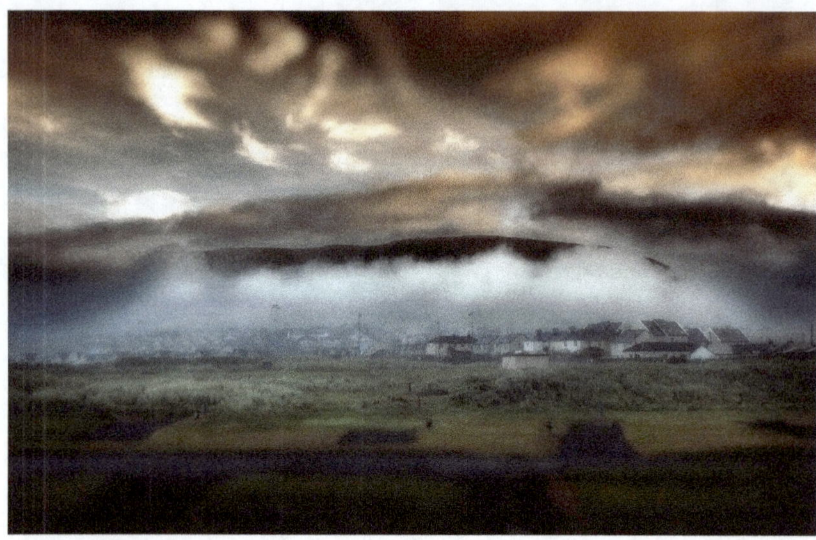

Off Season at the Camping and Caravan Park at Strandhill Overlooked by Knocknarea, County Sligo – Image: Paul Butler, December 2013.

Photographic Note: With photography, sometimes, you are just in the right place at the right time, though it pays to visit and revisit an area. The low cloud had been stuck on Knockarea all day, and the scene was pretty bland. Suddenly the cloud started to break, and the mountain came into view as I walked through the deserted caravan park. I got a couple of images before the cloud completely dispersed. The empty caravan berths and the cloud breaking create a dramatic and desolate feeling and the houses huddled at the base create a sense of hibernation.

The warrior Queen Maedbh is synonymous with Connacht; here is a small extract from an account written in 1888 by Lady Jane Francesca Wilde:

> Maeve, the great queen of Connaught, holds a distinguished place in Bardic Legends. When she went, to battle, it is said, she rode in an open car, accompanied by four chariots – one before, another behind, and one on each side – so that the golden assion on her head and her royal robes should not be defiled by the dust of the horses' feet, or the foam of the fiery steeds; for all the sovereigns of Ireland sat crowned with a diadem in battle, as they drove in their war-chariots, as well as in the festal and the public assemblies.[13]

13 Lady Jane Francesca Wilde, 'Queen Maeve': <https://www.libraryireland.com/AncientLegendsSuperstitions/Queen-Maeve.php> (1888).

Walking on the long strand from the village of Strandhill, you face the wild Atlantic Ocean and to the west, the coastline towards Dumoran Strand and Aughris Head. To the north of Strandhill is Benbulbin, a large flat-topped rock formation that is part of the Dartry Mountains. Benbulbin is a protected area, designated as a County Geological Site by Sligo County Council. In my opinion Benbulbin is more impressive than the famed 'Table Mountain' in Cape Town, South Africa, which I have had the privilege of visiting. Surrounded by hills, rivers, lakes and woodlands, Strandhill is an absolute gem of a place. To trek this ancient landscape is so good for the soul; you have the sea in front of you and the mountains behind. People of all ages, mostly with dogs in tow, head towards the sea ramp, ready for a brisk walk on the strand. The dogs strain, bursting to get off the leash and break into wild running in pursuit of an erratically thrown tennis ball or stick. Screaming children run in all directions, and couples walk slowly into the distance, soon becoming tiny figures against the headland.

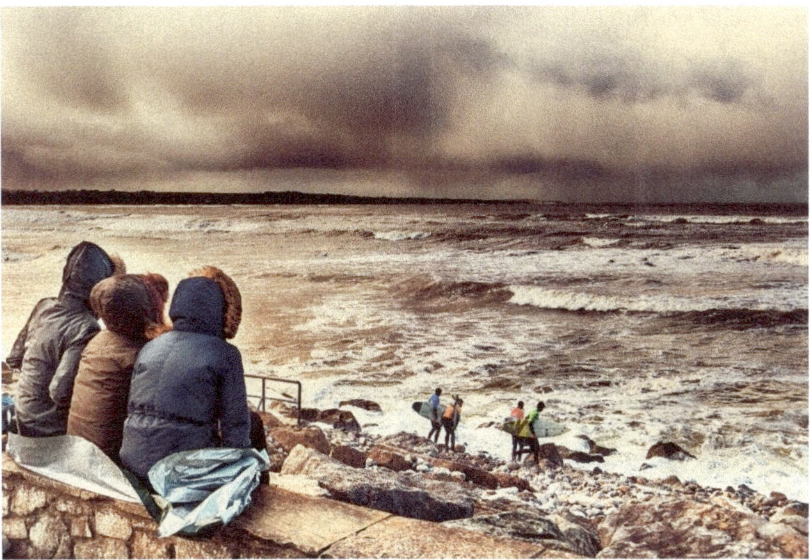

Watching the Surfers on a Cold and Windy Day, Strandhill, County Sligo – Image: Paul Butler, March 2016.

The waters are considered wild and dangerous, and swimming is forbidden at Strandhill Beach due to shifting sands and strong underwater currents; however, there is rarely a day that you will not find surfers waiting for an appropriate wave. The car park facing the sea is always busy with camper vans and cars, with wet suits drooped over the roof and surf boards standing to attention. The hardy souls get ready to enter the frothy fray as wrapped up onlooker's shiver against the strong wind and huddle in groups.

Through the seasons: Autumn to winter

A debate has raged in rural Ireland around the planting of state forest and their effect on the local wildlife and in some cases on people's mental health. The following article appeared in the *Irish Independent* in November 2018: 'Forestry has become a major part of the rural landscape and life in Leitrim. Almost 19pc of the County is covered by trees, mostly Sitka spruce.[14]' In September 2019, a government report on forestry in Leitrim confirms dominant use of Sitka spruce and campaign group criticizes 'over-reliance' on conifers in plantations.[15] I have noticed that when the forest was cleared around our area a few years ago, the amount of light permeating the landscape increased dramatically, inducing wildflower to recolonize the clearing and for a more diverse colour pallet to evolve.

14 Claire Fox, 'Leitrim and the Gigantic Forest Debate': <https://www.independent.ie/business/farming/forestry-enviro/forestry/leitrim-and-the-gigantic-forest-debate-37545279.html> (24 November 2018).

15 Kevin O'Sullivan, 'Report on Forestry in Leitrim Confirms Dominant Use of Sitka Spruce': <https://www.irishtimes.com/news/environment/report-on-forestry-in-leitrim-confirms-dominant-use-of-sitka-spruce-1.4005658> (3 September 2019).

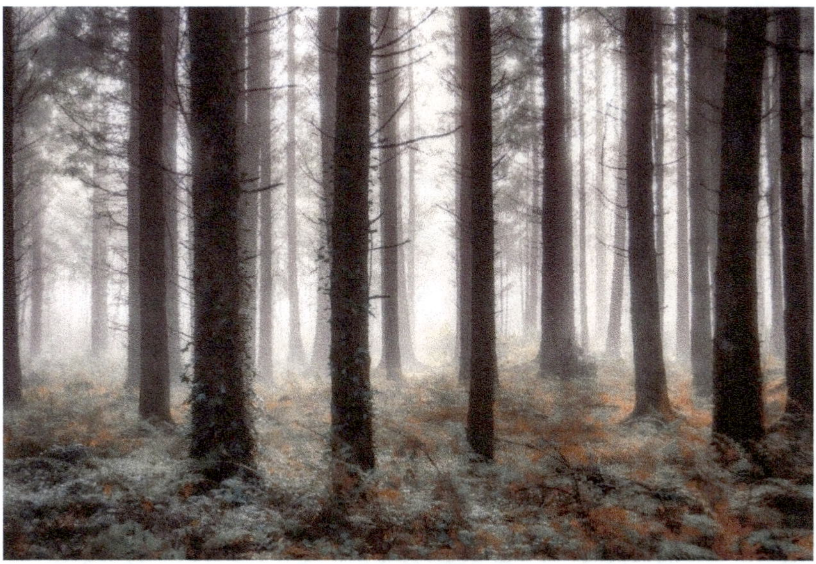

October Fog in the Wood, Farnocht, County Leitrim – Image: Paul Butler, November 2010. Photographic Note: Low October fog creates a mythical feel which greatly enhances the silence of this scene.

Reading through McGahern's short stories, one encounters descriptions like the following:

> There was no longer the dripping on the dead leaves, the wood clamped in the silence of white frost except for the racket some bird made in the undergrowth. [*CE*, 'Christmas', p. 19]

The concern for people surrounded by these plantations is that they really dominate the local environment. In some ways this contradicts the belief that getting out and walking in the woods has such a positive effect on your mental health. This I agree with, however, as if you must live in an area surrounded by these plantations, the loss of light can influence your sense of well-being.

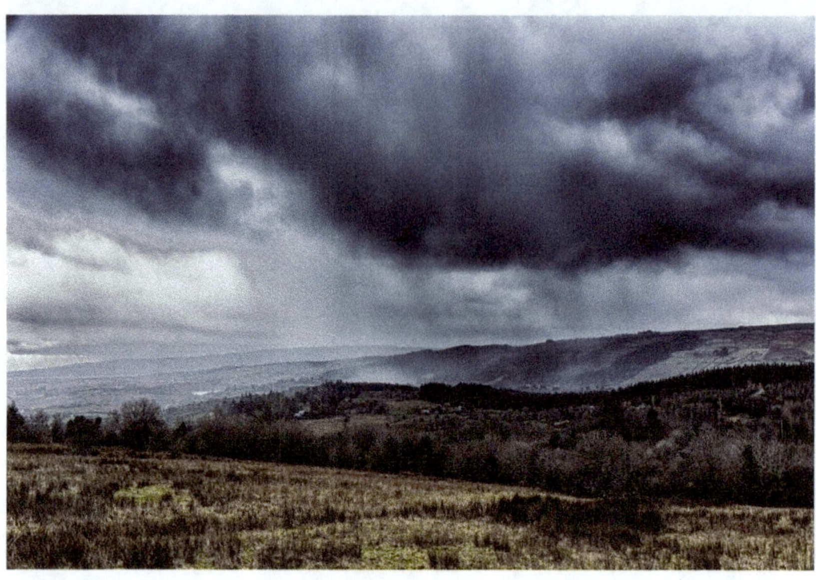

Rainclouds over a Commercial Forest Plantation, Close to Lough Allen, County Leitrim – Image: Paul Butler, March 2021.

As our life started to gather momentum in Leitrim, more and more photographic opportunities spread out before me. In early autumn with the dense Sitka spruce plantations carpeted in a morning mist, the inner darkness suddenly illuminates with shafts of golden light that reveal old native wood, hidden by the lake. I sling the camera over my shoulder and push through the low-lying branches to break out onto the lake shore to watch a large, bruised and bulging cloud roll across the sky. There is a certain heavy stillness that greets you when you scramble through state forestry. Nothing stirs within, and the light is reduced to a faint glow. The deep pile of dead pine needles is soft underfoot. Because of the density of tree planting, it is not inviting for wildlife or plant life, and the silence is deafening. The reward only arrives when you break through to the old native woodlands still hugging the breezy shoreline of Lough Rinn, their vibrant moss clad trunks and still leafed beech trees, an Aladdin's Cave of colour. The state forestry company, Coillte, cleared many local wood belts a few years ago and the newly planted saplings are starting to rise and outmanoeuvre the local fauna. At this moment of writing, the area is bathed in extra light and should remain so for the foreseeable future, though within the re-planted areas the saplings are now growing rapidly. When localized fog sits close to the ground, it creates the most atmospheric scene: everything slows, delicate moisture coats the grass and hedgerows and when that fog is accompanied by a freeze, the senses heighten to the sound of a crunch underfoot, or the squawk of a jay as it bolts from the trees flying low over the high fields parallel to the access road close by our home. McGahern once more provides an apt and evocative description:

> The weak winter sun had thawed the fields soft enough to course the hare on, and though it still hung blood-orange above the hawthorns on the hill the rims of the hoof tracks were already hardening fast against their tread. [*CE*, 'All Sorts of Impossible Things', p. 90]

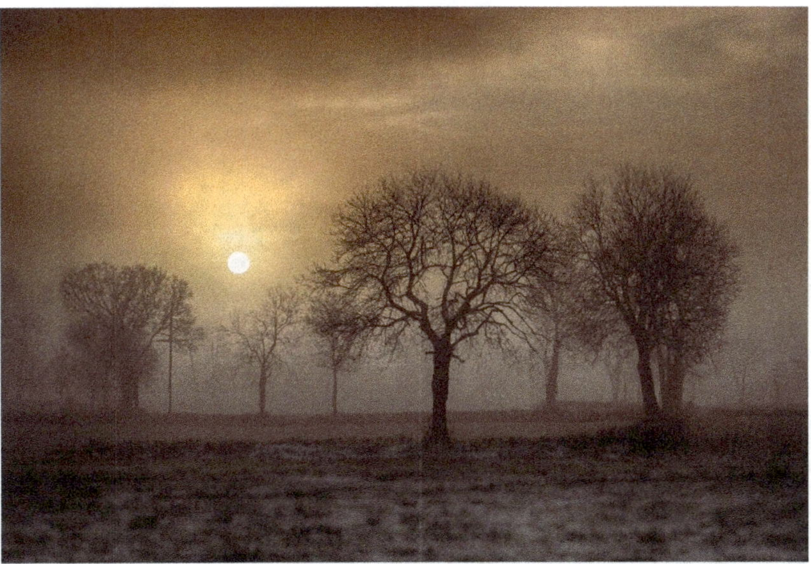

Frost on McGarry's Field, Farnocht, County Leitrim – Image: Paul Butler, January 2021.

Photographic Note: Freezing fog and the landscape takes on a ghostly aura and the trees take a human form.

Even the heavy days of winter with constant grey sagging cloud has the effect of creating a neutral light on the falling leaves and leaf litter carpet. The scene 'Setting Sun over the Cemetery' is of a small access road that runs past the graveyard at Farnocht, close to our home. When we get a decent snowfall, like this one in the image which was recorded in December 2010, the powdery snow has a fantastic dampening effect on background noise. The silence is absolute, and I always walk slowly and head up towards the mound on which the Lime Kiln stands, which is further down this access road. The graveyard, church and Lime Kiln are all formerly part of Lough Rinn Estate and are marvellous pieces of architecture. When you climb the mound and look out over the large white-covered field below, its majestic oak and whitethorn trees guarding the centre, it is breathtaking. No sound. No sounds at all save for the soft 'phump' as my feet sink through soft snow to the grass beneath.

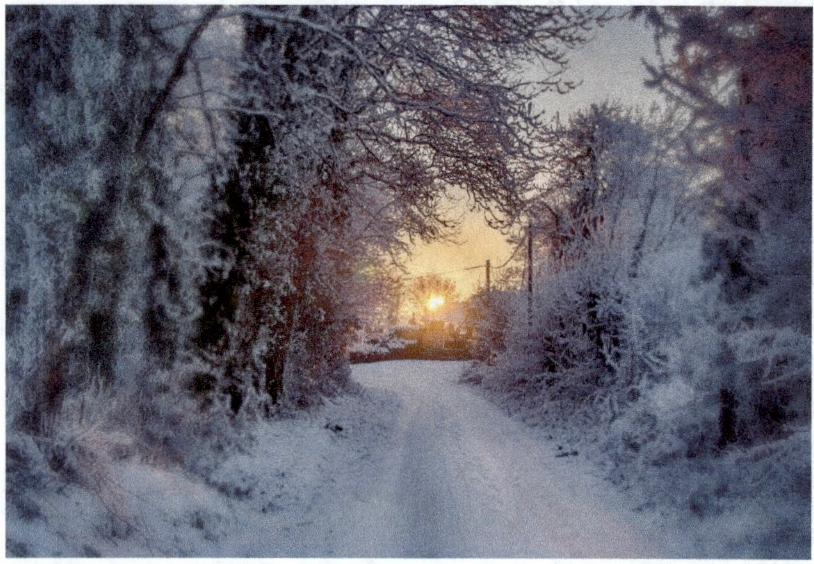

Setting Sun over the Cemetery at Farnocht, County Leitrim – Image: Paul Butler, December 2010.

Each day is different: the sky is never the same; the water on the lakes sparkles in new ways. With the winter redwings calling in the night sky, I feel fresh and ready to start again. I know that this is my home – a place I share not just with the people of Leitrim but also with McGahern and all his readers who commune with the pictures and scenes he evokes. I am often asked why I moved to Leitrim. Setting aside the long journey to my place of work in Dublin, the rewards are plain to see, literally. The images that accompany this chapter, taken during the four seasons of the calendar year, I hope will bear witness to the rich tapestry of what surrounds me when I return from work each evening. Stepping out of the car to be greeted by the cats and dogs, a clear and fresh night sky overhead, I let my breath wisp away into the night. Very recently I was speaking with a good neighbour about Leitrim and the landscape. He is a born and bred Leitrim man and part of the farming community. He asked me if I would ever think of moving back to the city now that our child was reared. I told him honestly that I could not. Leitrim is my home.

CHAPTER 3

A sense of place

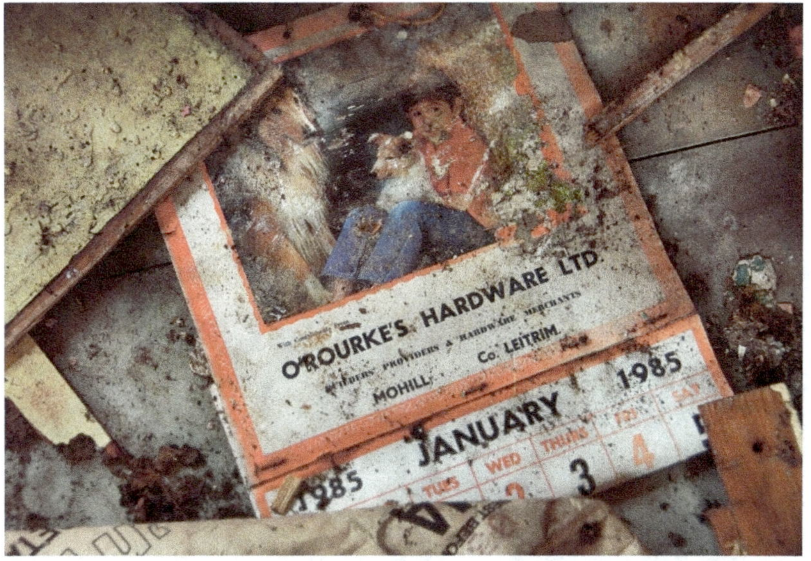

Butchers Calendar, Gortletteragh, County Leitrim – Image: Paul Butler, April 2011.

The Great Famine had such a terrible effect on the small Leitrim population that you are more likely to meet someone with Leitrim roots outside of Ireland rather than within Ireland. It devastated Ireland, with Leitrim suffering in a particularly bad way. The population of the county declined from 155,297 (Census 1841) to 111,897 (Census 1851). And thereafter it kept on declining. According to the Census of 1991, the population of the county had dwindled to 25,301. That is a drop of over 130,000 people in

150 years! The good news though is that according to the Census of 2016, the population of Leitrim rose by 32,044.[1]

Capturing a sense of place is a difficult and essential part of McGahern's literary undertaking. The following is an insightful definition from Terrain.org of a 'sense of place': 'Either the intrinsic character of a place, or the meaning people give to it, but, more often, a mixture of both. Some places are distinctive through their physical appearance, like Newgrange; others are distinctive, but have value attached to them, like the Cliffs of Moher. Less striking places have meaning and value attached to them because they are "home", and it is argued that attachment to a place increases with the distinctiveness of that place.'[2]

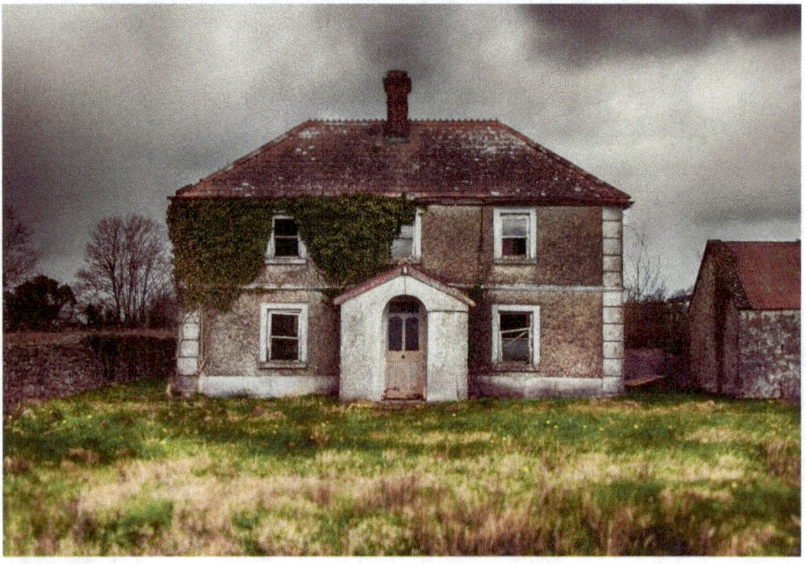

Farmhouse (Now Demolished), Oghil, Drumlish, County Longford – Image: Paul Butler, April 2014.

1 Central Statistics Office, 'Census Data': <https://data.cso.ie/>.

2 Simmons B. Buntin, 'What Is Sense of Place?': <https://www.terrain.org/ecomedia/q1/definitions.htm>.

This beautiful old 'Farmhouse' once resided just off the R198 Drumlish to Ballinalee Road in County Longford. It was a very imposing home and was on my photographic 'to do' list for a long time. One day I finally visited and obtained some fantastic images of the interior and the exterior. The house was demolished, and, in its place, a completely new dwelling now resides. It was a shame to lose such an imposing and what I thought to be a very architecturally pleasing structure. The poet Seamus Heaney related to place as follows: 'It is this feeling, assenting, equable marriage between the geographical country and the country of the mind.'[3] This would correspond to McGahern's treatment of place: it is one that is full of tenderness, while demonstrating an awareness of how people can be moulded in a negative way by their environment, depending on their experience of 'place'. What does it mean to experience a place? This question was put to architect Aishwarya Murari:

> You experience all 'places' (actually it should be: you experience all 'spaces'), your bedroom, living room, study, school, roads, alleys. Everything. The general definition for the word 'place' is: a specific location. You would experience any place if you were present there physically. The difference is in observing it or observing what is happening in it.[4]

As a place, Leitrim is the least densely populated county in Ireland. According to the Western Development Commission, Leitrim has a landmass of 158,885 hectares with a population density of 20.17 persons per square kilometre. The population of the county has grown by 5 per cent from 32,044 in 2016 to 35,087 in 2022.[5] There are no universities within the county, and just like swallows who must migrate, when finishing secondary school, students move to the bigger cities and towns to continue their education and in most cases when their studies are complete, they go elsewhere in search of employment. Financial services such as AvantCard and Bank of America are based in Leitrim, and the tourism industry in

3 Seamus Heaney, 'A Sense of Place (1977)', in *Preoccupations: Selected Prose* (London: Faber & Faber 1980), p. 132.

4 Quora, 'What Does It Mean to Experience a Place?': <https://www.quora.com/What-does-it-mean-to-experience-a-place> (2015).

5 Western Development Commission, 'Leitrim': <https://www.wdc.ie/County-profiles/leitrim/> (2016).

also is a big employer. In addition, forestry, food, the creative sector and farming, all add to the social fabric of the county. However, while I may find Leitrim beautiful, peaceful and invigorating, it has been remarked to me on many occasions that for those born and reared locally there is also a great desire to get the hell out of the place to see the world and experience life. The following quote reminds us of what is happening today in rural Ireland with the closure of post offices, Garda barracks and the disappearance of so many public houses. The short, sharp piece from a McGahern story, 'Wheels', accurately portrays how the heart is being ripped out of small rural communities: 'Quiet as a graveyard', he took up. 'And stare at beauty every day and it'll turn sicker than stray vomit. The barracks shut now, a squad car in its place' [*CE*, 'Wheels', p. 10].

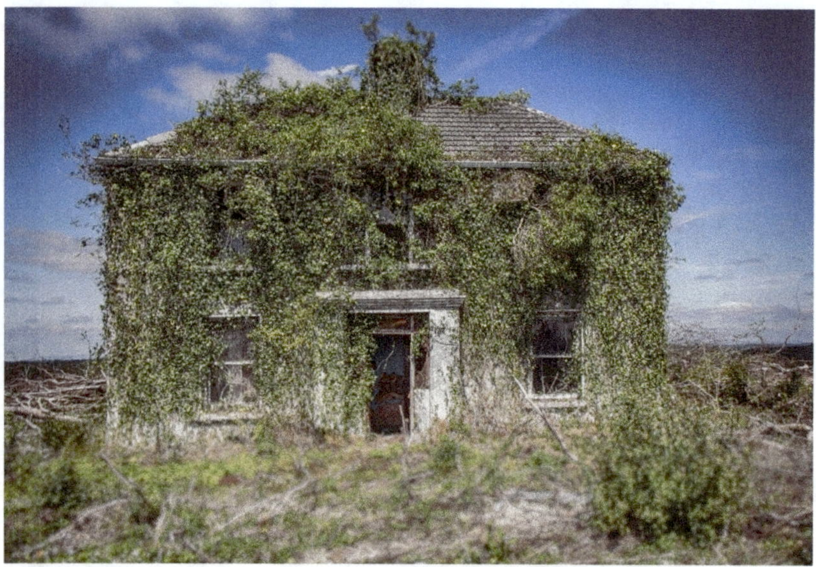

Ivy-Clad House Cloonee, County Leitrim – Image: Paul Butler, July 2019.

Photographic Note: The house 'Ivy Clad' recently became visible to the world after spending close to forty years completely entombed within a commercial forestry plantation. Everything was left in situ and the trees were planted right up to the front of the house. Situated on a steep rise, this farmhouse is in the parish of Gortletteragh in County Leitrim, enjoying a commanding view over the surrounding countryside. The front of the house faces towards Drumlish in County Longford, in the province of Leinster. It was a very fine setting for a home, and it could be again.

Certain abandoned dwellings that I revisit have now gone, wiped clean from the landscape, just like the scene 'The Pink Door', a beautiful old pink shop front. I photographed this welcoming and characterful shop front in June 2013 in Strokestown, which is a heritage town in County Roscommon. You pass through Strokestown when heading towards Mayo on the N5. The town can be a bit of a bottleneck, particularly during peak traffic times. And ironically enough, access to Strokestown Park House and the National Famine Museum is in the centre of the town. I had tried on numerous occasions to get a clear shot of the shopfront, but there were always cars parked in front as the Percy French Hotel is very close by. This shop front no longer exists; the building has been converted into a modern pharmacy. I really admire the peeling and faded pink façade, the intimate net curtains and the simple symmetry of the entrance. I think there is something very French about this scene, and as I said earlier, something very inviting. Who will remember its simplicity and beauty, I wonder? But at least it is captured for posterity. This image now adorns the cover of the collection *Patrimoine/Cultural Heritage in France and Ireland*, co-edited by Eugene O'Brien and Eamon Maher (Peter Lang, 2019).

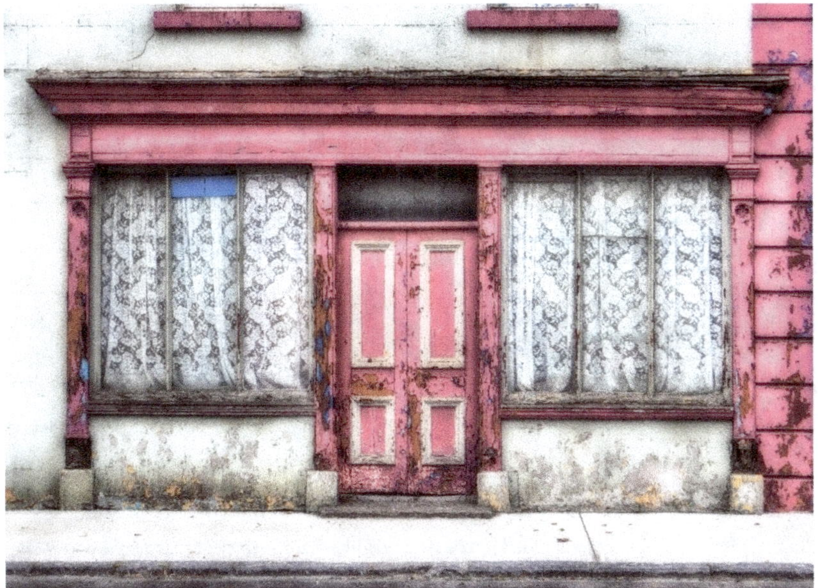

The Pink Door, Strokestown, County Roscommon – Image: Paul Butler, June 2013.

In my view, the recording of abandoned buildings and their interiors which are between eighty and hundred years old is extremely important, particularly if the buildings are destined to be bulldozed into oblivion. The Irish state has reached the centenary of its foundation, and these buildings and artefacts have been part of that journey. In fact, many were built while Ireland was still a colony of Britain. The buildings, no matter what they look like, are part of our founding history and cultural heritage, so, as they disappear so does the connection with our past. Demolition of these old homes, one could argue, is a form of 'destruction of memory' and cultural sabotage. At this point in our history, should we not be forced to protect our built past, which is part of our architectural heritage no matter how unattractive it may look? Our colonial past also left us with many fine stately homes, and they are part of our national identity. We are lucky that not all were burnt to the ground during the fight for independence.

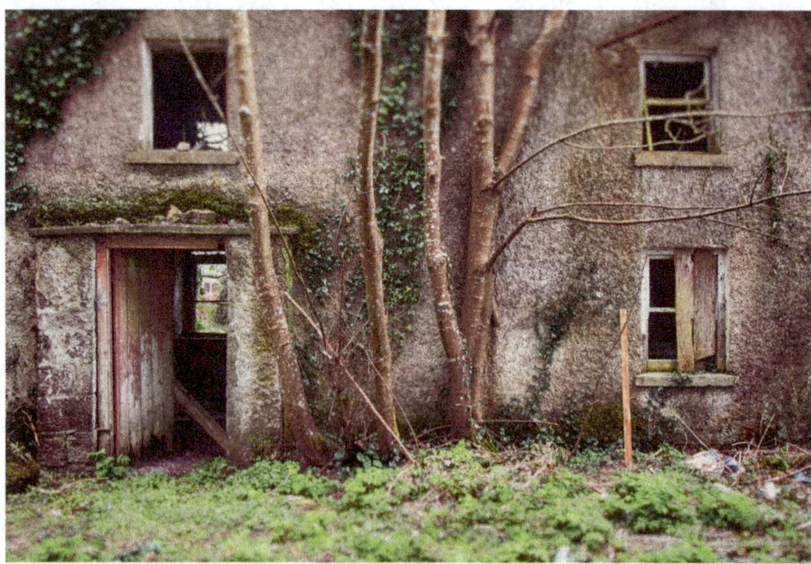

Once a Home, Newcastle, County Longford – Image: Paul Butler, March 2014.

Photographic Note: Nature has added its own stamp. I like that the shapes created by the trees and the root structure suggesting a reclaimed ownership on these former dwellings.

If one were to further label my work, it could be looked upon as a form of social archaeology, with everyday objects allowing me to provide the viewer with a brief glimpse of a previous life. In relation to the scene 'A Dish Scrubber', recorded in 2016, it asks many questions of this well-used dish washing brush: How many times a day was it used? Was there tension in the kitchen regarding chores? The rust patterns suggest to me that it was well-used. When it was placed on the sill, did they realize that it would be the last time they would use it? This quote which is attributed to American photographer Aaron Siskind elaborates on my style of visual recording and expression: 'Photography is a way of feeling, of touching, of loving. What you have caught on film is captured forever … It remembers little things, long after you have forgotten everything.'[6] That is what I try to achieve when recording the ordinary; I always allow the possibility of a back story and leave it wide open for interpretation.

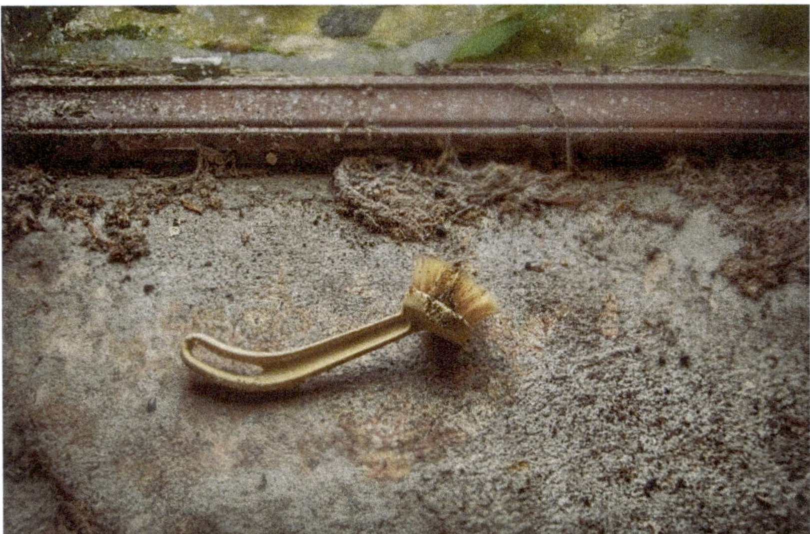

A Dish Scrubber, Breanross South, County Leitrim – Image: Paul Butler, April 2016.

Photographic Note: I warmed up this image slightly with a warm orange filter, as the window light was very cold due to low hanging grey rain clouds which caused a slight blue cast to fall on the scene. In post-production, a small percentage of High Dynamic Resolution (HDR) was added to illuminate detail into the stone sill.

6 Aaron Siskind, 'American Photographer': <https://www.britannica.com/biography/Aaron-Siskind> (4 February 2021).

A further observation by Bohrer reinforces my view that what I capture in my imagery is a visual record of a fast-disappearing past:

> Through photographs we preserve the past and looking for the past is the very job of the archaeologist. But what are we looking at in an archaeological photograph? Archaeological photography is often largely deserted, to be scanned with a forensic gaze, towards finding evidence of what once took place.[7]

I want to use the following movie scene to illustrate my point. It may seem an odd inclusion, but it contains some dialogue relevant to my point. The lines and the scene from *Indiana Jones, Raiders of the Lost Ark* (screenplay by Lawrence Kasdan) have always stayed with me. If you have not seen the movie, allow me to quickly to set the scene. Dr Indiana Jones, a justly revered archaeologist played by Harrison Ford, is searching for the 'Ark of the Covenant'. At the same time, he is trying to stop the Nazis getting their hands on it. In this scene set in a backstreet bar in Cairo, Jones, in shock and mourning, is proceeding to get steadily drunk. He believes that his love interest, Marian, has just been killed in a truck explosion as they tried to evade local assassins and Nazi agents. At the bar, Jones is approached by Nazi agents and is forced to get up and go meet his arch nemesis. Emile Belloq, played by Paul Freeman, is a French archaeologist who is working for the Nazis. It is obvious that the two archaeologists have a history. Belloq is also looking for the Ark of the Covenant. Sipping a drink and smoking a shisha pipe, he looks up and smiles sardonically from under his white fedora as Jones staggers in front of him. It is a very tense scene.

> BELLOQ: 'Look at this [Belloq holds up a silver pocket watch] it's worthless. Ten dollars from a vendor in the street. But I take it, I bury it in the sand for a thousand years, it becomes priceless!'[8]

That is how I feel when I photograph the ordinary. Those items we bypass and overlook, they are the everyday. To me they are priceless, and I want to record them before they disappear into dust. As I said, I am

7 Frederick N. Bohrer, *Photography and Archaeology* (London: Reaktion Books, 2011).

8 Lawrence Kasdan, *Raiders of the Lost Ark*: <https://www.imdb.com/name/nm0001410/?ref_=tt_ov_wr> (1981).

fascinated with old and abandoned homesteads; they are a treasure trove of lives lived in a particular area at a particular time. When photographing in situ, the curiosity of the surroundings and the objects remaining act as a guide for my camera. The novelist William Thackeray once remarked: 'The two most engaging powers of a photograph are to make new things familiar and familiar things new.'[9] As stated, many times, I am drawn to the many old and abandoned houses that dot the landscape in this part of north-west Ireland. I feel the sensation of that emptiness, which affects me. There is something about these silent losses and the fabric of lives once lived that moves me deeply. There are times when I must physically leave a space, as it can become overwhelming. I connect with what I see in front of me because I feel as if I empathize with the soul of that building. Or maybe it is a strong form of self-reflection that causes this sensation to amplify. And then quite soon after leaving, there is usually a strong pull to go back inside and stay a little while longer. To the question 'Does your house have a soul?', Laurie Stone replies:

> You think they're just wooden structures. They're containers, made to hold people and possessions. Houses don't have souls. At least that's how I felt until I drove by my old home of ten years. That's when my heart broke.[10]

9 William Makepeace Thackeray, 'Biography': <https://archive.org/stream/williammakepeace01melv/williammakepeace01melv_djvu.txt>.

10 Laurie Stone, 'Does Your House Have a Soul?': <https://www.lauriestonewrites.com/2015/08/13/do-houses-have-souls/> (13 August 2015).

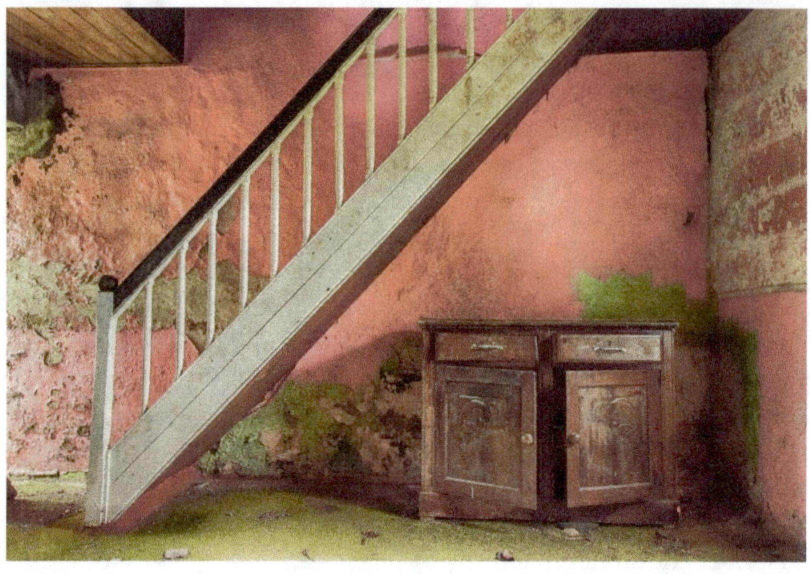

Farmhouse Interior, Oghil, Drumlish County Longford – Image: Paul Butler, April 2014.
Photographic Note: I really like the strong symmetry of the white stairs and we have an old sideboard cabinet, offering secrets from a forgotten time. And the pink walls slowly peeling to reveal an old green colour. Both colour tones seem to have been very popular at the time and is visible within a lot of old homes. During the 1950s, pastel colour schemes that were popular included pink, mint green, turquoise, pale yellow and blue.

And as I referred to in my introductory section, many of the homes and landscapes I explore relate to the time of John McGahern, one of Ireland's foremost writers. He was also a son of Leitrim and I, as a photographer living in Leitrim, understand his world in possibly a different way from other readers. This fascination with old and abandoned houses offers a glimpse of a life lived and opens us to so many interpretations. Add to that my desire to search for hints of a past, as if I'm playing the role of photographic archaeologist recording a way of life that is fast disappearing.

In his short story 'Oldfashioned', McGahern notes with some sadness the decline of the old ruling aristocracy. This passage blends with the scene 'Lakefield House' which I recorded in 2013.

> The Protestants had so dwindled that there was no longer a living in Ardcarne; the old Georgian parsonage had been closed, its avenues of great beech trees, the walled orchard, the paddock and lawn and garden, all let run wild. [*CE*, 'Oldfashioned', p. 249]

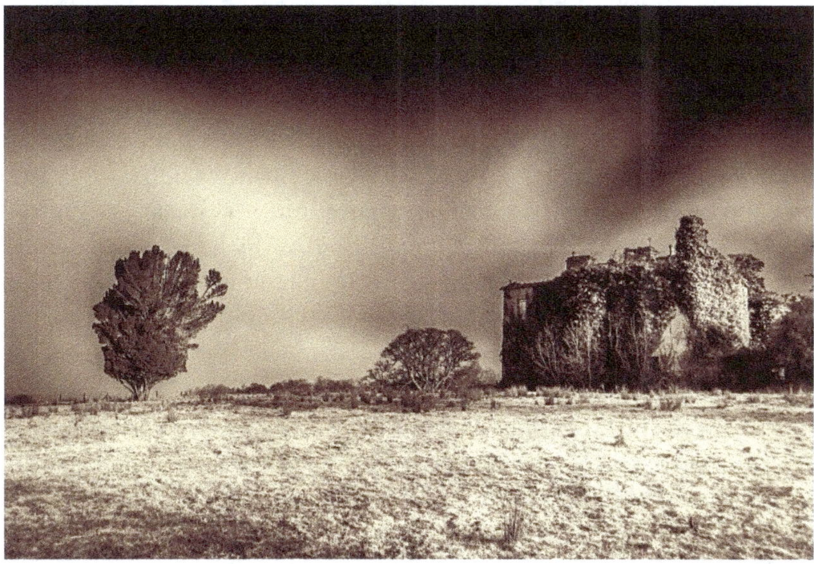

Lakefield House, Breanross North, County Leitrim – Image: Paul Butler, January 2013.

Photographic Note: In post-production, I added a layer and converted it to High Dynamic Resolution (HDR). I then converted the image to black and white infrared and increased the red and blue filtration to dramatize the sky and make the buildings and landscape assume a ghostly appearance. This treatment I feel alludes to the ghosts of the past.

This shell that was once Lakefield House sits on the eastern shore of Lough Errew, not far from the former Lough Rinn Estate. The fine cut stone yard buildings are still in excellent condition. The view from the old house towards Lough Errew is quite beautiful. The house is listed on the NUI Galway *Landed Estates Database* (I provided images of the property for the database):

> Lakefield House was associated with the Crofton family since the mid eighteenth century. A new house was constructed between 1771–1798. At the time of Griffith's Valuation it was leased by Duke Crofton from Hugh Carmichael, M.D. and was

valued at £25. The house continued in Crofton ownership until 1931 when the estate was purchased by the Land Commission.[11]

One beautiful sunny evening in August 2020, I was out driving and doing a bit of investigating. I turned onto a tiny access road situated in the townland of Tully, County Leitrim. Along this road I discovered the heritage site which is the birthplace of Margaret of New Orleans: 'A young Leitrim woman who became one of the most celebrated philanthropists in New Orleans history. But she wasn't some wealthy widow – her late husband left her nothing. So, Margaret started out, very much, as an entry-level philanthropist.'[12] After taking a few images at this heritage site, I drove on and further along the road I discovered an old farmhouse, long since abandoned. Lacking windows and having absolutely no interior except for cattle-trodden floors and the walls covered in moss, I dared not venture up a seriously dodgy-looking staircase. I have an agreement with my wife that when I am out investigating an old building I avoid going upstairs unless I can guarantee that the stairs are safe. I do abide by this, mostly. I moved outside the old building and after poking around a very overgrown garden, I noticed in the adjoining field the blackish blue roof of an old car sticking out from among the rushes like a small beached whale.

11 Lakefield House, 'Landed Estates Database': <http://landedestates.nuigalway.ie/LandedEstates/jsp/property-show.jsp?id=483> (18 May 2011).

12 Eoin Butler, 'The Girl from Leitrim Who Became the "Angel" of New Orleans':<https://www.irishtimes.com/life-and-style/abroad/the-girl-from-leitrim-who-became-the-angel-of-new-orleans-1.2964329> (10 February 2017).

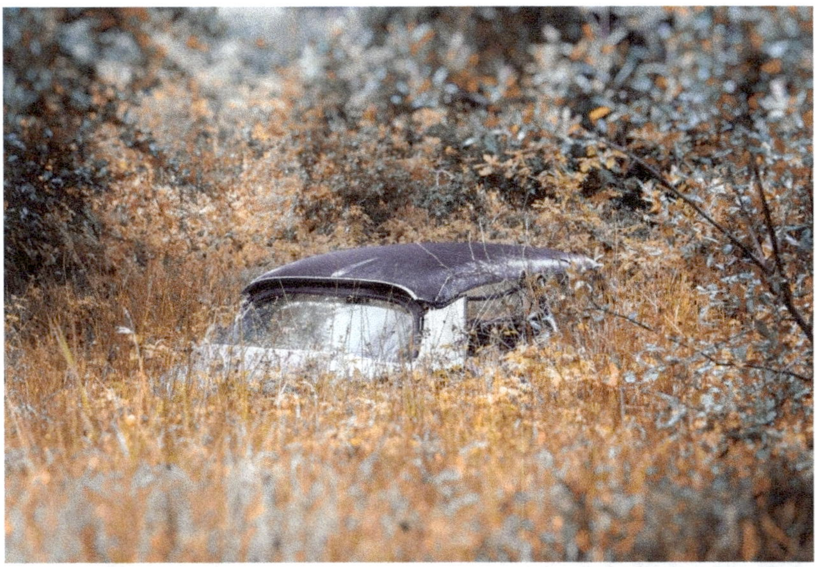

Rusting Old Citroen DS, Tully South, County Leitrim – Image: Paul Butler, August 2020.
Photographic Note: I gave this image an extreme (warm) colour correction in post-production to emphasize nostalgia, heat and romance.

From what I could discern, it looked like a big old luxury Citroen DS. I remember this type of car vividly, as a farmer we know had one, and it was so comfortable to sit in, with the chassis nearly touching the ground. There was, and still is something very cool about these big old classic French cars. What struck me about the scene 'Rusting Old Citroen DS' was how nostalgic and romantic it felt. What kind of life did this car and its owner have, I wondered? My musings went like this:

> I visualized the driver, cruising these country lanes on a summer evening, elbow on the window opening with a cigarette in hand. In the passenger seat, a sun-glassed lady sat right far back smiling as her cigarette smoke filtered gently from velvet red lips. On the radio sweet music floated up towards the evening sky. Their eyes meet, as the hedgerow blurs through the windscreen. A faint blue haze of exhaled cigarettes accentuates dust particles, offering endless possibilities of love on an open road.

Yet again, it is amazing what little treasures you stumble upon and what stories you visualize when you go wandering. I really like this image, and it was on display as part of a group exhibition in Athens.

Another subject I am really fascinated with are old gates, especially their workmanship. I photographed 'The Maker of the Gate', which belongs to a neighbour of ours, in 2011. The gate is well over a hundred years old, and I really like that the person who made it etched his name 'Reilly' on the gate tongue. It is another little call from the past. The gate needs a fair bit of remedial work though, as it is slowly falling apart.

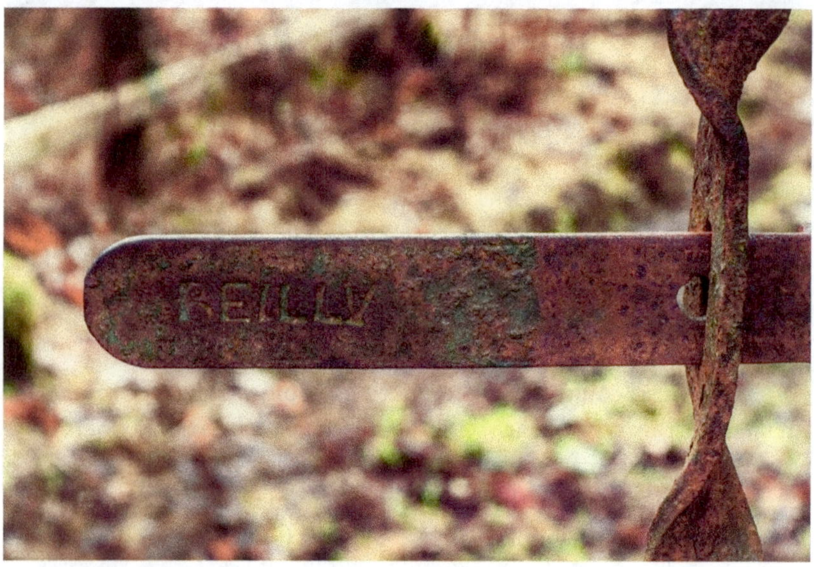

The Maker of the Gate, Farnocht, County Leitrim – Image: Paul Butler, January 2011.

And in many of the old homesteads I have photographed, there are always many bits and pieces of a life that once was. The image 'Forgotten Swing' I photographed in 2010, and it just cries out with so many memories of what a home once was. I came across this old, beautiful and somewhat sad swing in the overgrown garden of the former estate manager's house in Lough Rinn. This house has been idle for a very long time. It is a majestic residence with floor to ceiling windows and a secret garden. For every time

I gaze upon it, I can hear childhood sounds and voices. And the questions follow. How many times did it sail through the air, how many times did it offer a place of sanctuary, a place to think things through? The swing encapsulates the cycle of a young life; the joy of an eternal childhood filling the air with laughter and squeals. Or maybe it was a sad and slow swing which brought dark memories flooding into the mind. The little swing is now still, though memories remain rooted within the moss-covered seat. I choose 'Forgotten Swing' to end this section on place-exteriors, because it reinforces that emptiness, especially for parents who watched their swallows fly the nest.

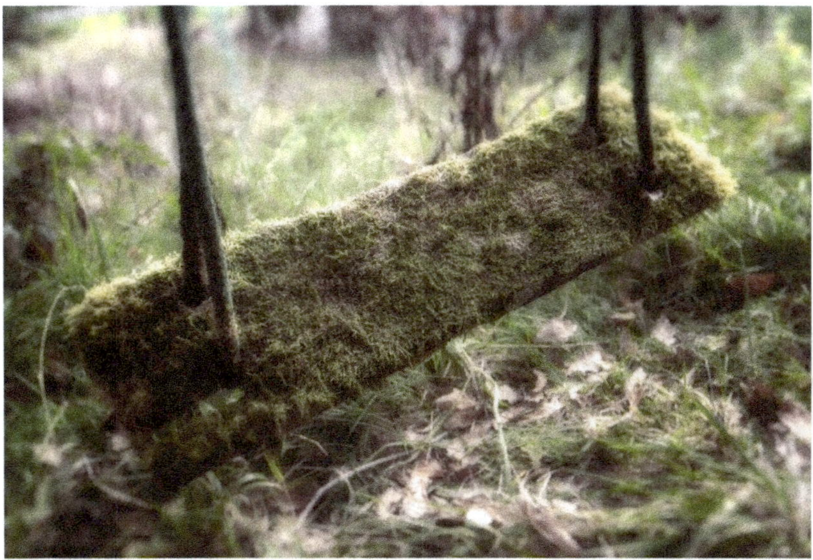

Forgotten Swing at the Former Estate Managers House, Rinn, County Leitrim – Image: Paul Butler, October 2010.

Interiors

I believe that McGahern's words and my imagery fit together like a good pair of gloves. The following passage from one of McGahern's short stories, 'Love of the World', accurately describes a typical day in a remote area of the county and his words whisper across those quiet country lanes, 'Not many people like this quiet. There's a constant craving for every word of every sound and sighting and any small happening' [*CE*, 'Love of the World', p. 336].

I remember vividly the absolute thrill I felt from this first time I entered an old home in 2011 and recorded the scene, 'Calendar at the Kitchen Window'. The rotting front door was ajar and hoof prints led into the parlour. Cattle had already made themselves comfortable and there was mud and empty cattle feed bags strewn around some of the rooms. I felt like I was entering a secret world, untouched for a long time. The hall entrance and adjoining rooms were covered in mud and hoof marks– which would lead one to assume that a farmer allowed his livestock to wander in and out. As is common practice, the house was probably purchased along with a parcel of land. Or maybe the original owner had passed away or was infirm, and it all remained intestate. I revisited this house over several weeks. The passage below describes perfectly the popularity of these calendars, which held a privileged position within the home, 'Within the deep walls on the lake, a butcher's calendar of the year before was hung' [*RS*, pp. 17–18].

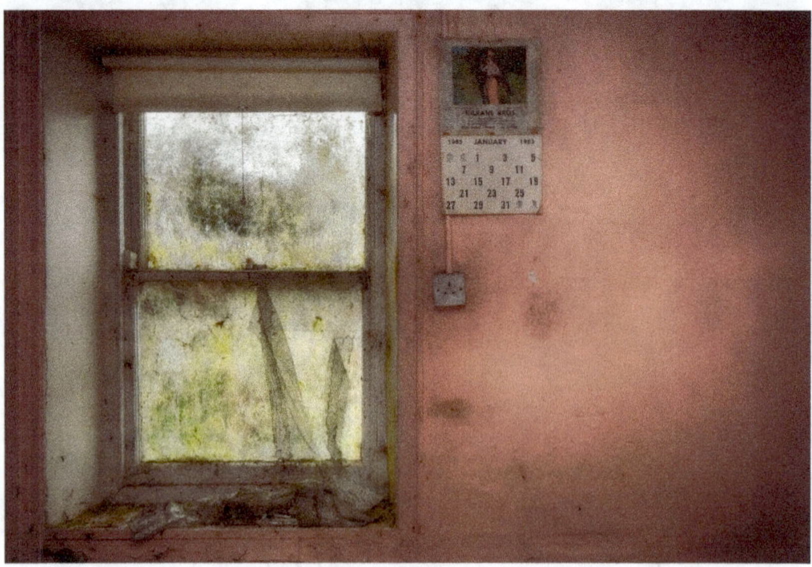

Calendar at the Kitchen Window, Gortletteragh, County Leitrim Image: Paul Butler 2011.
Photographic Note: And once again we note the 1950s pink wall paint.

The butcher's or hardware shop calendar was such a common item to be found in most kitchens. The 'Calendar at the Kitchen Window' dates from 1985. These calendars for loyal customers usually, if not always, had a picture of a child with either a dog[s] or a horse[s], as in this calendar. This particular one was associated with Paddy Kilrane, a cousin of my wife and a butcher based in Mohill. Paddy only stopped trading a couple of years ago, and the shop now lies empty and is for lease. And on the main street another butcher closed a few years ago, like a lot of premises in Mohill. In an nice twist, Kilranes Butchers just like its old calendar, houses only memories.

Update November 2022: On a positive note, the house in 'Calendar at the Kitchen Window' has been renovated. And a new butcher's shop is soon to open on the Main Street in Mohill.

I have often felt conflicted when documenting abandoned dwellings and landscapes, questioning whether I was doing this for the right reasons. For example, was I trying to frame an image to give my specific viewpoint? The answer to that is an emphatic 'No'! I want to share my portrayal of the beauty of the ordinary. My intentions are genuine, and this book is a simple documentary journey through a wonderful silent county and of a world that is slowly fading away. It is not some voyeuristic trip to fulfil the latest social media thrill. I love to share the ordinary, and if it gives the viewer a special feeling or moment, that is what matters most to me. The following quote credited to the legendary French photographer Henri Cartier-Bresson does help articulate what I am trying to achieve: 'One eye of the photographer looks wide open through the viewfinder, the other, the closed, looks into his own soul.'[13] There is a definite auto-ethnographic element to my approach, as through my images and McGahern's words, I plunge into the depths of my soul. McGahern's description of interiors, the real smells and sounds within the houses and his careful and minimal use of words to set up a scene were all so deliberately scripted that I cannot avoid seeing it in photographic or filmic terms. The interior and the items found within are the true soul of the home, or, in my case, what is left of the soul. In a sense, the character of the homes I have photographed harks back to a simpler time, usually reflected in the remaining contents.

13 Henri Cartier-Bresson, 'The Foundation': <https://www.henricartierbresson.org/en/hcb/>.

This image 'Powers & Jameson Whiskey Bottles' chimes with the following passage from McGahern's short story 'Swallows'. It allows you to drift into the scene, opening the parlour door from a cold evening into the warmth and the smell of a turf fire. The composition of the old cabinet with the whiskey bottles – constant contradiction of a solitary and quiet pious life with the need for some sort of social release. The torn wallpaper with brown backing is of the old, embossed pattern type. When this paper was hung, it would last a generation and was very tough to remove. However, a lot of these old houses suffered from dampness, and the weight of the paper would result in it falling off, of its own accord. And the piece of ivy working its way inside the old house and reclaiming everything. You knew the importance of always having a bottle in the press in case an important visitor arrived unexpectedly:

> The Sergeant went and took a bottle of whiskey and two tumblers from a black press in the corner, its glass covered with a faded curtain, joking uncomfortably, 'I call it a medicine-press', as the Surveyor opened the violin-case on the table. [*CE*, 'Swallows', p. 125]

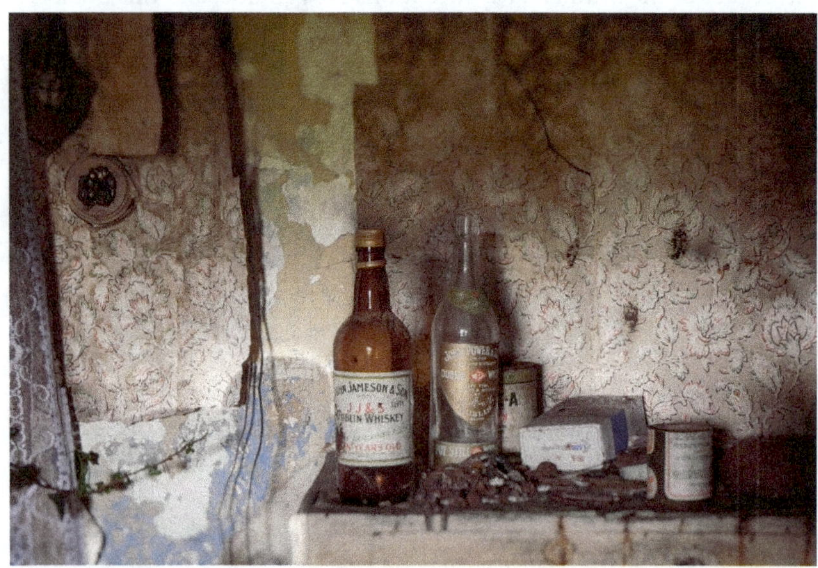

Powers & Jameson Whiskey Bottles at Curraghroe, County Roscommon – Image: Paul Butler, April 2016.

Photographic Note: It was evening time, and there was beautiful light flooding in through the old sash windows. I used quite long exposures with the aperture set about f22 to get as much detail as possible.

I have encountered plenty of empty alcohol bottles within the old houses I have visited. Mostly they are scattered across the floor, or some may be the result of a secretive drinking den. The two bottles in the image 'Powers & Jameson Whiskey Bottles' were recorded in situ and are without a doubt part of the original home. To me, they create a sense of welcome and warmth. I was amazed at the number of everyday items lying around this house in Curraghroe, County Roscommon, and interior scenes from this abode feature throughout this book. The land surrounding this house was bought and the house came with it. It was slowly falling into disrepair. Inside, everything was strewn around, even though the owner had died a few years previously, it still had a lived-in feel. Outside, a lovingly restored stone shed stood opposite the house. I had a great long chat with the owner/farmer when he discovered me on site taking pictures. Earlier I had asked a local woman if it was ok to go in. Obviously, neighbourhood watch is quite active in this area. The farmer wanted to sell the house with the stone shed and thought I might be interested. He could easily have chucked me out, but when I explained what my project was about, he allowed me to carry on.

The scene 'Rusted Key of Many Memories' portrays an old key sitting on the kitchen windowsill; it must had lain there for over thirty years. The creeping ivy and soft window light add real atmosphere to this scene. Obviously, it opened one of the inner doors, but which one?

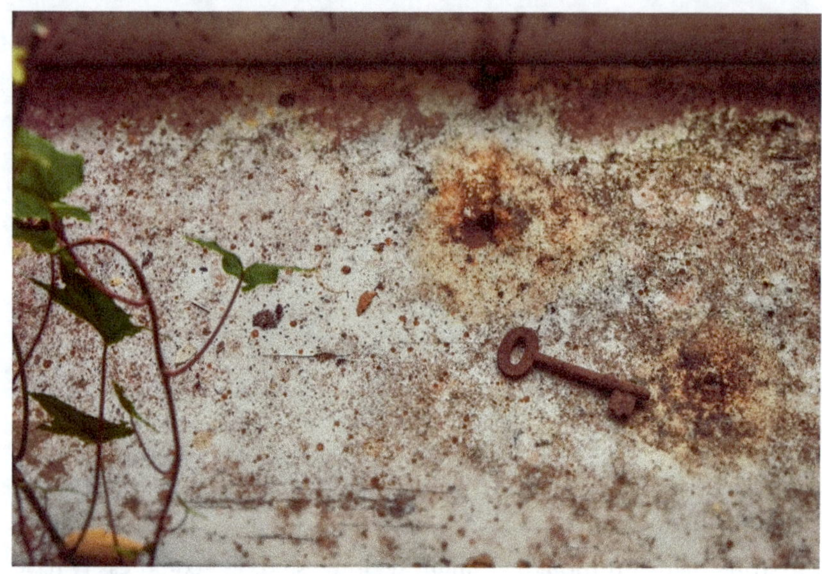

Rusted Key of Many Memories, Cloonee, County Leitrim – Image: Paul Butler, July 2019.

And once again I refer to another observation from Cartier-Bresson:

> In order to give a 'meaning' to the world, one has to feel involved in what one frames through the viewfinder. This attitude requires concentration, discipline of mind, sensitivity, and a sense of geometry. It is by economy of means that one arrives at simplicity of expression.[14]

In a 2002 interview with Robert McCrum in the *Guardian*, McGahern was asked, 'Who do you think influenced you as a writer?'[15] I think McGahern's response does give an insight into how he built up his scenes:

> McGahern – 'I think that each of us inhabits a private world that others cannot see. The only difference between the writer and the reader is that the writer is able to dramatize that private world. But that private world, once it's dramatized, doesn't live again until it

14 Ibid.

15 Robert McCrum, 'The Whole World in a Community': <https://www.theguardian.com/books/2002/jan/06/fiction.features> (6 January 2002).

> finds a reader. When I start to write, words have become physical presence. It was to see if I could bring that private world to life that found its first expression through reading. I really dislike the romantic notion of the artist.'

McGahern did not want to make any exaggerated claims about how he found his artistic inspiration. The emphasis on 'seeing' is key to my reading of McGahern as a visual writer. I found his way of 'seeing' the world had a big influence on my view through the lens and I, as stated earlier, find myself, out of respect, recording these scenes for posterity.

The following piece which appeared in the *Irish Times* is very poignant, reinforcing a time in everyone's life when one generation moves on and says goodbye to what has gone before. Entitled 'Closing the Door One Final Time on the World Where I Was Born' and written by Michael Harding, it contains this observation:

> Gathering up the discarded ornaments and junk, I thought I saw my mother again. Little Lotus came with me to my mother's house recently. The house had been sold and I wanted to bid farewell, and to close the door for one final time on the world where I was born. I checked empty rooms, knowing that in a few weeks the locks would be changed, and the property handed over to a new owner. A few discarded ornaments lay about the floors and on the tables in various rooms. An old silver teapot on a shelf in the kitchen. An amber sugar bowl in the sink. A papier mâché cat under the stairs that I gave my mother for Christmas in 1994.[16]

16 Michael Harding, 'Closing the Door One Final Time on the World Where I Was Born': <https://www.irishtimes.com/life-and-style/people/closing-the-door-one-final-time-on-the-world-where-i-was-born-1.2969785> (21 February 2017).

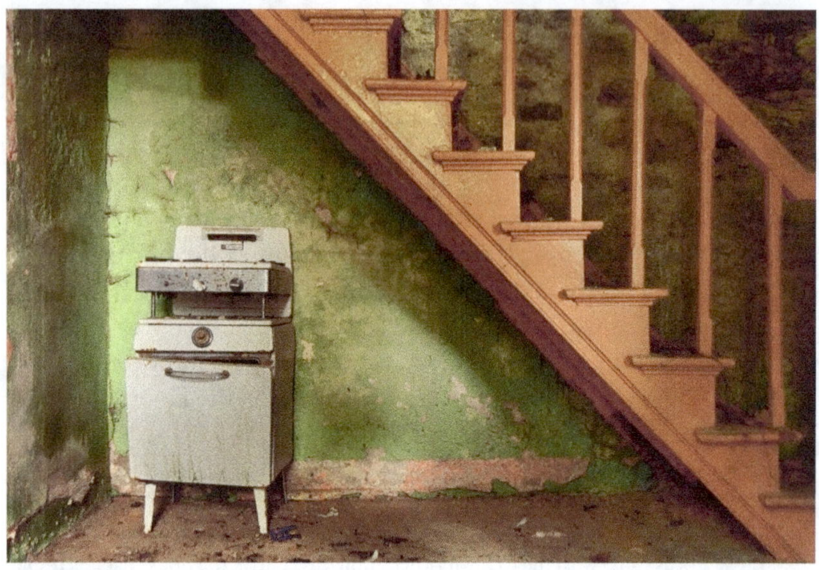

The Gas Cooker, Near Ardagh, County Longford – Image: Paul Butler, September 2013.
Photographic Note: The stair in this image creates such a sharp angle and beautifully frames the little gas cooker. Note again the 1950s green paint, a common scullery colour for that time.

Harding has been living close to Arigna, County Roscommon, in a remote part of County Leitrim, and was initially from County Cavan. His work, with its strong emphasis on place, is close to the preoccupations of McGahern. In McGahern's short story, 'Wheels' the image 'The Gas Cooker' , blends with the ritual of getting dinner ready. One can nearly smell and taste the rashers and hear the egg spitting as it fries slowly on the pan: 'He drummed an idle rhythm with the bone of the knife on the cloth until she put the plate before him, fried eggs, and bacon, a yellow well of butter in the middle of the creamed potatoes' [*CE*, 'Wheels', p. 7].

In *A Private World*, McGahern refers to the country tradition of *ceilidh*, which is a social gathering or unplanned visit involving dancing and storytelling when people drop in, sometimes unexpectedly:

> People were very neighbourly; there was a whole community around here then. You'd never know who would turn up or when. Sometimes you mightn't see somebody for a couple of days even, but then you might see five or six people in the one day. And you just have to stop writing then and it's not something I ever paraded anyhow. [*PW*]

In an essay, 'Eulogizing a home: How to Say Goodbye to a Place with Memories', Kelli Kehler states: 'We say that it's the memories and people that make a home, not the things in it or the structure itself, yet when we're forced to leave a treasured home behind, it doesn't merely tug at the heartstrings – it damn near severs them.'[17] That is a feeling I tune into when I explore these old houses and find artefacts and remnants. In the image 'The Child's Lost Wellington Boot', I often wondered if there had been a happy childhood or had some sad event befallen the infant? The deep isolation of the boot within the wooden box creates more questions than answers. And within these small simple rooms, I once again come across a world of unknown stories.

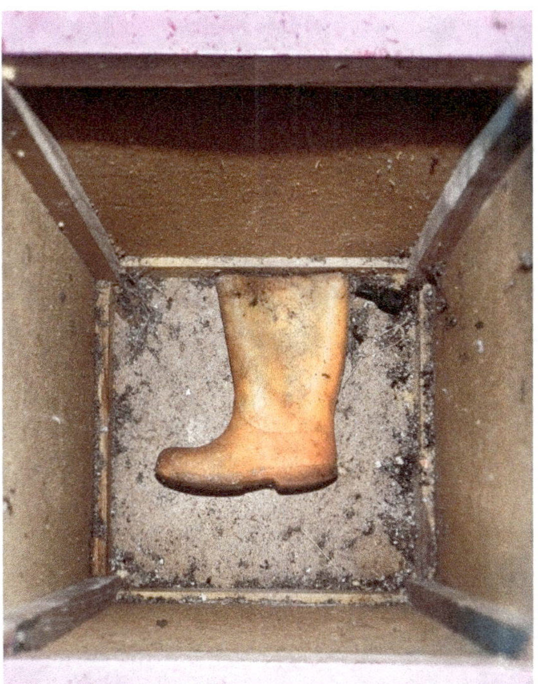

The Child's Lost Wellington Boot, Gortletteragh, County Leitrim – Image: Paul Butler, April 2011.

17 Kelli Kehler, 'Eulogizing a Home: How to Say Goodbye to a Place with Memories': <https://www.designsponge.com/2015/02/eulogizing-a-home-how-to-say-goodbye-to-a-place-with-memories.html>.

The following piece by Frederick N. Bohrer reinforces my view that what I record in situ is a visual record of a fast-disappearing past:

> Through photographs we preserve the past and looking for the past is the very job of the archaeologist. But what are we looking at in an archaeological photograph? Archaeological photography is often largely deserted, to be scanned with a forensic gaze, towards finding evidence of what once took place.[18]

And the first two lines from a translation of the poem, 'Memories Are a House',[19] by Avot Yeshurun, bring out the atmosphere of memory within these forgotten dwellings:

> Memories are a house.
> Time is a roof.

'The March of Modernity' was recorded in the village of Scramoge, County Roscommon, and I use the term 'village' quite loosely. Scramoge consists of a tiny public house, a church and, thanks to the madness of the 'Celtic Tiger', a couple of large developments of houses more suitable to a Dublin suburb. Scramoge is just off the N5 Dublin to Mayo Primary Route, four kilometres from the heritage town of Strokestown, County Roscommon.

18 Frederick N. Bohrer, *Photography and Archaeology* (London: Reaktion Books, 2011).

19 Avot Yeshurun, 'Memories Are a House': <https://www.poetryfoundation.org/poetrymagazine/poems/50964/memories-are-a-house> (1989).

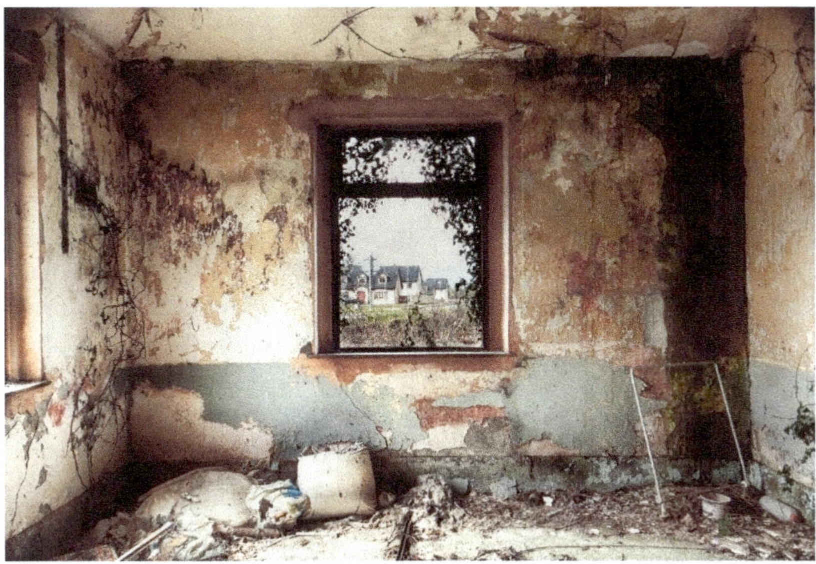

The March of Modernity. Scramoge, County Roscommon – Image: Paul Butler, April 2016.

There was a coldness and lack of feeling within this place, and not just in a physical sense. The house itself exuded an air of sadness. It was as if my radar could not pick up a sensation of happiness, only emptiness and sadness. The following passage from McGahern's short story 'A Slip Up' is quite sad and thoughtful. Its tone of obvious displacement, regret and loneliness adds existential depth and meaning to the image. The main protagonist's trauma and loss of 'sense of place' is tangible as he turns to dreams to cope with a cold and anonymous place:

> Every morning since he retired, except when he was down with that winter flu, Michael walked with Agnes to Tesco's, and it brought him the feeling of long ago when he walked round the lake with his mother, potholes and stones of the lane. [*CE*, 'A Slip Up', p. 85]

Within this scene I wanted to guide the viewer towards the relentless march of modernity with the new 'suburb' visible through the rotting window. I still cannot figure out how the planners allowed a big development to be built in the middle of rural countryside. This image also adorns the cover of the 100th edition of the *Reimagining Ireland* book series, *Reimagining Irish Studies for the Twenty-First Century*.[20] I am very fond of the story, 'A Slip up'; it feels very real, and I can actually see it. I had the pleasure of attending two plays based on an adaption of the story: the first was in the Dock Arts Centre at Carrick on Shannon, County Leitrim, and the second was in Ballinamore Library, also in County Leitrim. Both were very poignant and moving portrayals. This theme has stayed with me as I can clearly visualize a displaced elderly country man standing lost, afraid and alone in an alien environment. The story reminds me of the many Irish who had to emigrate and helped keep our country's economy alive. With little education and their working lives spent, they have nothing to return to. They were alone and set adrift on the sea of loneliness.

The village of Scramoge in County Roscommon was a great example of the worst excesses of the building boom. As explained earlier, the village consists of a church and a tiny public house, dwarfed by a couple of enormous housing developments built during the Celtic Tiger. For a long time, the houses were completely empty, and the development was kept manicured, generating the impression of a film set. In recent times, most of the houses are occupied, though a shop and office development facing onto the road remains only partly in use. The crossroads at Scramoge were also the scene of an ambush during the War of Independence (1921) in which three British soldiers and an RIC Officer were killed. Two Black and Tans were also taken captive and shot dead. In response, three IRA volunteers and a person not involved were executed.

In the image 'Cattle & Sheep Cures for all Ills', I was fascinated with the mix of remedies sitting on the scullery shelf within the old house in Curraghroe, County Roscommon. Judging from the array of bottles, the farm may have had both sheep and cattle. The land in this area is flat and looks decent enough for animal grazing. Curraghroe is on the R371 from Roosky, in Roscommon (via Scramoge) to Lanesboro, in Longford.

20 *Reimagining Irish Studies for the Twenty-First Century*, edited By Eamon Maher and Eugene O'Brien (Oxford: Peter Lang, 2021).

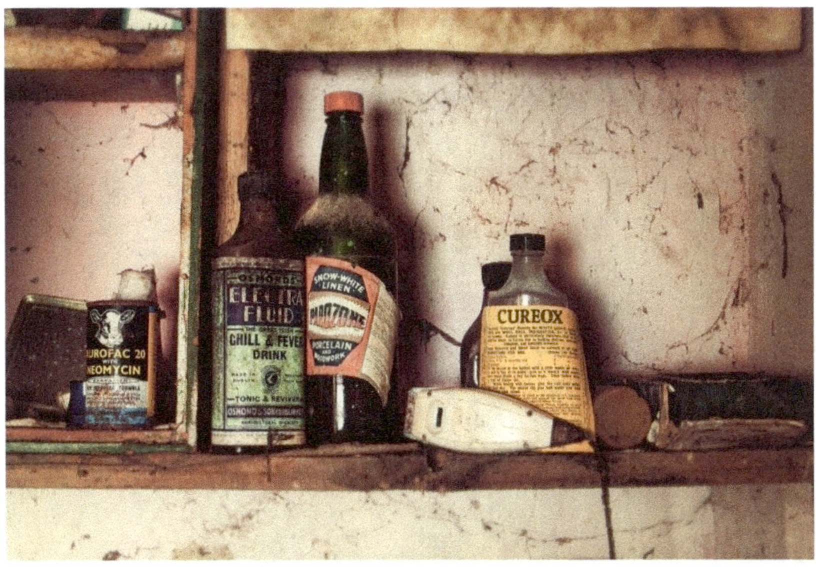

Cattle & Sheep Cures for all Ills, Curraghroe, County Roscommon – Image: Paul Butler, April 2016.

As for the bottles in the image, after a bit of investigating, I could find no reference to Electra Fluid the Great Irish Fever & Chill Drink. However, according to the National Library of New Zealand, I discovered that Osmond's Electra Fluid has been around as Osmond & Son in New Zealand Ltd, and they were manufacturing veterinary chemists with a head office in Grimsby, England, and Wellington, New Zealand, in the early years of the twentieth century (1900 to 1920).[21] It also seems that some version of the company still exists with an address in Shropshire, United Kingdom.[22] Parazone Bleach is still available today. Aurofac 20, a cattle antibiotic, was discontinued in 2005. Cureox, according to the label, seems to have been for Wool Ball Indigestion, which I presume is a condition sheep would get?

21 Osmond & Sons, 'Manufacturing Veterinary Chemists': <https://natlib.govt.nz/records/22845945?search%5Bi%5D%5Bname_authority_id%5D=-154800&search%5Bpath%5D=items> (1900).

22 Osmond's Website: <https://www.osmonds.co.uk/>.

I recorded a quintessentially Irish scene 'The Dresser' for its character on a sunny evening during April 2016. As was tradition, the good China delph set would have been kept in this cabinet.

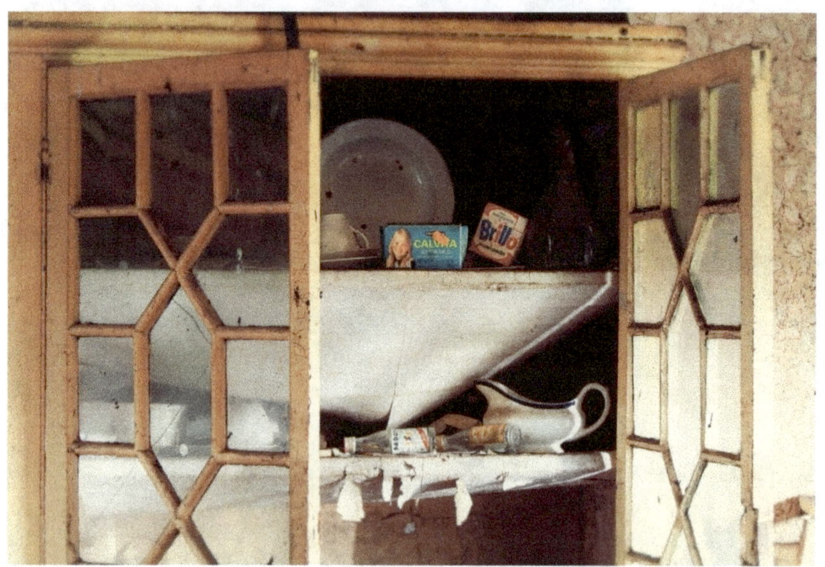

The Dresser, Curraghroe, County Roscommon – Image: Paul Butler, April 2016.

The box of Brillo scouring pads were as much a necessity then as they are now. I remember vividly having to use a large amount of elbow grease as the scouring pad oozed pink soap, trying valiantly to remove burnt potato skins from the bottom of a large pot. And here again we see a few miniature bottles of Paddy's and Powers Irish whiskey. The Calvita Cheese box was a staple growing up, a forerunner to today's easy single cheese slices. And this product is still going strong. I remember it had the consistency of rubber and was wrapped in very thin foil coating that stuck to the cheese, especially if it softened due to heat. I recall it being slathered onto cream crackers that went damp and limp unless eaten quickly, and it possessed a vivid sickly sweet taste. And as for the image of the young girl on the Calvita box, in 2012, RTÉ Radio's Ryan Turbridy tracked down the original Calvita girl.[23] This image of an old dresser portrays a sense of life and hustle and bustle, from having 'the dinner' to having 'the tea'. I am a great admirer of these kitchen dressers. This scene is timeless and generates a great deal of warmth and nostalgia.

'The Lampshade' was from a little home that was once situated off the L1601, at the corner of Beeches Road, beside the former Shannon Key West Hotel in Roosky, County Leitrim. My attention had been drawn to this old house on numerous occasions and so, one Sunday afternoon in February 2014, I stopped to have a quick look around.

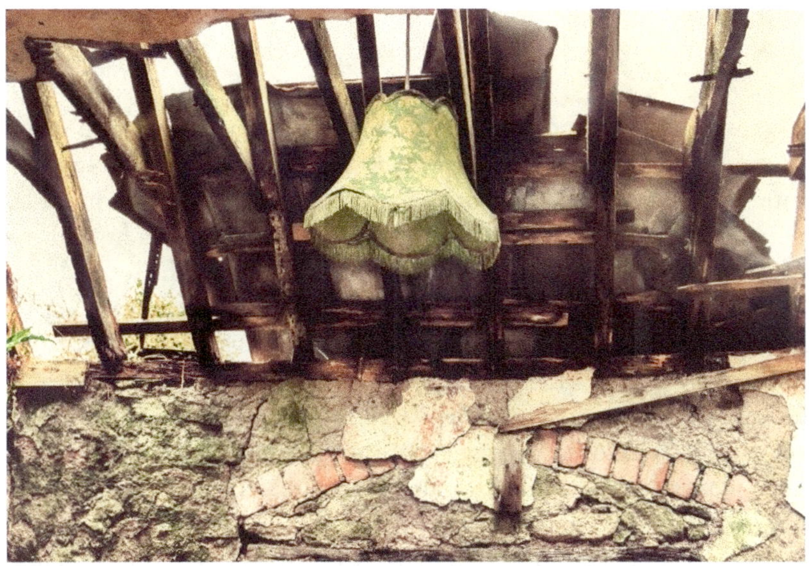

The Lampshade, Roosky, County Leitrim – Image: Paul Butler, February 2014.

The old place was ready to collapse at any moment, such was the state within. I found it nostalgic that the lampshade and ceiling coving had

23 Calvita Girl: <https://www.facebook.com/2fmofficial/posts/tubridy-2fm-tracked-down-the-calvita-girl-and-shes-looking-well-any-ideas-for-wh/124582471008981/> (18 April 2012).

stubbornly survived the elements. It adorned this ruined house with a sense of style and a form of defiance, indicating that at some stage in the past there was pride in this home. Lo and behold, within a couple of weeks, a bulldozer had razed the old structure to the ground. All that remains now is a low white concrete fence and the floor foundation – any trace of the home is wiped clean. I managed to capture some poignant images in this old structure and once again I feel grateful to have been able to capture a visual record of a home that once was.

Windows

It is always a joy to capture images within these old homesteads, the windows and their beautiful frames. Windows are the eyes of the house, the entrance to its soul, looking onto the world and inviting you inwards. Oh, the stories they could tell! It is usually the first part of a home I try to capture. If there is good light, it can really help open the scene. Hard light can create wonderful shadows, but it can be a juggling act not to lose detail in its glare. Cloudy or diffuse light gives me more opportunities to pick up close window detail and accentuate the most ordinary and delicate subtleties within. Funnelling the eye towards the light, with all your focus directed onto dreams, possibilities and many untold stories. The older and deeper walled windows of mud and stone cottages are a particular favourite. The window wells are so deep that they simply draw you in. It is clever that the wall cutting that surrounds the window frame expands wedge-shaped outwards back into the room, thus allowing for the maximum distribution and utilization of light. The detail of coving around a window well and the simple beauty of old sash windows hark back to a different time when care, detail and much pride was placed in such small utilitarian things. You would pay a fortune to have sash windows and shutters in your home now. The scene 'A Deep Window of Secrets' is a very fine example of this style. Here we see once again the use of that beautiful and soulful soft pink.

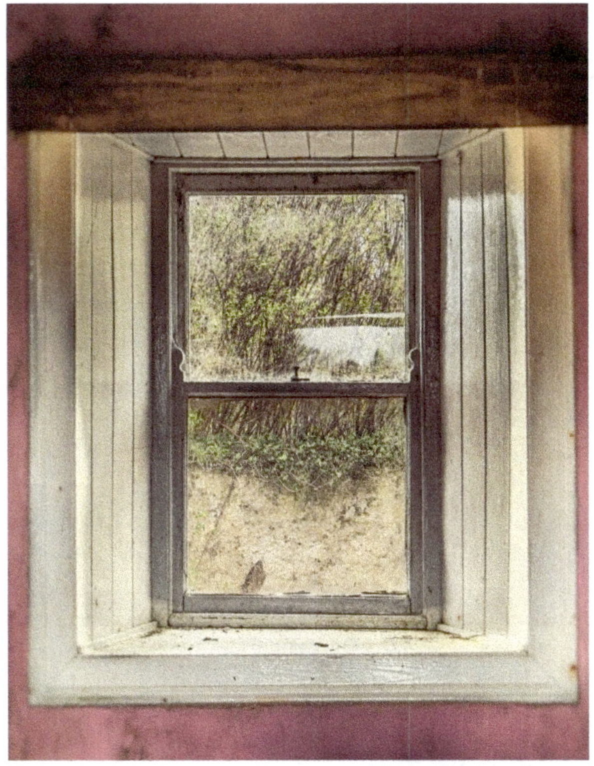

A Deep Window of Secrets, Oghil, Drumlish County Longford – Image: Paul Butler, April 2014.

I found this interesting piece regarding the history of glass and how the word *window* originated. 'Vinduaga' is an old Norse word meaning both 'wind' and 'eye'. The Ancient Romans were the first people to make use of glass in their windows. Of course, it was only the wealthiest citizens who could afford to enjoy glass windows. The first Roman windows were installed in Italian villas about 2,000 years ago.[24]

24 Amanda Littlejohn, 'Who Invented Windows and Doors?': <https://owlcation.com/humanities/Who-Invented-Windows-and-Doors> (2019).

Within the scene 'The Net Curtains', I have often wondered how many times someone stood in front of this window looking out onto the world. What were their thoughts? Did the window act as a barrier for a sad and lost soul wishing to escape to a freer world? Or did the window give comfort and act as a shield from a great and fearful unknown? And then again, not wanting to be voyeuristic, did a couple just lie on the bed and enjoy soft warm evening sunlight filter through dust particles? I admire the fact that the net curtains remains in place. It is wonderful that the curtains still offer a sense of privacy. And because the net curtains help to diffuse the light, helps the still affixed faded green wallpaper is allowed to subtly glow. The framing of this window calls to a past life, and is captivating with its blurred welcome, enticing you with unknown stories. It is a special appeal which surrounds the personality of old windows, they are the gateway to separate worlds.

Now, we take the following passage from McGahern's short story, 'The Wine Breath', and let it breathe life into this bedroom window scene:

> Somewhere, outside this room that was an end, he knew that a young man, not unlike he had once been, stood on a granite step and listened to the doorbell ring, smiled as he heard a woman's footsteps come down the hallway. [*CE*, 'The Wine Breath', p. 120]

Curtains: The deliberate framing of the net curtains allows diffused light to seep into the central portion of the frame, narrowing the view towards the outside, inviting the viewer to ponder.

Window: The grimy and dirty windows blurring the view invite the viewer to engage in a moment of melancholy or nostalgia.

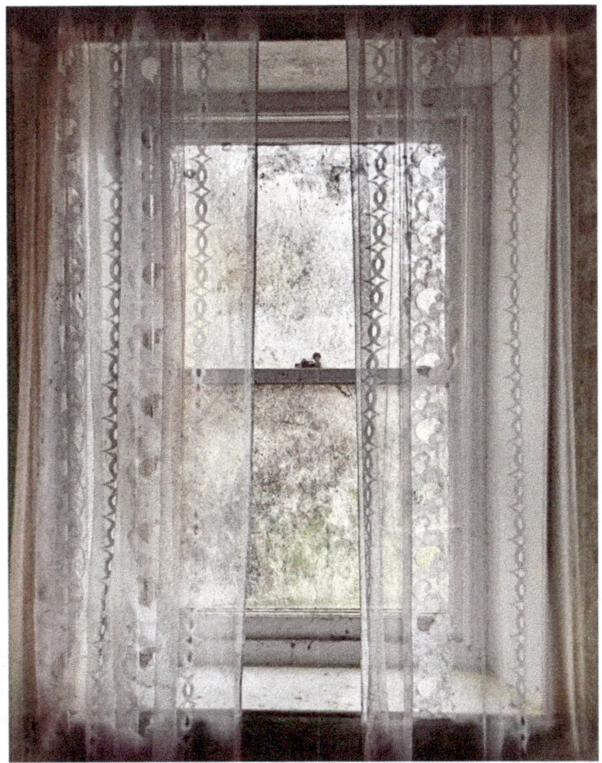

The Net Curtains, Gortletteragh, County Leitrim – Image: Paul Butler, April 2011.

Photographic Note: This room was incredibly dark. I always record the original image in RAW format. RAW format (.NEF) file is an image file format that allows you to record every bit of data in a scene, so that when you want to process a digital image you have greater latitude to enhance/balance the image, pull detail from the shadows and decrease highlights and so on. The file type most people would use to when taking an image is a (.jpg) file. It is a compressed version and allows for practically no alteration to shadows or highlights, what you see is what you get. I could in post-production bring up as much shadow detail as possible without affecting the light balance of the window frame. However, as you can see there is lot of 'noise' in the image ('noise' makes it looks like a very grainy image). This 'noise' is due to the very high ISO (film speed) used. I was hand holding the camera, and I had to use a very fast shutter speed. It would have been better to use a tripod and make a long exposure, but needs must, and I was tied for time.

And in a further connection to the window scene 'The Net Curtains' I refer to this beautiful piece taken from the website 'As I have understood him' with the words credited to Algerian-born French philosopher Jacques Derrida: 'We may now define trace as the sign left by the absent thing, after it has passed on the scene of its former presence. Every present, in order to know itself as present, bears the trace of an absent which defines it.'[25] This is very apposite for this window scene 'The Net Curtains', which does provide a 'trace' of a relived past in the present.

The scene 'Within Reach' with its broken windowpane and white pony was recorded in August 2011. It is a personal favourite because I am drawn to decay and destruction, though not in a negative sense. I am drawn because decay contains a hidden beauty. And this scene creates such impact, the rotting window frame and peeling paint signifying unfulfilled dreams. The broken glass directs your gaze onto an off centred white pony, offering freedom, adventure and the unknown. All these signifiers, an alluring contradiction, that you few chances in life, so take them when they come, for they are soon lost. Or do nothing. I really like that this scene contradicts and jars. I now illuminate the scene further with this passage from *The Barracks*:

> She was determined to grasp at a life of her own desiring, no longer content to drag through with her repetitive days, neither happy nor unhappy, merely passing them in the wearying spirit of service; and the more the calls of duty tried to tie her down to this life, the more intolerably burdened it became. [*B*, p. 15]

25 Jayant Prasad, 'Derrida: The Father of Deconstruction': <https://newderrida.wordpress.com/2007/11/19/some-key-terms/> (2007).

'Within Reach' adorns the cover of *The Reimagining Ireland Reader: Examining Our Past, Shaping Our Future.*[26] And as of November 2022, this ruined cottage is currently 'For Sale'.

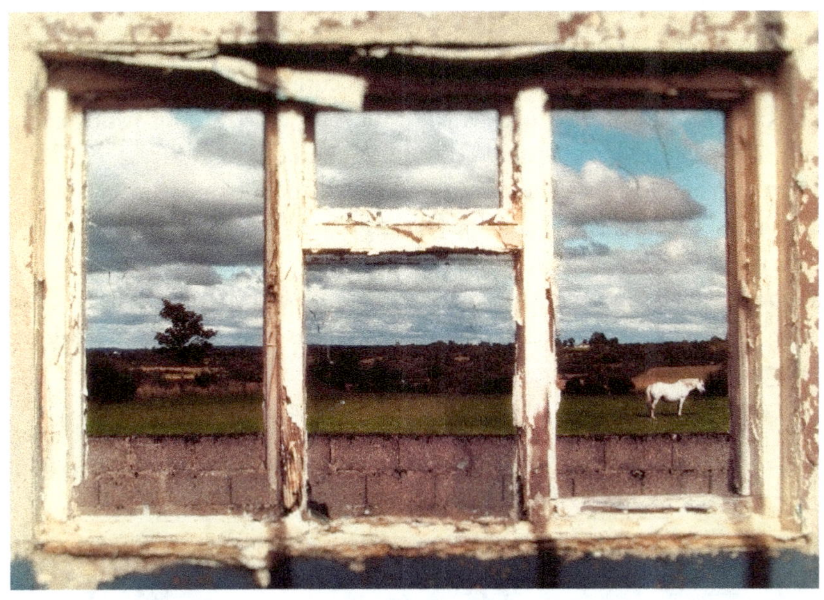

Within Reach, Beihy, Fearglass, County Leitrim – Image: Paul Butler, August 2011.

Photographic Note: Just to confirm that the white pony was 'not' added in post-production. This scene is exactly as I recorded it. I had to move numerous times as I could not get a practically straight on shot of the window frame. I had very little wriggle to play with. You can see that the frame is a little off horizontal. I had noticed the pony standing in the field so I eventually got into a position where I could place the pony as if it was leaving the frame.

Another time I was out driving on a grey and miserably wet Sunday in April 2016. On numerous occasions I have passed a very run-down and damp cottage not far from Bellantra Bridge, over the Black River, on the road from Mohill in County Leitrim to Drumlish in County Longford. The cottage had

26 *Reimagining Ireland: Examining Our Past, Shaping Our Future*, edited By Eamon Maher (Oxford: Peter Lang, 2018).

never really piqued my curiosity, until I noticed that it was now 'for sale', and decided that before it was cleared out I would stop and have a look around. I opened the latch, it did not budge, so I put my shoulder to the door and gave it a little shove. The door scraped along bare stone flagstones into what I presumed would be an empty shell, only for me to discover old furniture, cookbooks and other items strewn around. Off this main room was a closed door with its brown paint well faded. I was curious and I turned the rusty old knob gave it a little shove, which it didn't need. The door swung open and sitting before me was an old travel chest and the scene 'Travel & Tales'. Forgotten and forlorn on a small wooden table beside the window, a wonderful scene unravelled as I imagined having to drag the trunk around on your travels. Or more likely than not, you would have packed all your belongings as you had no choice but to leave Ireland to find work. This was before the time of the compact wheelie bag. And I use this passage from *Memoir* to bring alive the reality of one of those journeys:

> In the 1950s a half-a-million people emigrated from this small country, nearly all of them to Britain, far more than in any other decade in the entire century. [*M*, p. 209]

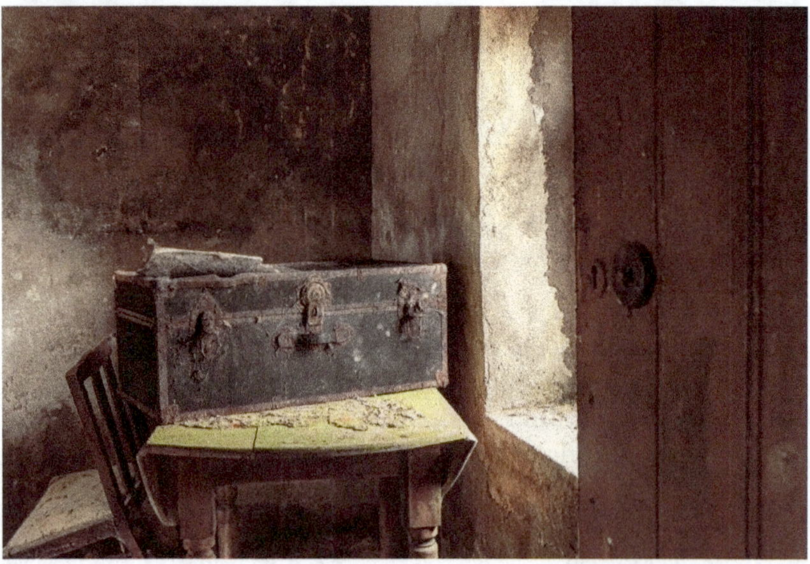

Travel & Tales, Drumshambo South, County Leitrim – Image: Paul Butler, April 2016.

Photographic Note: I adjusted the table to help illuminate the scene with the north-west facing window to allow as much clean light fall onto the travel chest.

The low cloud really helped soften the light, which is ideal for portraiture. The brown rusted handle and clasps clash beautifully with the neutral plastered walls which are complimented by the green mould slowly colonizing the table. Overall, the earthy colours are quite pleasing to the eye. I had noticed that some remedial work had been attempted on the window well. There is a deep silent beauty about this scene and the timeless imaginative journeys it evokes. It is wonderful that by recording these fading scenes some eventually end up as book covers. They are frozen in perpetuity and that makes me feel very happy indeed. This image of the old travel trunk now adorns the cover of *Essays on John McGahern: Assessing a Literacy Legacy*.[27] I also contributed a chapter and a series of images to this publication.

Within the scene 'The Good Suit' recorded in 2011, the lines from a McGahern short story, 'The Country Funeral', stimulate the senses; you can smell cigarette smoke trapped within the room. And once again I like the fact that the net curtains are still in place. The rusty latch on the window frame was not for budging as years of paint have sealed it tight. And hanging from the wardrobe, were the good Sunday clothes.

27 Eamon Maher and Derek Hand (eds), *Essays on John McGahern: Assessing a Literacy Legacy* (Cork University Press, 2019).

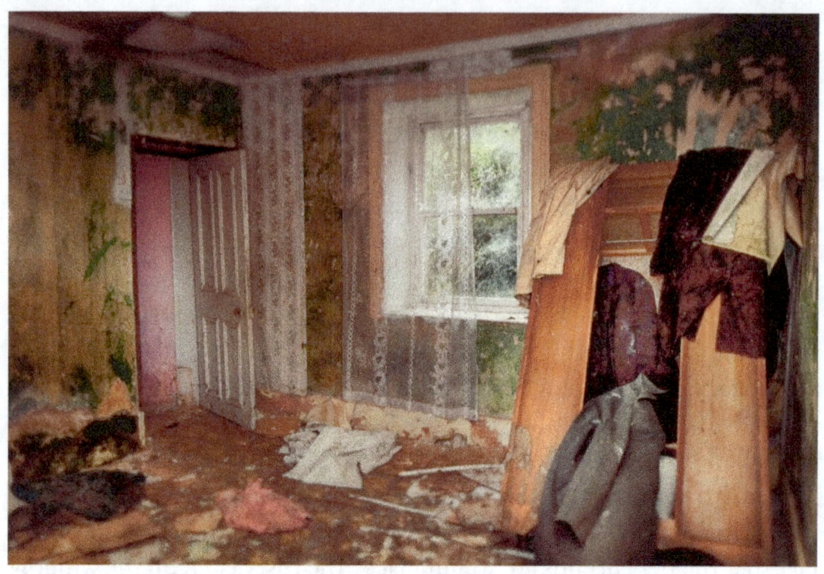

The Good Suit, Gortletteragh, County Leitrim – Image: Paul Butler, April 2011.

> In the house Philly went from room to room to let in fresh air but found that all the windows were stuck. [*CE*, 'The Country Funeral', p. 394]

In April 2021, I managed to gain access to a unique and derelict house, not far from our home. It had been boarded up for many years. I refer to it as 'The House of Windows'; it has floor to ceiling windows on the front of the house. The name 'LM Kearney and date 28/06/56' was drawn on one of the bedroom walls. A story I had heard was that a former owner may have worked for the Department of Agriculture. This may explain the large windows, designed to let in as much light as possible for the benefit of the many plants. The house built from mass concrete, is to be completely renovated.

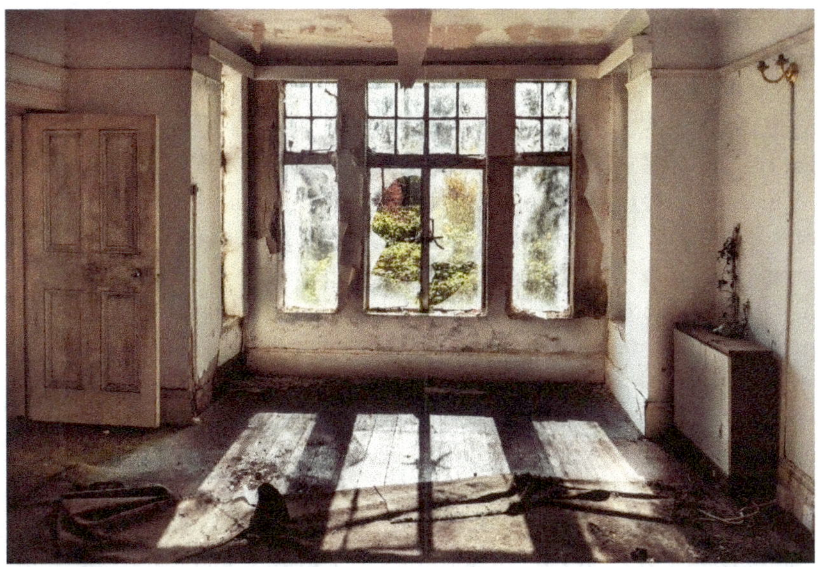

The House of Windows, Gortletteragh, County Leitrim – Image: Paul Butler, April 2021.

The structure itself is in poor condition and a substantial amount of remedial work will be required. But it will be a very fine house if it is renovated in a style fitting its character, especially if the large metal window frames are reconditioned. This old house is all about windows; it is all about the light.

The High Nelly bicycle as a primary mode of transport

In the County of Leitrim there were only 169 cars in 1915.[28] One can assume that by the 1940s there were still quite scarce, particularly with the Second World War and the Emergency in full swing. In 2003, Christy

28 CSO, 'Life in 1916 Ireland': <https://www.cso.ie/en/releasesandpublications/ep/p-1916/1916irl/economy/tp/> (2014).

Tiernan, the postmaster at Farnocht, passed away at the ripe old age of eighty-nine. A wonderful tribute was published in *The Hogan Stand*: 'In 1936 Christy Tiernan purchased a hackney car – a 14.9 Ford. Christy's hackney service was very much in demand during the Second World War. He transported expectant mothers to the maternity hospital and was as accurate as a register when it came to dates of birth in the area. The price of the fare to the All-Ireland semi-final in Croke Park in 1947 was a cut price of £6 a car.'[29] The economic war with Britain from 1932 onwards had further depressed the Irish economy so that the bicycle was the most popular mode of transport along with the extensive rail network that still existed during that time. The reason I include this small section on the bicycle is that I constantly stumble upon old rusting bicycles among many of the houses I have photographed. They too [bicycles] have their history and the vivid description of the McGahern's father cycling in the wind and rain on his rounds is described within McGahern's work's including *The Barracks, The Rising Sun* and his short stories. Here are a few lines from *Memoir* regarding his father cycling from the barracks in Cootehall, Roscommon, to the family home at Aughawillan, Leitrim, 'I remember him most of all arriving out of wet dark nights, his black cycling cape and pull-ups and black sou'wester hat shining with rain' [*M*, p. 69].

The scene 'The Vicious Collie' encapsulates the solitary cyclist and that slower and easier approach of travelling from place to place. I captured this image on the road just outside our house on a cold and misty January morning. Next door, an elderly neighbour possessed a bad-tempered collie. We were all afraid of her; she showed a lot of signs of instability. Being a working dog, she should have been on a farm and not left outside a house all day unattended. Sometimes she was chained up, abandoned and alone, and you could hear her howls as she tried to break free.

29 Hogan Stand, Leitrim: <https://hoganstand.com/County/leitrim/article/index/38808> (28 February 2003).

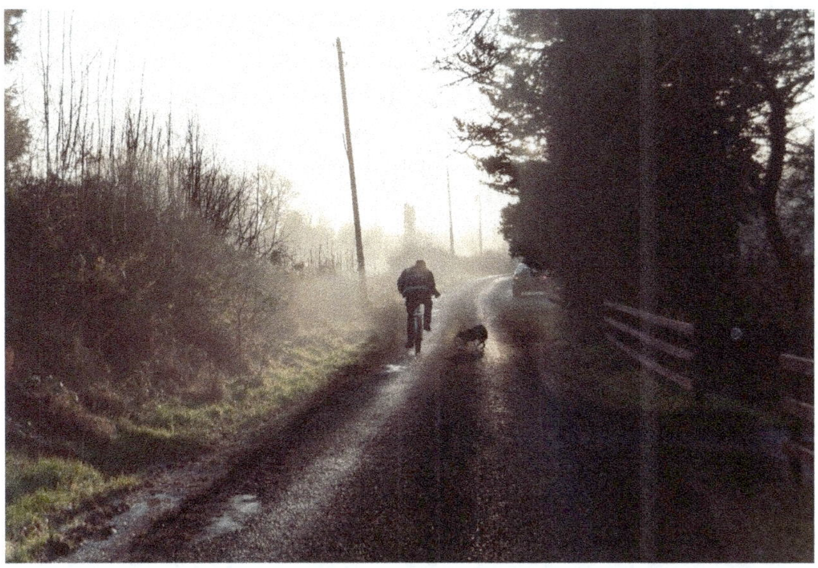

The Vicious Collie, Farnocht, County Leitrim – Image: Paul Butler, January 2014.
Photographic Note: I always felt that this image worked best with a strong black & white contrast.

Every time I headed out on a walk, I really needed to keep my wits about me. That morning the cyclist passed by with his head down as I walked out our gate. Luckily, I had my camera thrown over my shoulder. I turned and watched as the cyclist was slowly consumed by the mist. I spotted the dog hiding behind the hedge waiting for the unsuspecting victim. However, this cyclist was obviously used to the unexpected and showed no surprise as the dog ran out and snapped at his heels. He calmly cycled on deftly raising his legs, avoiding any attempted nips. The morning fog added to the drama of this scene. I captured the scene just as the dog made one more attempt to bite. Sometimes you are in the right place at the right time. This image is now the cover of *The Rainy Day*, by Martin Keaveney, a collection of short stories about farmers: young and old, cunning, foolish, greedy, generous, talented and forgotten.[30] And as noted in this piece from

30 Martin Keavney, *The Rainy Day* (Castlebar: Mayo Books 2018).

Ireland's Own: 'It was not unusual for people to travel over thirty miles at a time to a nearby town on business, or to attend a football or hurling match. Michael Collins rode around his High Nelly, an anonymous figure to his enemies in the early 1920s.'[31] Overlooked and discarded, the bicycle was an essential and mostly the only cost-effective and practical way for connecting from place to place.

The old Cavan & Leitrim narrow gauge railway

Cavan & Leitrim Railway was a narrow gauge network that ran from Dromod to Mohill and onto Ballinamore and Arigna. A branch also ran from Ballinamore, County Leitrim to Belturbet in County Cavan. This branch line ran close to the McGahern homestead, stopping at Garadice Halt. The branch line closed in 1959. In *Memoir*, McGahern fondly remembered taking the train to Ballinamore as the station at Garadice would have been a short walk from their house.

> Most Saturdays I went to town on the train with my mother. [*M*, p. 71]

31 Mary Conliffe, 'My Mother's High Nelly': <https://www.irelandsown.ie/just-a-memory-my-mothers-high-nelly/>.

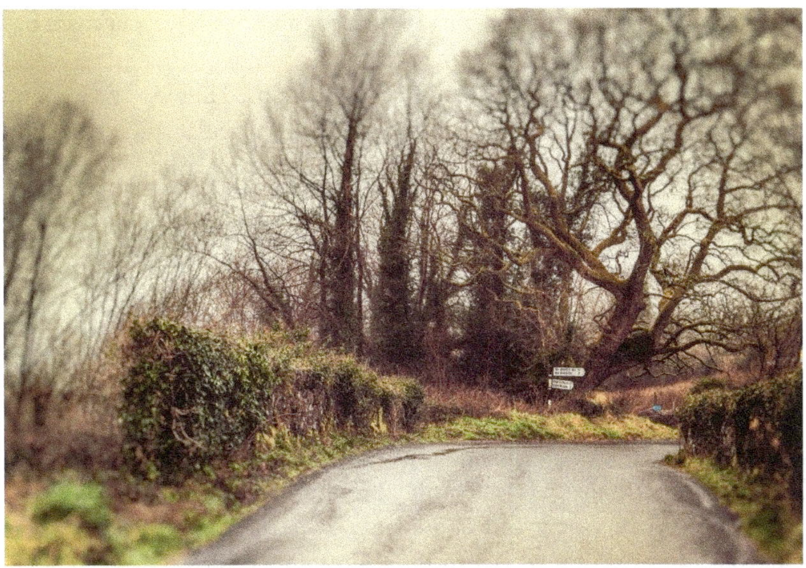

The 3-Arch Masonry CLR Railway Bridge Close to Aughawillan, County Leitrim – Image: Paul Butler, February 2019.

The bridge over the old branch line was over one kilometre from the homestead in Corramahon. As you approach the bridge from the townland of Corramahon, the road gently rises, and swings left towards Ballinamore. It is near this turn you would have found Garadice Station where a young McGahern would have got the train. Garadice is approximately five kilometres from Ballinamore. The station at Garadice was in operation from 1887 until 1959 when the line closed. Today, the old branch line is a very sad state, and one of the old station buildings is on private property, surrounded by woodland. There are plans to turn the old narrow gauge route into a Greenway along the complete length of the original Cavan & Leitrim Railway line from Mohill to Belturbet. Here is a short piece about the railway line from the Rev. Roger Farnworth's 'The Cavan and Leitrim Railway': 'The Cavan & Leitrim Railway was a 3ft (914 mm) narrow gauge in the counties of Leitrim and Cavan in the northwest of Ireland. It ran from 1887 through until 1959. It survived because it carried coal from the mine at Arigna.'[32]

The Arigna mines in County Roscommon closed in 1990 and in 2003 reopened as the Arigna Mining Experience. The spectacular entrance setting to the interpretative centre with views across the north midlands towards Lough Allen are compelling: 'Coal mining provided much needed work in a region of poor agricultural land, it is often said: "There was money in Arigna when there was no money elsewhere." '[33]

The train station at Dromod is on the main Dublin-Sligo rail line, and the Cavan & Leitrim Narrow Gauge Heritage Museum sits opposite this busy station. Facing the main station car park you will find the beautifully quant red brick station house belonging to the old narrow gauge and alongside is a small transport museum. A one-kilometre stretch of narrow gauge track with an operational engine and livery serve as a tourist attraction.[34] A very poignant quote fro*m That They May Face the Rising Sun* illustrates the importance of the train towards the economic reality for this area. At that time in our young nation's history, emigration was rife, and remittances kept the country afloat:

> The train from Dromod. Two drinks in the bar across from the station waiting for the train that you'd be as well without. There's nothing to celebrate seeing someone going. [*RS*, p. 95]

32 Roger Farnworth, 'The Cavan and Leitrim Railway': <https://rogerfarnworth.com/2019/05/09/the-cavan-and-leitrim-railway-a-short-history-and-a-look-at-dromod-station/> (19 May 2019).

33 Arigna Mining, 'A Tradition That Runs Deep': <https://www.arignaminingexperience.ie/history/>

34 Cavan and Leitrim Railway, 'Museum': <https://www.familyfun.ie/cavan-and-leitrim-railway/>.

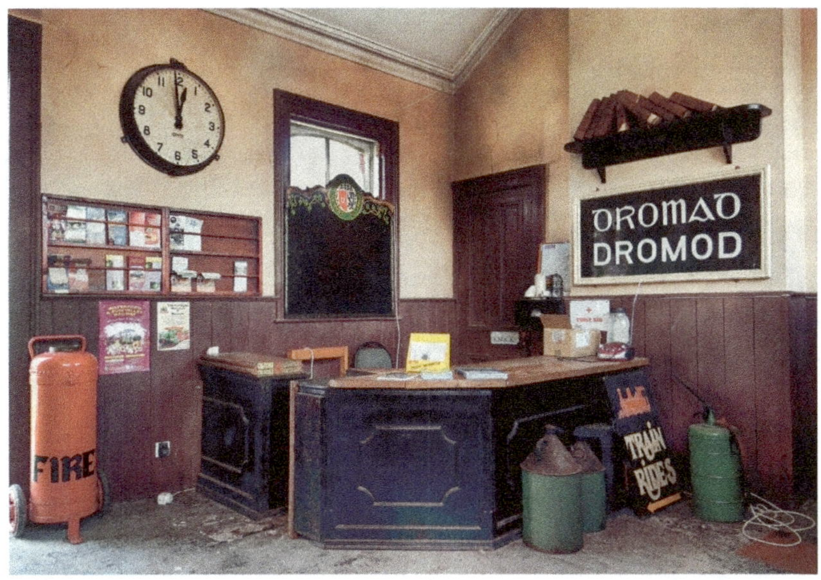

Original Waiting Room at the Cavan and Leitrim Railway Heritage Museum, Dromod, County Leitrim – Image: Paul Butler, June 2013.

A wonderful article in the *Irish Times* by Rodney Edwards noted thus: 'Sixty years since Border rail transport ran out of steam', bemoans the closure of rail network similar to the Cavan & Leitrim Railway, 'Willie Gault, a guard with Sligo, Leitrim, and Northern Counties Railway, boarded the train from Enniskillen, Co Fermanagh, to Manorhamilton, Co Leitrim, and back one last time on September 30th, 1957. The closure of over 200 miles of railway connections disappeared and it had a significant impact on many rural towns such as Bundoran, Clones, Enniskillen, Omagh, Sligo and Armagh, and many small villages in between.'[35]

35 Rodney Edwards, 'Sixty Years since Border Rail Transport Ran Out of Steam': <https://www.irishtimes.com/news/ireland/irish-news/sixty-years-since-border-rail-transport-ran-out-of-steam-1.3232191> (25 September 2015).

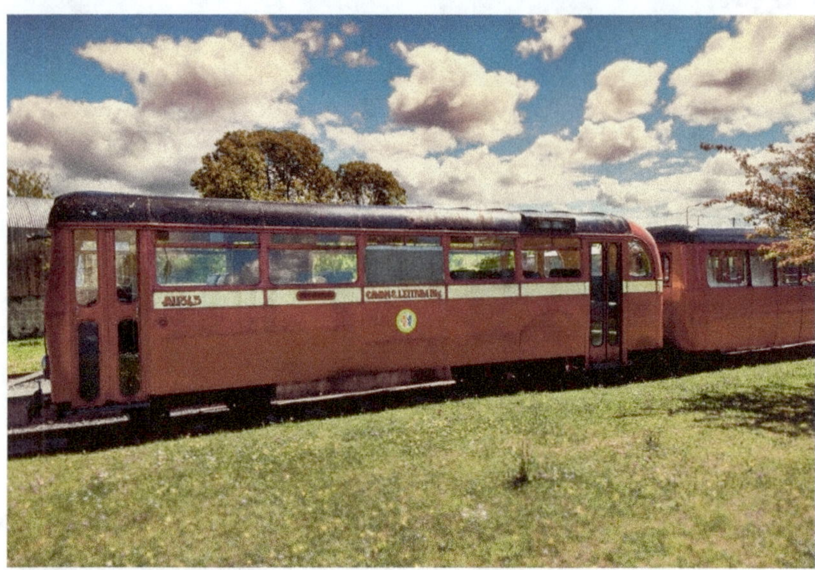

Railbus at the Cavan and Leitrim Railway Heritage Museum, Dromod, County Leitrim – Image: Paul Butler.

And when you include the partition of Ireland and the closure of rail lines in west Ulster, this all had a devastating effect on cross-border rail services, especially in the north-west of the country. Donegal lost all its rail connections. It is hard to believe that in Ireland up to the 1930s the island was covered with so many rail routes it was possible to travel the length and breadth of the country by train.

Landmarks

MJ Henry's Bar, Cootehall, County Roscommon, mentioned in *Memoir*, is one of a few of McGahern's fictional places, and it is visible from inside the church; in fact, the church is right opposite the pub. One can visualize sneaked glances as Sunday Mass droned on and on, the desire must have quickened for a pint and a quick catch-up on local gossip before 'the dinner'. The importance of the pub as an integral part of the locality is alluded to in *Memoir*, Every night Master Glynn went to Henry's bar, where he was popular with his old pupils [*M*, p. 29].

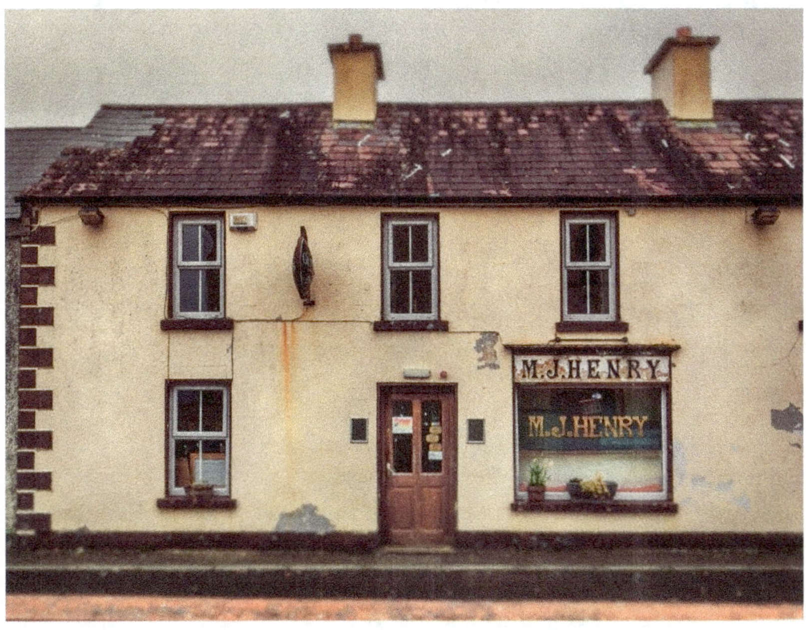

MJ Henry's Bar, Cootehall, County Roscommon – Image: Paul Butler, April 2018.

I came across this interesting article in the *Irish Times* which refers to McGahern and to Mohill: 'Author John McGahern described Mohill, Co Leitrim as beautiful "in its plain way", and said the first sign that winter was over was when he saw bags of seed potatoes and bundles of cabbage plants on the corner outside Luke Early's bar on Main Street.'[36] Shopping and market days drew McGahern to Mohill. He had a great fondness for the place.

36 Marese McDonagh, 'Mohill Was a Dead Town but It Is Reinventing Itself': <https://www.irishtimes.com/news/ireland/irish-news/adapting-to-survive-mohill-was-a-dead-town-but-it-is-reinventing-itself-1.3671955> (23 October 2018).

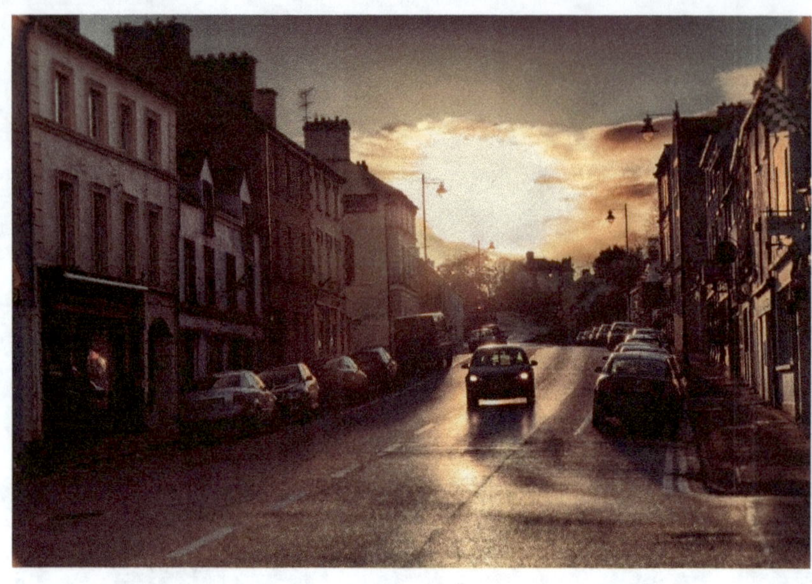

Main Street, Mohill, County Leitrim – Image: Paul Butler, October 2014.

The scene 'Paddy McManus at work' in a small garage in Ballinamore, County Leitrim, is relevant to this section. The image was recorded in the actual garage mentioned in *That They Face the Rising Sun*. To this day, it is still known as 'The Shah's Garage'. 'Their ways and habits helped. The Shah liked to rise early. Frank Dolan seldom got out of bed before midday but would work late into the night' [*RS*, p. 132].

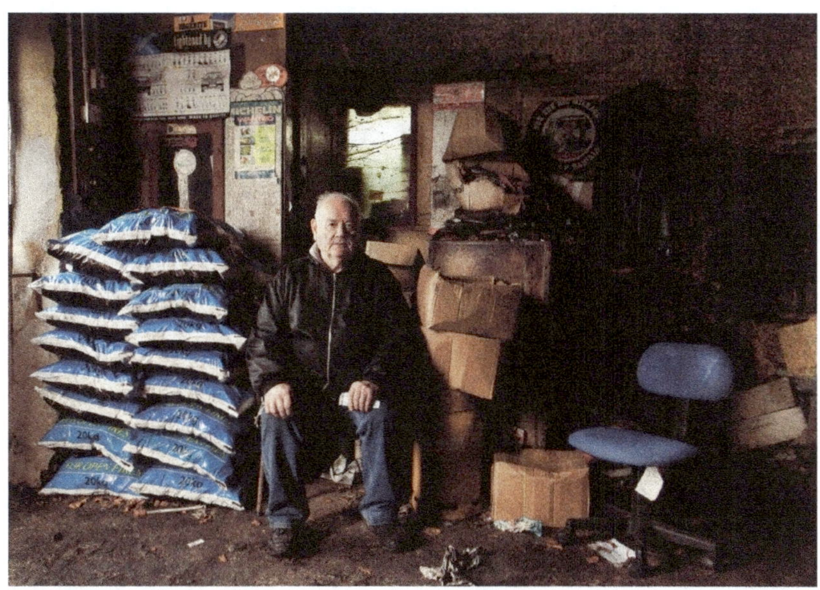

Paddy McManus at Work in the Shah's Garage, Ballinamore, County Leitrim – Image: Paul Butler, October 2013.

The reason it gained the nickname 'The Shah's Garage' was that during the global oil crisis[es] of the 1970s, they were one of the few garages in the area able to provide petrol and diesel for their favourite customers. I recorded this image of Paddy McManus, cousin of John McGahern, in October 2013 when Paddy still worked part-time at the garage.

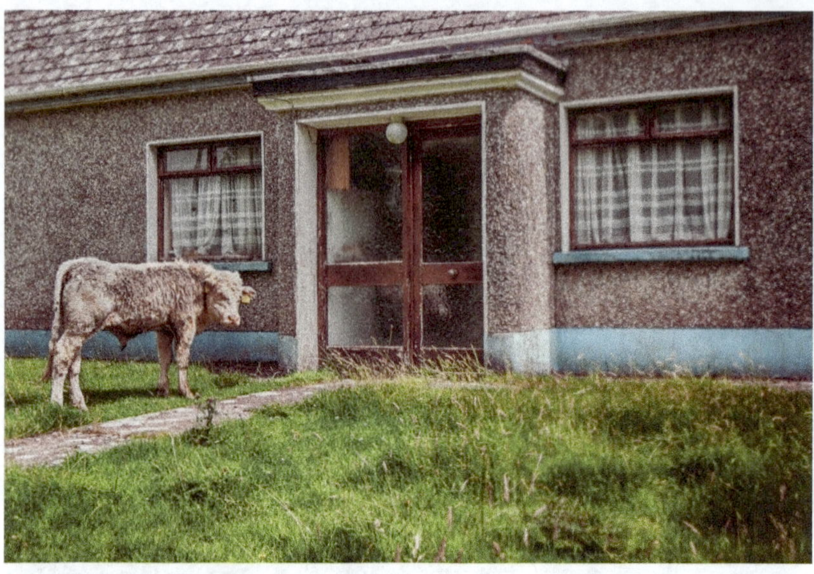

Home for Lunch, Near Cornacarta, Elphin, County Roscommon – Image: Paul Butler, July 2016.

Some of our neighbours have cattle on a few acres. They are occasional farmers as other full-time employment is necessary to supplement the farm grant. These grants help keep these smallholdings alive, allowing most farmers to act as custodians of the land. You will come across many small fields clogged with reeds and waterlogged. And during the winter, a few cattle are still strewn around muddy fields, and in some cases a solitary beast standing to attention. As previously mentioned in the section on Landscape, the soil is poor in Leitrim and not conducive to crop growing.

As an exception, not far from our house is a large dairy herd, but that is unusual as you will mostly find smallholdings with just a few cattle sold on for beef.

Quoting from a 2013 report from *Agriland*, it was found that within Connacht the average herd size is 32 cows. In the Ulster counties of Donegal, Monaghan and Cavan, the overall average herd size is 43 cows. The lowest average herd size noted was in Leitrim at 24.9 cows.[37]

37 Tom O'Callaghan, 'Regional Divide in Herd Sizes': <https://www.agriland.ie/farming-news/analysing-herd-sizes/> (25 October 2013).

I will end this chapter with this image of 'The Lonely Chair' recorded in July 2019, symbolizing what is lost and the emptiness still inhabiting this area. This house where the chair resides is located within 'Ivy Clad House' which appears close to the beginning of this chapter. As detailed earlier, the house was hidden within a Cóillte plantation for over thirty years and now is revealed. In this scene, I really like the window draped naturally with ivy as nature reclaims the building; time moves forward. The soft light entering the room creates gentle pastels. This little brown chair, waiting or hoping for someone to return and once again sit and look out onto the wonderful view of the north midlands. What becomes of this house on the hill? I hope it is not allowed to fade away. The only limit is our imagination.

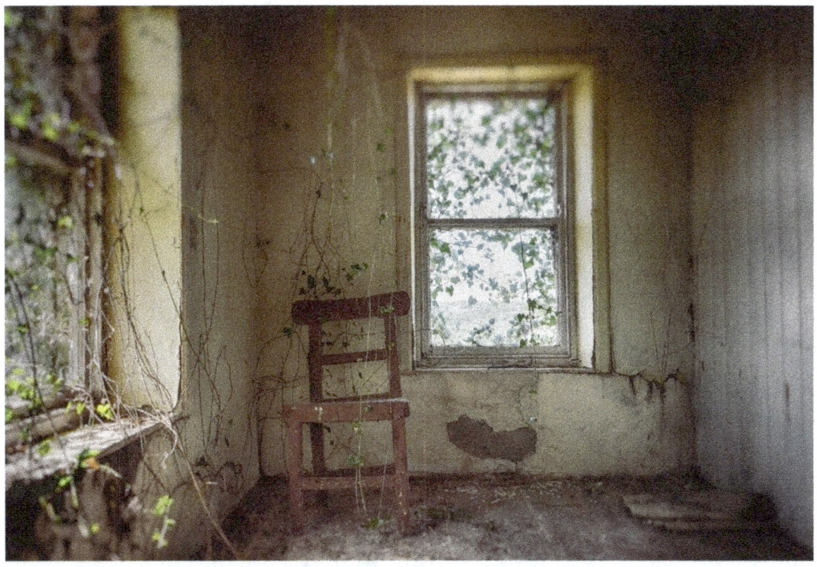

The Lonely Chair, Mucknagh, County Leitrim – Image: Paul Butler.

I shall leave the last word on this chapter to John McGahern, who said in an interview with Hermione Lee: 'I think that each of us inhabits a private world that others cannot see.'[38]

Addendum: Leitrim and the economic crash of 2008

After talking about dwindling Protestants and the abandonment of houses and land within the fading world of McGahern, this addendum is important within the context of cyclical economic hardship for Leitrim. During McGahern's time, for many it was immigration, or stay put and exist off the bare fields, and, with luck, maybe some paid employment.

However, for a few golden years in the noughties, the decline halted – it was a building boom and party time in Ireland. In Leitrim, due to the incentivized tax break for the north Shannon region (known as Section 23),[39] houses and developments shot up like mushrooms all over the county. The good times had come to Leitrim. Unfortunately, it suffered from badly planned, ill-suited and pretentious developments not suited to this little quiet county. Following the global economic crash in 2008, Leitrim again became neglected with swathes of the county littered with ghost buildings and estates. And just like the decline of the aristocracy, the abandonment and depopulation of the county began once again. It would have been interesting to get McGahern's view on this; alas it was not to be. John McGahern died in 2006, just a couple of years before the country imploded as the Celtic Tiger was brought to its knees. When the economy spectacularly tanked, the north-west of Ireland, which includes Leitrim, was one of the worst affected areas. And according to the Census of Population 2016,

38 Hermoine Lee, 'In Conversation with John McGahern': <https://lannan.org/images/lit/john-mcgahern-040407-trans-conv.pdf> (7 April 2004).

39 Section 23 Tax Relief: <https://www.revenue.ie/en/tax-professionals/tdm/income-tax-capital-gains-tax-corporation-tax/part-10/10-11-01.pdf> (Updated 2022).

for every 1,000 people in Leitrim there were 112 vacant homes.[40] The *Irish Times* reported that rents in Leitrim increased dramatically due to people leaving the cities during the Covid pandemic.[41] And in the first quarter of 2022, rents were on average 24.8 per cent higher than a year previously. The cycle continues for this little county.

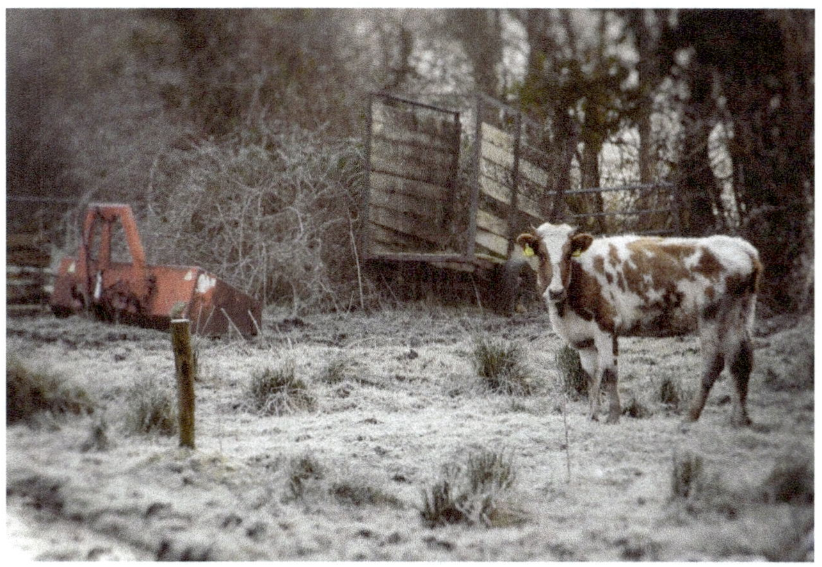

Gabriel's Cow, Farnocht, County Leitrim – Image: Paul Butler, February 2018.

40 CSO, 'Census of Population 2016 – Profile 1 Housing in Ireland': <https://www.cso.ie/en/releasesandpublications/ep/p-cp1hii/cp1hii/vac/>.

41 Marese McDonagh, 'Leitrim Rents Driven Up by People Leaving Cities during Pandemic': <https://www.irishtimes.com/news/ireland/irish-news/leitrim-rents-driven-up-by-people-leaving-cities-during-pandemic-1.4726167> (12 November 2021).

CHAPTER 4

Ritual

Dana Radler in her article 'A Lifetime Memory Quest: Identity, Places and Characters in John McGahern's *Memoir*' notes in relation to certain characters that McGahern depicts: 'For all the characters in *Memoir*, life revolves around religious practice, each day starting with a prayer and all major events being referred to as marked, influenced or decided by God.'[1] Eamon Maher develops this point in some more detail:

> In some ways, the Catholic Church of McGahern's youth worked hand-in-glove with the emerging state and together they controlled a docile population who were happy to do what they were told most of the time.[2]

Religious themes flow through McGahern's work, from his description of the Rosary in *The Barracks* to the significant details surrounding the rituals of death in his short story 'A Country Funeral'. The smells, colours and rituals are plainly visible on the pages of his work and in the visual vignettes that he supplies. Religion constituted a major part of rural life in the middle decades of the past century (and still does in some communities to the present day) and though the Catholic Church has recently seen a significant decline in its reputation, faith remains a big part of in the lives of people living in Ireland.

In an article that he wrote on this subject entitled 'The Art of Memory in the Work of John McGahern', Peter Declan Guy notes, 'McGahern's

1 Dana Radler, 'A Lifetime Memory Quest: Identity, Places and Characters in John McGahern's *Memoir*': <https://www.researchgate.net/publication/328969147_A_Lifetime_Memory_Quest_Identity_Places_and_Characters_in_John_McGahern's_MEMOIR> (December 2015).

2 Eamon Maher, *'The Church and Its Spire': John McGahern and the Catholic Question* (Dublin: Columba Press, 2011), p. 16.

short stories combine historical facts and sociological observations with fictive elements and personal recollections, thus producing an alternative history of his epoch.'[3]

The scene 'Crumbling Frame of Saint Anthony & the Infant' blends with the following lines from *Memoir*. I use this scene to illustrate the innocence and absolute trust McGahern felt surrounded by:

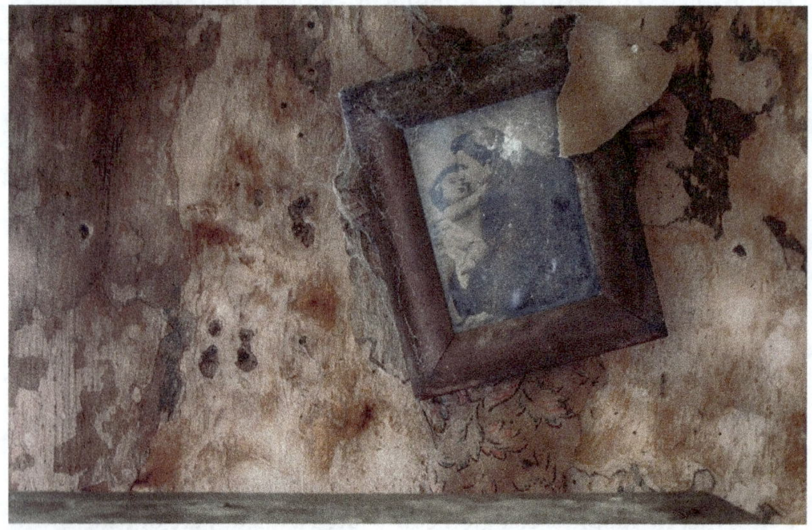

Crumbling Frame of Saint Anthony & the Infant, Curraghroe, County Roscommon – Image: Paul Butler, April 2016.

> Between this hell and heaven, purgatory was placed. Descriptions of it were vague, probably because all of us expected to spend time there. [*M*, p. 11]

The aged brown hues allude to a different era and the muteness of this scene guides you towards a sensation of an immutable place. McGahern

3 Peter Declan Guy, 'The Art of Memory in the Work of John McGahern' (Academia) Unpublished paper.

acknowledges the debt he feels he owes his exposure to Catholicism and its rituals in his essay 'Love of the World':

> I have nothing but gratitude for the spiritual remnants of that upbringing, the sense of our origins beyond the bounds of sense, an awareness of mystery and wonderment, grace and sacrament, and the absolute equality of all women and men underneath the sun of heaven. [*LW*, p. 133]

So, it can be taken as a given that religion, and particularly Catholicism, informed McGahern's work to a significant degree. The rituals associated with it, along with the local customs and practices of the people to whom he gives life in his art, are by extension core to his aesthetic goals. McGahern was acutely aware that the influence on Catholicism was all-pervasive during his youth. It was part of the fabric of life at the time. Such a commitment (even if it was at times superficial, almost pagan) does not disappear overnight. It lies hidden in people's psyche; affects the way they think and act.

Religion and McGahern's early years

Leitrim sits within the diocese of Ardagh and Clonmacnoise; this diocese is entirely within the Republic of Ireland and spreads across the counties of Longford, Leitrim, Cavan, Offaly, Roscommon, Sligo and Westmeath. Regarding the history of the diocese: 'Ardagh was erected as a Diocese by the Synod of Kells (1152) and was made a suffragan of Armagh. In the thirteenth century a dispute arose as to whether it was subject to Tuam or Armagh. Gregory IX ordered an investigation in 1235 and it was resolved in favour of Armagh'.[4] In 1961 in Ireland, 94.9 per cent of the population were Catholic – this was the highest percentage ever recorded. Leitrim may still be considered by some a religiously conservative area; however, during the abortion referendum, the result for the constituency

4 Diocesan Office, 'Historical Reference: Merging Together': <https://ardaghdiocese.org/historical-reference-merging-together/> (3 March 2022).

of Sligo-Leitrim was: 'Yes' – 59.38 per cent and 'No' – 40.62 per cent. During the vote for amendments to the divorce legislation, Sligo-Leitrim returned a 64.94 per cent 'Yes' vote.

In contrast, the result for legislation for same-sex marriage was possibly a bit skewed, with Leitrim being spilt in two and attached to different constituencies. North Leitrim-Sligo voted 'Yes' – 53.57 per cent. South Leitrim-Roscommon voted 'No' – 51.42 per cent. This was the only constituency to vote against the proposal and was heavily criticized. However, when one looks deeper at the voting pattern for this constituency as mentioned in The Journal.ie website: 'All of this criticism comes despite the fact that more people voted "Yes" in Roscommon-South Leitrim (17,615) than in both Donegal North-East (16,040) and Donegal South-West (15,907) and that fewer people voted "No" in Roscommon-South Leitrim than in 13 constituencies.'[5] So in effect, Leitrim voted 'Yes' in all referendums and is not that religiously conservative.

This 'rose-tinted' form of Catholicism stayed with McGahern throughout his life: its pageantry and mystery appealed to, and nourished, his artistic imagination. He remarked in *Love of the World* that he lived in a 'theocracy in all but name' and described the Ireland of his youth and early adulthood in the following terms: 'Churches in my part of Ireland were so crowded that children and old people who were fasting to receive Communion would regularly pass out in the bad air and have to be carried outside' [*LW*, p. 149].

During the 1940s and 1950s, Christian Brothers, nuns and priests were recruited at a very young age. The new recruits were often from poorer families who felt honoured to see their children become men and women of the cloth. They would be people who were respected, looked up to, sought out for guidance. Growing up in Ireland during McGahern's era, sexuality and freedom of thought were heavily repressed with the Church dominating practically every facet of life. Despite the War of Independence and the aspirations contained in the 1916 Proclamation, a rigid form of Roman

5 Paul Hosford, 'Why Did Roscommon-South Leitrim Vote No?': <https://jrnl.ie/2121899> (24 May 2015).

Catholicism came to the fore. The struggle for independence resulted in one power block (the British Empire) being replaced by another (the Catholic Church and a compliant political class) in the twenty-six counties.

McGahern alludes to this in *Memoir*:

> The Church controlled nearly all of education, the hospitals, the orphanages, the juvenile prison systems, the parish halls. Church and State worked hand in hand. [*M*, p. 210]

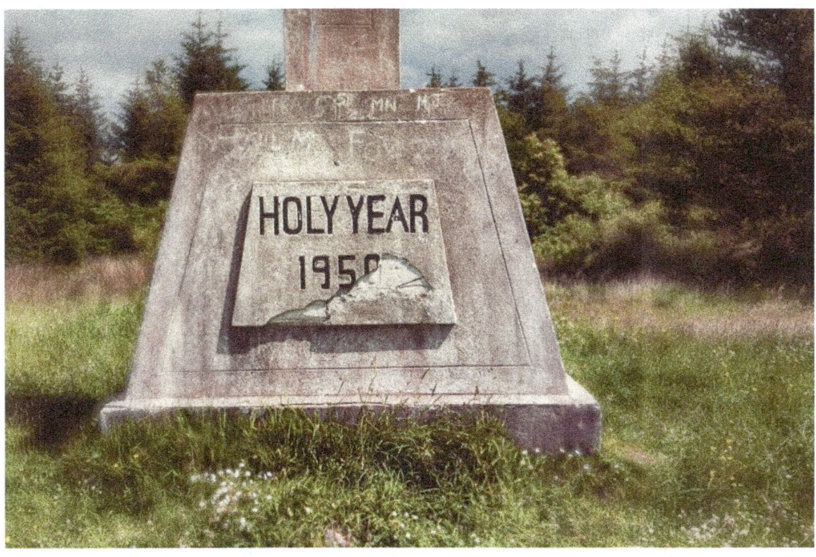

Marian Year Cross, Sliabh Bawn, County Roscommon – Image: Paul Butler, June 2014.

Photographic Note: This concrete Holy Year Cross sits atop the second peak (254m high) at the Sliabh Bawn Amenity Area. And now since the wind farm and amenity area have opened this Marian Cross has been painted white and repaired. Personally, it looks awful as the original grey colour gave it character and an agelessness.

Clearly, this was a very different society to the one that pertains to Ireland now. Everything was skewed in favour of men, and women were left in horrific pain during childbirth and often suffered lifelong injuries after giving birth. In the interview with Eamon Maher already referred to,

McGahern observes how religion underscored the foundation of his childhood:

> The rosary was said every evening. I always liked that sentence about the medieval churches, that they were the bible of the poor. The Church was my first book and I would think it is still my most important book. At the time, there were very few books in the house.[6]

These observations are far from being completely negative. McGahern also emphasized the beautiful ceremonies and the way in which religion offered distraction from the backbreaking work and austere lives of the people. He also notes how alongside the oppressive monolith that was the Church, popular devotions flourished, none more prominent that the key role that was played by the cult of the Virgin Mary. McGahern also refers to the power of the Church in the essay, 'Saving Grace', published by the *Guardian* in 2006 shortly before his death:

> I grew up in what was a theocracy in all but name. Hell and heaven and purgatory were places real and certain we would go to after death, dependent on the Judgement. Churches in my part of Ireland were so crowded that children and old people who were fasting to receive Communion would regularly pass out in the bad air and have to be carried outside. Not to attend Sunday Mass was to court social ostracism, to be seen as mad or consorting with the devil, or, at best, to be seriously eccentric.[7] (Note: this quote also appears in *Memoir*.)

A passage from *The Barracks* written in 1963 clearly illustrates a similar view to 'Kitchen Interior', recreated a thousand times over in so many homes across the country. McGahern created his rooms from memory as in the lines below. You will notice that there is a great deal of reverence in this image, as all items flow in a pattern from the Sacred Heart downwards towards the parents of the house and then outwards towards their home.

6 'Catholicism and National Identity in the Works of John McGahern', p. 72.

7 John McGahern, 'Saving Grace' (Essay): <https://www.theguardian.com/books/2006/apr/08/featuresreviews.guardianreview30 > (2006).

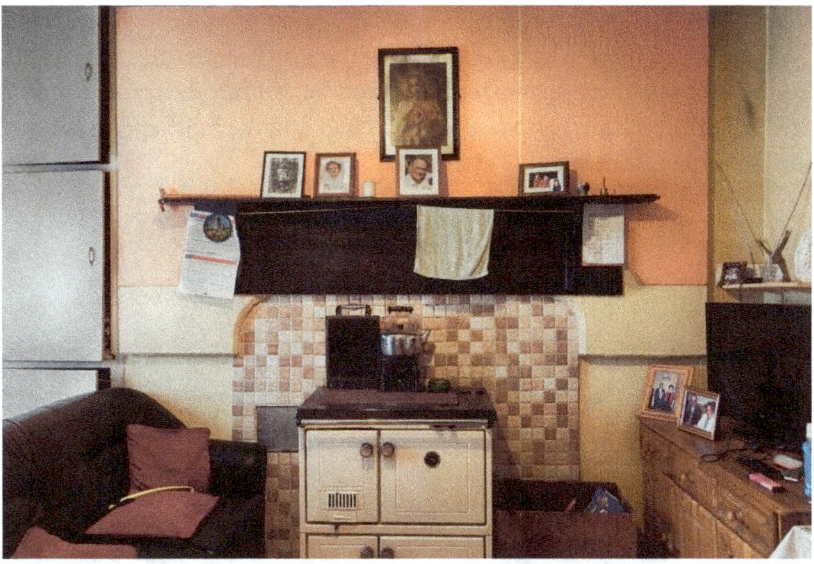

Kitchen Interior, Trish Carrigy's Old Family Home, Aughagreagh, Banninalee, County Longford – Image: Paul Butler, September 2014.

Photographic Note: A long exposure helped to gather the low warm tungsten light and no artificial light used. In post-production, a colour correction on the window light removed a slight blue cast. In addition, the colour correction of overhead tungsten helped reduce the overall yellow colour cast. A wide aperture of 27mm allowed me to encompass the full interior. To counter lens distortion a correction filter within Photoshop removed this.

And when we add the passage from *The Barracks*, we can enhance the colour and warmth of the scene in 'Kitchen Interior':

> The bright golds and scarlets of the religious pictures on the walls had faded, their glass glittered now in the sudden flashes of firelight, and as it deepened the dusk turned reddish from the Sacred Heart lamp that burned before the small wickerwork crib of Bethlehem on the mantelpiece. Only the cups and saucers laid ready on the table for their father's tea were white and brilliant. [*B*, p. 1]

Growing up in Leitrim, McGahern looked upon religion and his mother as being somehow melded. She had a deep spirituality that impressed her son. And within the image 'Mother & Child', recorded in the old kitchen at Curraghroe, County Roscommon, there are lines from *Memoir* that reinforce that closeness, evoking as it does the unshakeable bond that McGahern shared with his mother. Within the scene 'Mother & Child', the realistic grasp of the child's hand on the mother's cloak adds further embellishment:

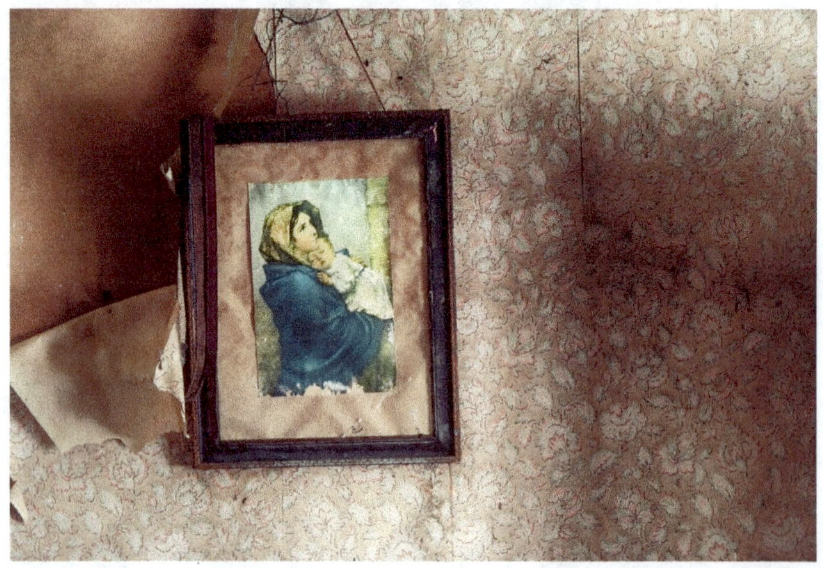

Mother & Child, Curraghroe, County Roscommon – Image: Paul Butler, April 2016.

> Heaven was in the sky. My Mother spoke to me of heaven as concretely and with as much love as she named the wild flowers. [*M*, p. 10]

The scene 'Mother & Child' in a photographic analogy is a kind of double exposure, using a photograph of an old religious image hanging on a wall to visualize a powerful bond. Even though the cheap religious print hanging on the wall has faded over time, there is emotion reflecting from the scene. The old brown string stubbornly holding the picture in place after so many years, in some ways, reinforcing that this dream will never fail. And the torn and faded wallpaper drawing you to the revelation of a bare wall, thus creating that notion of stripping back everything you know and everything you feel to one fundamental emotion and bare desire. This 'want' is what McGahern always deeply desired – the need to return to that deep unconditional love. This image 'Mother & Child' does represent what a young McGahern would have taken as truth and trust from his mother. His absolute devotion of his mother and need for her constant attention are noted by Dana Radler:

> Frequently though those intricate and fine or hard emotions are not revealed directly, but through the memorization of physical movements and gestures, as in the scene evoking briefly and humorously a boy's increasing jealousy to his own siblings: 'I was a single star until the twins arrived, and I became insanely jealous of the natural transfer of attention.'[8]

The passing of Susan McGahern had such a profound effect on him; it was more than just a death; it was a massive loss from which he never fully recovered. The visualization of the Virgin Mary in 'Mother & Child' holding a sleeping child is seen as comforting, and the loss of a sanctuary of love and tenderness is felt – our long journey through life to its conclusion:

> We come from darkness into light and grow in the light until at death we return to that original darkness. [*M*, p. 360]

McGahern and the rituals of the Church

The church was the focal point of the surrounding area, a reassuring presence with a quietness which appealed to McGahern's mother, Susan. The space allows her to think and then there is the calming effect of prayer, especially the rosary, which grew into her life, the exquisiteness of the ceremonies that were held there. In 'The Church and Its Spire', McGahern bemoaned how in Ireland we chose to abandon Gothic church architecture, whose tall spires raised people's glance from the avaricious earth and invited thoughts of the transcendent, in favour of the Romanesque, with

8 Radler, 'A Lifetime Memory Quest'.

'the low roof, the fortress, the fundamentalists' pulpit-pounding zeal, the darkly ominous and fearful warnings to transgressors' [*LW*, p. 145]. In *Memoir*, he recounts how unimpressed he was with certain aspects of the Church of his early childhood in Aughawillan, County Leitrim. When going to Mass, he would have walked the two kilometres from home with his mother and siblings, past the school where his mother taught.

As an altar boy, McGahern had an opportunity to see first-hand all that went into the preparation and celebration of Catholic religious services such as baptisms, weddings, funerals and, most notably, the Eucharist. The atmosphere in the church would have been very different to the one he was accustomed to at home, and it held an undoubted appeal to him. He associated the softer, more spiritual side of religion with his mother, and McGahern was excited at the prospect of serving at the altar as this was a further link in the chain with his mother. However, there were also ceremonies conducted that are now quite archaic as remembered by McGahern in *Memoir*:

> As an altar boy in red and white with a lighted candle I took part in many ceremonies of 'churching'. [*M*, p. 52]

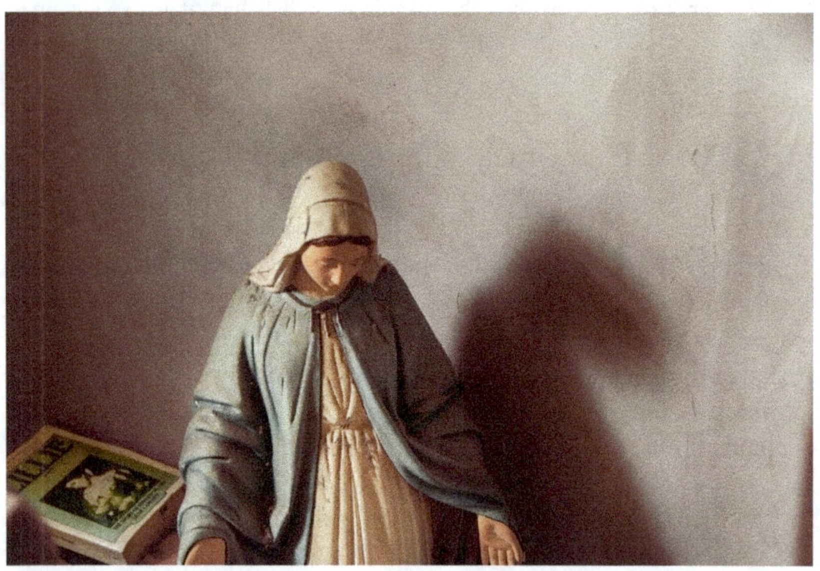

Statue of Mary in the Dining Room, Aughancliffe, County Longford – Image: Paul Butler, May 2017.

There is some confusion as to what 'churching' was. A useful resource I find is *History Ireland* and on their archival website I came across the following article that attempts to explain some aspects concerning this ordeal:

> The medieval church practised 'churching' as a rite of purification and thanksgiving for the safe delivery of a woman after the birth of her child. It marked the end of the 'green month' of the woman's confinement and her resumption of normal domestic life and sexual relations with her husband. At the Reformation nonconformists rejected churching, but Catholic and Anglican churches continued the practice into the late nineteenth century. It was universal at all social levels – even Queen Victoria was churched.[9]

Thankfully, the practice of 'churching' has disappeared in Ireland, even though it still pertained up until a few decades ago. How a woman who had brought a baby into the world, the most natural and sacred of all acts, could have needed purification afterwards is difficult to comprehend. It probably had a lot to do with the Church's view of sexuality as being invariably linked to sin, even within marriage. I had chosen the image 'Statue of Mary in the Dining Room' to symbolize the ritual of 'churching' because of the way that the head of the statue is bowed, epitomizing the futility of another ridiculous attempt at the subjugation and humiliation for women. This scene visualizes how wronged a woman must have felt over this ritual. However, the slight smirk on the mouth of the statue does promote a delicious irony or should I say, 'two fingers' to the whole ritual of 'churching'. In this image 'Statue of Mary in the Dining Room', you will notice a novel titled *Lillie* (in the bottom left corner of the scene). This novel tells the story of Lillie Langtry, who became the mistress of the future King Edward VII (while he was Prince of Wales) from 1877 to 1880. Lillie also took several other lovers, including Prince Louis of Battenberg, the Prince of Wales's future nephew-by-marriage, who possibly fathered her only child.[10] The fact the novel is visible in the image 'Statue of Mary in the Dining Room' offers an amusing juxtaposition.

9 Fiona Fitzsimons, 'History Ireland – Churching': <https://www.historyireland.com/churching/> (February 2020).

10 Lillie Langtry, 'British Courtesan and Actress': <https://www.encyclopedia.com/women/encyclopedias-almanacs-transcripts-and-maps/langtry-lillie-1853-1929>.

The Rosary, Mass and Confession

Like so many Catholic countries, a familiar item in Ireland were, and still are, rosary beads. They are our form of worry beads and are an essential part of the ritual of the Rosary. According to the *Catholic Exchange*:

> The origins of the rosary are rather sketchy at best. The use of prayer beads and the repeated recitation of prayers to aid in meditation stem from the earliest days of the Church and has roots even in pre-Christian times. Evidence exists from the Middle Ages that strings of beads were used to help a person count the number of Our Fathers or Hail Marys recited. Actually, these strings of beads became known as *Paternosters*, the Latin for "Our Father."[11]

For a young McGahern, religion formed an essential part of family life in the household. In some ways, the rituals could be a comfort, which was so important for its time. And McGahern directly references the rosary beads in *The Barracks*:

> The eternal medals and rosary beads were waiting on the spikes of the gate for whoever had lost them. [*B*, p. 14]

11 William Saunders, 'Origins of the Holy Rosary': <https://catholicexchange.com/origins-of-the-holy-rosary>.

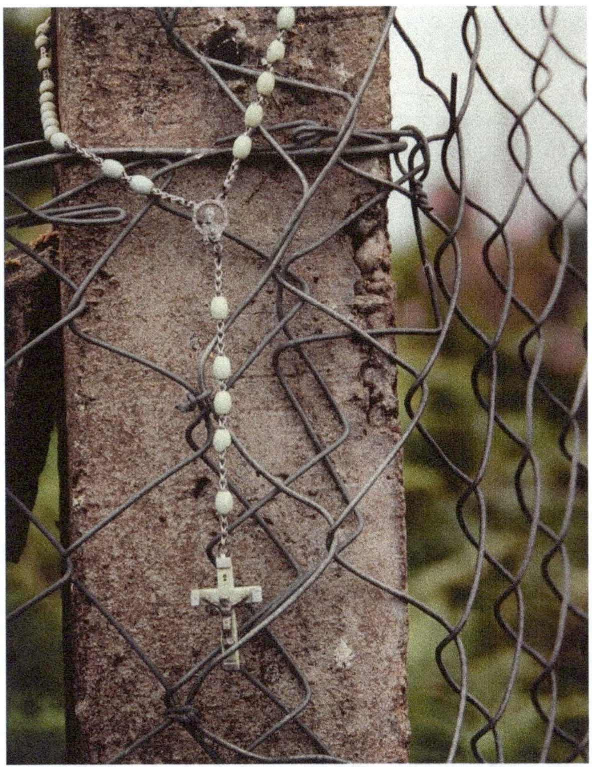

Rosary Beads at the Dublin/Sligo Rail Crossing at Aghnamona Bog Nature Preserve, County Leitrim – Image: Paul Butler.

Photographic Note: This image contains a burnt sienna effect which I added in post-production to globalize the scene; it could easily be South America or Russia, wherever you choose.

I recorded the image of the 'Rosary Beads' in situ at the railway crossing in Aghnamona Bog, County Leitrim, while waiting for the train from Sligo to Dublin to pass. This small road across the bogland takes you to the village of Roosky.

Mass and other ceremonies were such an important part of McGahern's childhood, and attending them with his mother and her absolute joy at the solitude she experienced gave him much delight. In contrast,

McGahern's depiction of Elizabeth Reegan's approach is commented on by Eamon Maher:

> Elizabeth is probably untypical of many of the women of her acquaintance in that she spent a period nursing in England, where she discovered a different approach to religion and to life. Her affair with Halliday, a depressed doctor with a very bleak outlook on existence, taught her that there are many different types of pain and that it is up to the individual to cope as best he or she can with the hand that is dealt them.[12]

McGahern regularly remarked on his mother and father's different approach to religious devotion, the father being more of the harsh, authoritarian mind-set, whereas the mother was far more spiritual and gentler. The following lines illustrate his father's deliberate exploitation of religious devotion to bolster his own position: 'In his shining uniform he always walked with slow steps to the head of the church to kneel in the front seat. She would slip quietly into one of the seats at the back' [*M*, p. 47].

And while Elizabeth Reegan would not allow herself to become part of a labour pool for the parish priest in *The Barracks*, McGahern creates that sense of solemnity and beauty of his mother's observance in what Elizabeth expresses: 'She'd been brought up in fear of God but what remained most powerful in the memory was the church services, always beautiful, especially in Holy Week' [*B*, p. 123].

Rituals were indissociable from religion and as such, they were scripted into daily life. You will sense the change in McGahern's tone from the heavenly adoration of his mother to the factual description when talking about his father's ritual of shaving. The razors in the image 'Ritual of the Razor & Religion' implies so much tension and menace in direct contrast with the gentle and iconic faces of Mary and Jesus gazing upwards.

12 Eamon Maher, '*The Church and its Spire*', p.37.

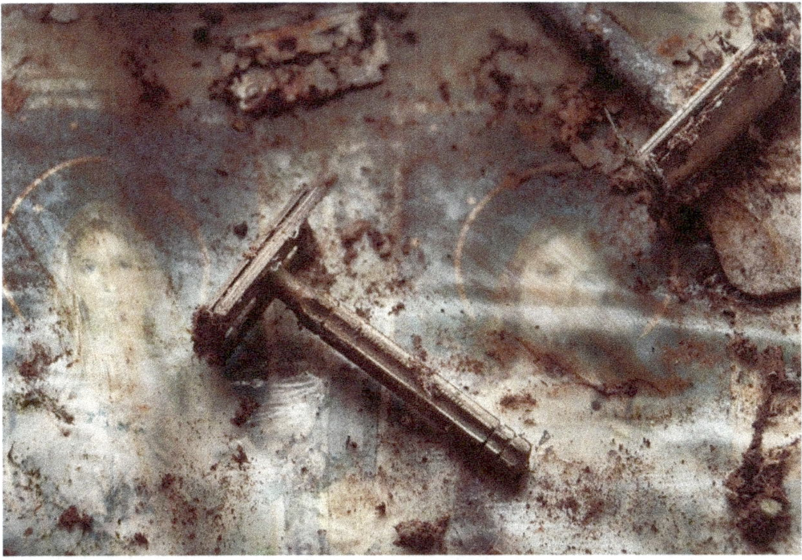

Ritual of the Razor & Religion, Gortletteragh, County Leitrim – Image: Paul Butler, April 2011.

Photographic Note: I was delighted to discover this scene on the sill in the old cottage. I had to rub off some of the grime from the faces to make them a bit more obvious. I was pleased with the soft light diffused by the grime on the sash window.

McGahern's description of his father shaving in *Memoir* conveys the same sense of tension and menace:

> While he sharpened his open razor on a leather strap that hung from the wall, we'd pour the shaving water into a basin that stood in a tall, rusted, iron stand in front of the scullery window. [*M*, p. 32]

If we compare the passage above with the following lines from *The Barracks,* we see how McGahern has embellished the ritual of shaving and further ramps up the tension felt by the children observing Reegan:

> He [Sergeant Reegan] took down the plain wooden box that held his shaving kit from the top of the medicine press and opened it on the sewing-machine to get his cut-throat razor and he stroked it over and back the strip of fine leather tacked to the side of the press. [*B*, p. 43]

The image of the razors is another personal favourite, and it is one of the earlier images I created for this project. The dust and dirt covered religious card under the razors lying on the old sill says so much about this important ritual. Closing my eyes, I remember my father using that type of razor and I can still smell the warm soapy water. I can still hear the blade scraping against the hard stubble on his skin.

One often has the impression when reading McGahern's fiction and prose writing that the adherence to Christianity was as much a thing of habit and social pressure as a genuine commitment to a particular form of faith. People went along with what society expected of them. They conformed outwardly, while continuing to doubt a lot of the dogma that was preached from the pulpit. McGahern admitted on numerous occasions that everyone looked forward to the parish missions with the Redemptorists, especially because of the fire and brimstone sermons that were given. It was all great drama and excitement during those times and an occasional touch of the religiously exotic elicited great excitement in their otherwise dull lives as he mentioned in *Memoir*:

> Every few years Redemptorists came to the village like a small band of strolling players and thundered hell and damnation from the pulpit. [*M*, p. 202]

My own views on organized religion have changed over the years. Brought up in the Catholic tradition, I did attend Mass as a child, but stopped in my late teens. I would consider myself closer to nature, from which I get my spiritual energy. I have no need or desire for enlightenment within a large gathering in a church. I am often reminded of a saying my father used when quizzed by my mother as to why he was not going to Mass: 'I'd be closer to God up in that greenhouse than I'd ever be in a church.' That also sums up my own position with regard to religion. These lines from *The Barracks* captures that fear of making the slightest sound, a fear of an autocratic Church, a fear of God and multiple doubts about oneself: 'She might have been kneeling in the queue in front of the confessional and her turn to enter into the darkness behind the purple curtain coming closer and closer' [*B*, p. 79]. John McGahern considered a vocation to the priesthood for a certain period. It was not unusual for young boys to choose that path in the 1930s and 1940s in rural Ireland in particular. It appears he looked on it as a form of attachment or fulfilling a contract he made to his mother. His love for her and his love of ceremony and rituals were as one. In *A Private World,* he refers to his calling:

> I thought for a long time that I'd be a priest. And the closer I got to that decision the more seductive and attractive the life of the world was. For my life when I was young the story of Christ and the ceremonies of the church and the seasons completely explained our lives and gave meaning to our lives. [*PW*]

Susan McGahern and the rituals associated with death

The publication of *Memoir* in 2005 ultimately confirmed that places, people and episodes previously encountered in the novels and short stories were close transpositions of the writer's own experiences. And within this section we see how McGahern translates his own experience into his writing. *Memoir* illustrates his mother's quiet nature. You really sense his strong admiration of her unquestioning faith, particularly as she sensed that her health was failing:

> 'God has given me near perfect health for forty years', she wrote to my father. [*M*, p. 47]

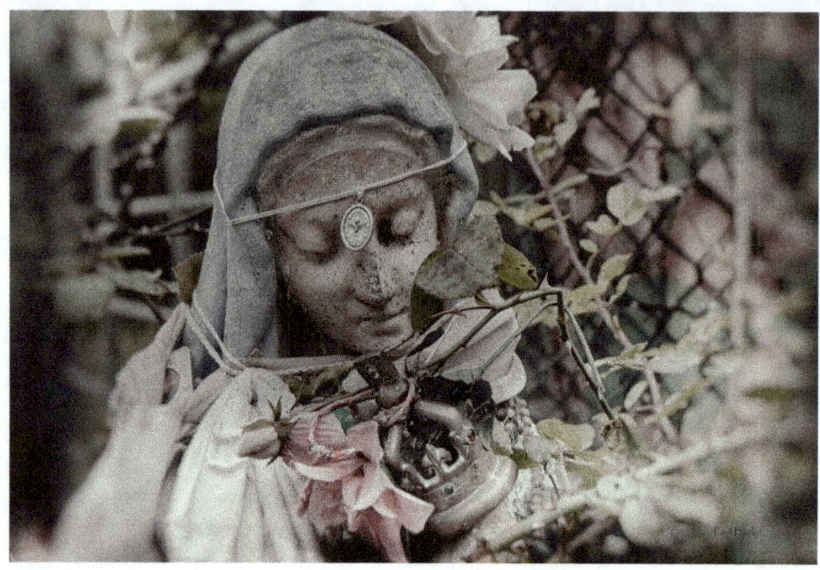

Serenity, Ogulla Shrine, County Roscommon – Image: Paul Butler, July 2016. Photographic Note: In post-production, I made the decision to place over this image a 'Victorian Plate Glass' treatment. I wanted this print faded, scratchy and historic to visualize McGahern's near ethereal experience of his mother that he wished to re-enter and re-emerge himself within. This post-production treatment is: 'The wet-collodion process, also called collodion process was an early photographic technique invented by Englishman Frederick Scott Archer in 1851. The process involved adding a soluble iodide to a solution of collodion (cellulose nitrate) and coating a glass plate with the mixture.'[13]

This image 'Serenity' is full of wisdom, innocence and uncertainty. I admire the ad hoc nature of the personal offerings adorning the small statue. The rose vine growing up and across the figure, signifying the beauty of growth and gentle flowering of time, while thorns represent a sharp rebuke unless you show those offerings due respect. All these juxtapositions occur as her downward gaze exudes grace and calmness. I feel it is a way to visualize McGahern's mental image of his mother. The following

13 *Encyclopaedia Britannica*, 'Wet Collodion Process': <https://www.britannica.com/technology/wet-collodion-process>.

lines from 'High Ground' further illuminate this scene, reinforcing that feeling of closeness, vulnerability and untouchability. Once again, we can sense through his words that close connection he shared with his mother, and the pedestal upon which he placed her:

> After the harshness of growing up, a world of love and beauty, of vague gardens and dresses, one woman in a gleaming distance seemed to be almost within reach. We would enter this world. We would make it true. [*CE*, 'High Ground', p. 190]

Referring again to McGahern's use of memory, Guy states: 'Memories do not simply link his characters to the past; they also enable them to review it and to reorganize it imaginatively. Memory and imagination provide comfort and shelter and are essential tools for survival and escape from a reality which is often painful and gloomy.'[14] Susan McGahern had a special relationship with God, one which transcended even what she felt for her husband and children: He was her Alpha and Omega, the source from which she sought solace at times of deep pain and worry. McGahern wrote with huge affection about his mother, blending memories and aspects of her personality into some of his female fictional characters. The scene 'Bedroom Interior' is so practical and feminine in its composition. The pinkish wall colour, the ironing board, the mirror, the crucifix and Mother Teresa are all there. Life with all its beauty and banality carried on for his mother even though she battled the incurable cancer. Her faith remained strong.

14 Guy, 'The Art of Memory in the Work of John McGahern.'

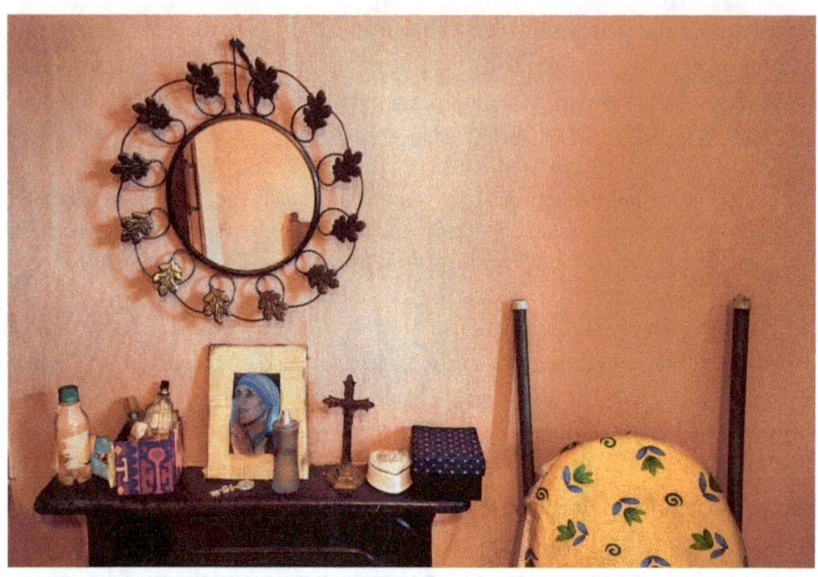

Bedroom Interior, Trish Carrigy's Old Family Home, Aughagreagh, Banninalee, County Longford – Image: Paul Butler, September 2014.

It is hard not to consider that McGahern was thinking of his mother coping with her cancer diagnosis in the following passage from *The Barracks*:

> She had naively trusted that she'd be given some sign or confirmation before the end, or that she'd discover something, something she knew not what, some miracle of revelation perhaps, but she had been given nothing and had discovered nothing. [*B*, 85]

McGahern's mother, who died when he was just ten years old, was a very devout woman whose dying wish was that her son would become a priest. This did not happen for many reasons, the main one being that it was the mother, and not the son, who had the vocation. And the further I attempt to visualize McGahern, the more I realize that the ritual of death and loss left an indelible mark. He was such a wounded soul.

There is a cut-stone estate cottage which was once part of the large Lough Rinn Estate. This building has a beautiful secret garden that is infinite, so full of nooks and crannies. This cottage sits opposite St Mary's

Church of Ireland, in Farnocht, County Leitrim. Within the garden, there is this crumbling garden ornament of a crying child being comforted. It sits by a little red bridge that guides you over a stream, well hidden within. I recorded 'The Crying Child' during the heavy snowfall of December 2010. This scene beautifully illustrates the following lines from *Memoir* that are so deeply moving as a failing Susan McGahern tries to help a young John McGahern understand that her time was nearing its end:

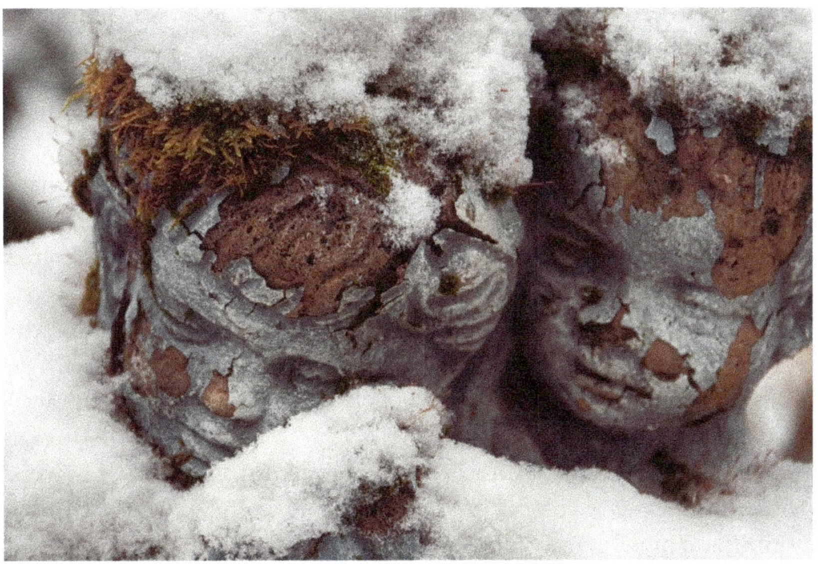

The Crying Child, Farnocht, County Leitrim – Image: Paul Butler, December 2010.

> 'I don't want you to be too upset if I have to go away. And I want you to do all that you can to help the others and to keep them together.' 'Go where?' 'If God calls me and I have to go.' [*M* p. 117]

Combining passages with the scene, 'Crying Child' portrays so much sadness and comfort, a fitting choice also for the passages from *Memoir* and *The Leavetaking*, encapsulating the phenomenal trauma and loss McGahern suffered as a child:

> 'I came to say goodbye, Mammy.'
>
> Her eyes were fixed on my face; she seemed to be very tired. I bent to kiss her. She did not move. I was bewildered. Both Maggie and the nurse turned away. [*M*, p. 124]

And in *The Leavetaking* we have the following description:

> "I'll say Masses for you when you're dead."
>
> "You'll say Masses for me when I'm dead," she repeated with a catch of a breath.
>
> "Lots and lots of Masses for you. You'll hardly have to spend any time at all in purgatory with all the Masses." [*L*, p. 28]

Elizabeth Reegan approaches death with an equanimity that owes something to the feeling that she had not been a bad person, that she had in general led a good life. McGahern's painful memories of his mother's passing and his own experience of attending many funeral ceremonies come into play within the next few passages. When the moment comes within *The Barracks* and Elizabeth Reegan passes, McGahern details the traditions associated with death: 'The priest and doctor were sent for, the body washed and laid out – the eyes closed with pennies and her brown beads twined through the fingers that were joined on the breast in prayer' [*B*, pp. 221–2].

And now McGahern creates that sad and intimate world of prayers, neighbourliness and respect in 'The Country Funeral': 'All through the evening and night people kept coming to the house while others who had come earlier quietly left' [*CE*, p. 389].

The image 'And Time Is Stilled' captures the inexorable passage of time frozen at a specific point that comes to life each time a person views the scene. The calendar is open on January 1960; the clock stopped at 5.48. These are specific temporal reference points, but the scene is normal, timeless and universal. The scene also takes on a particular life for me, with the marks on the calendar and the stopped clock. Who made those marks and ticked off the days?

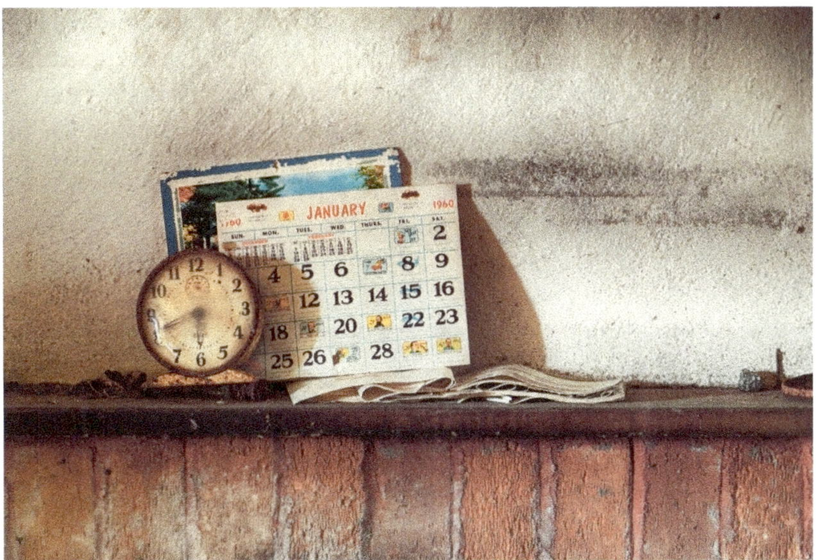

And Time Is Stilled, Curraghroe, County Roscommon – Image: Paul Butler, April 2016.
Photographic Note: As stated previously, this abandoned home in Curraghroe, County Roscommon, was an absolute treasure trove of imagery. This little scene on the mantelpiece is very poignant. The old Sweet Afton pack brings back many memories of my long-gone granny in Piltown, County Kilkenny, smoking those untipped cigarettes. And I note that the unwound clock and the calendar look fresh even after fifty plus years.

The following passage from McGahern refers to a specific tradition:

> An X was drawn through each day of every month until October was reached. On the twenty-second of October, the march of XX's across the days came to a stop. The twenty-third of October was the first clear day and all the remaining days of the year were unmarked. 'That was the day he died', Jimmy Joe said. [*RS*, p. 18]

The mourners are following customs that have been in existence for centuries in Ireland. They are present to lend their support to the bereaved, to celebrate the life of the person who has passed, to partake of the hospitality that is always supplied on occasions such as these. Where I live in south Leitrim, when a local person passes away it is touching to see the number of cars that arrive to offer condolences; it is as if the whole county knew the deceased. In addition, it saves the people having to go to the funeral Mass the next morning if they can get in quickly and be seen to offer condolences. I can hear the soothing church bell of Gortletteragh church carry across the fields as the death notices carry from the radio in the local shop. In *Memoir*, McGahern's personal memories meld with his imaginative interpretation to create this beautiful and sensitive evocation:

> They'd lift her from the bed and place her in the wood. They'd put the lid in place and turn the screws. Never would her face be seen again. [*M*, p. 131]

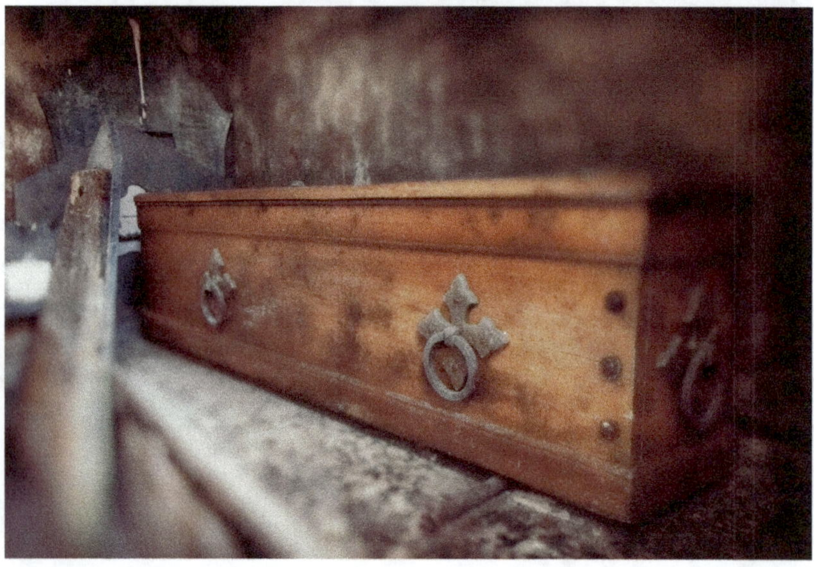

Placed in the Wood, Aughrim COI, Carricklom, Elphin, County Roscommon – Image: Paul Butler, March 2016.

And in *The Leavetaking*, we have a very similar description, as if McGahern were reliving that moment: 'They'd lift her from the bed, a feather: and place her in the wood. Quietly they'd turn the screws of the lid. Never in this world would her face be seen again' [*L*, p. 78].

And the slow and steady shuffling feet of the mourners through the snow within 'The Wine Breath', complement the following image 'The Pink Cross' of a snow-bound graveyard – 'all was silent and still there. Slow feet crunched on the snow' [*CE*, pp. 110–111]. The following piece, also from 'The Wine Breath', evokes how the priest while passing by a neighbour cutting beech trees and, on seeing the white sawdust, was transported back to a funeral ceremony during heavy snow thirty years earlier. The sawdust looked like a covering of snow; memory took it as a trigger to go back decades earlier.

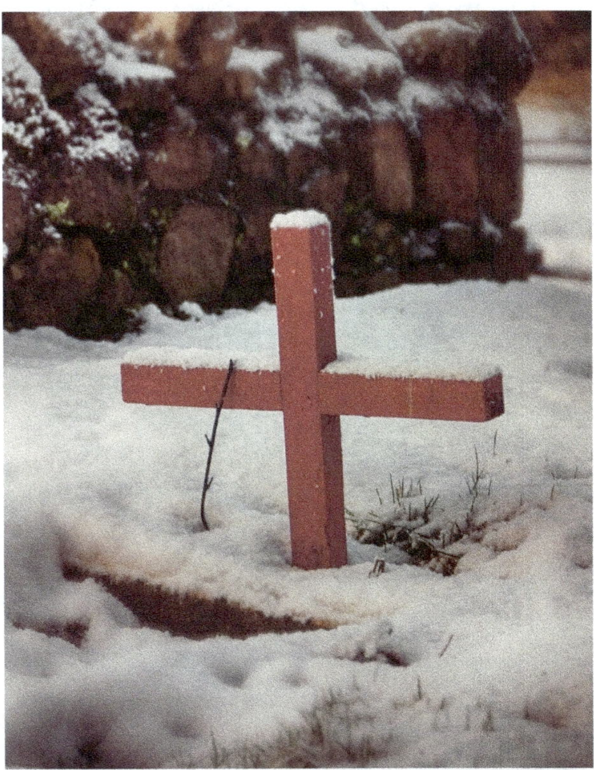

The Pink Cross, Farnocht Cemetery, County Leitrim – Image: Paul Butler, February 2018.

> This, then, was the actual day, the only day that mattered, the day from which our salvation had to be won or lost: it stood solidly and impenetrably there, denying the weak life of the person, with nothing of the eternal other than it would dully endure. [*CE*, 'The Wine Breath', p. 113]

Peter Guy makes the following observation: 'What also comes through in *Memoir* is the selective nature both of memory and of the art which is based on memory, in that the biographical materials that McGahern uses in his fiction are always the same ones and are harvested mainly from his childhood years.'[15] Guy elaborates on McGahern's use of memories by arguing that memory and imagination are the dimensions where happiness and eternity can be experienced. The old priest in 'The Wine Breath' feels that, unlike the solid, impenetrable and dull reality of 'the actual day', everything in that remembered day was so pure and perfect that he felt purged of all tiredness and bitterness and, was, for a moment, eager to begin life again: 'the day set alight in his mind by the light of the white beech, though it had been nothing more than a funeral he had attended during a dramatic snowfall when a boy, seemed bathed in the eternal, seemed everything we had been taught and told of the world of God' [*CE*, p. 180].

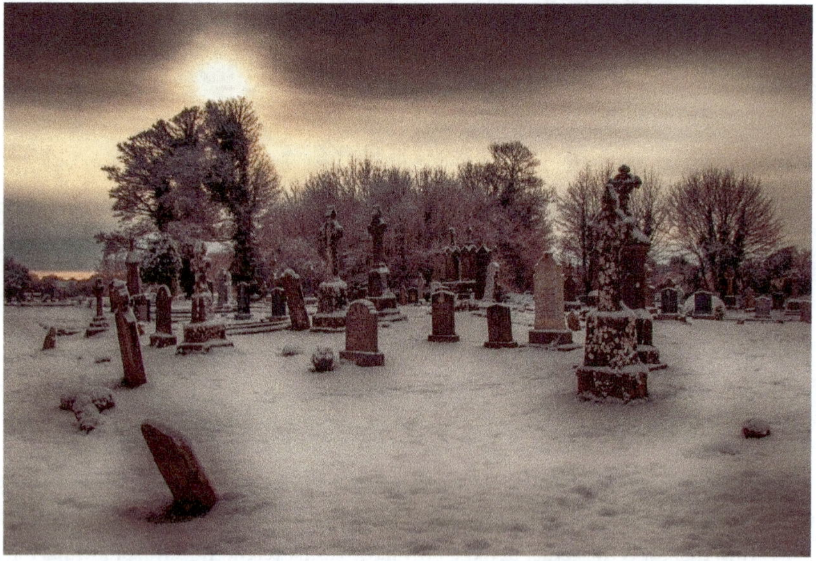

Farnocht Cemetery in Snow, County Leitrim – Image: Paul Butler, December 2010.

15 Ibid.

Moreover, in *Memoir*, McGahern goes into fine detail about the final placing of the coffin: 'The crowd circles the grave, the priest's clay falls on the boards. Heads are bowed as the quick shovelfuls thud on the hollow boards' [*M*, p. 133].

The simple touching description of gravediggers waiting unobtrusively to fulfil their duty in *The Pornographer* once more captures something of the special nature of funerals in McGahern's work:

> After the decade of the Rosary I was waiting for the shovels to start filling in the clay when the undertaker unrolled a green mat of butcher's grass and placed it over the grave. They'd fill in the grave as soon as the churchyard was empty, some barbarous notion of kindness. [*P*, p. 241]

There is an acceptance by McGahern of his own mortality in the following passage from *The Dark*, and it provides a similarly gloomy picture of the havoc wrought by death, which is placed with an evocative image 'November Sun at Farnocht Cemetery':

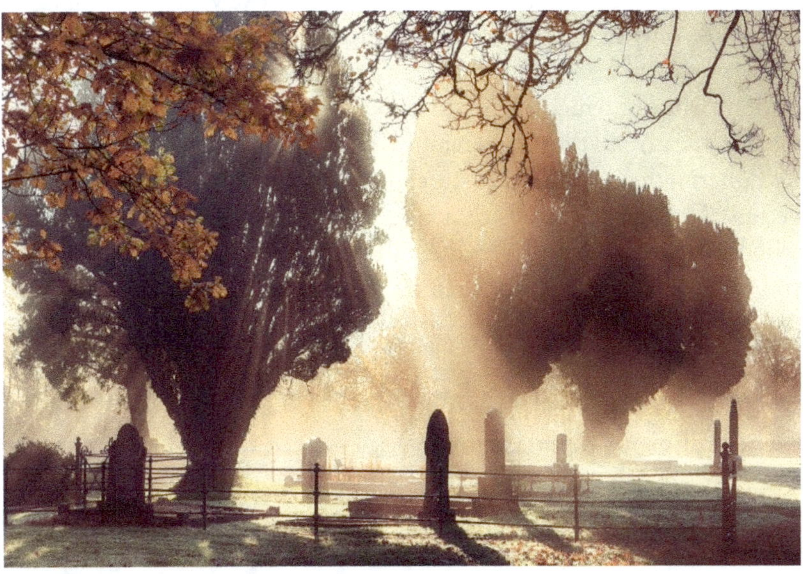

November Sun at Farnocht Cemetery, County Leitrim – Image: Paul Butler, November 2019.

> Through the window the stones of the graveyard stood out beyond the laurels in the moon, all the dead about, lives as much filled with themselves and their importance once as you this night, indecision and trouble and yearning put down equal with laughing into that area of clay, and they lay calm as you would one eternal night while someone full of problems and uncertainties would lie as awake as you in a room. [*D*, pp. 68–9]

In addition, and like the chapter on 'Place', the powerful respect of the memory of the dead. I equally use the following piece from *The Pornographer* as illumination for the scene and to reflect on the change that came over McGahern:

> We can no more learn from another than we can do their death for them or have them do ours. We have to go inland, in the solitude that is both pain and joy, and there make our own truth, and even if that proves nothing too, we have still that hard joy of having gone the hard and only way there is to go, we have not backed away or staggered to one side, but gone on and on and on even when there was nothing, knowing there was nothing on any other way. [*P*, p. 203]

McGahern seems to attribute an exclusively positive value to the imagination, not only in that it fills in the gaps of memory, but also because it allows that re-arrangement and that re-elaboration of personal recollections without which a work of art cannot function. And so, after his mother's death and the forced removal of the family from Aughawillan by his father to the barracks, the church in Cootehall, County Roscommon, became McGahern's favourite, acting as something of a sanctuary: 'The school, the library, the river, they all became a refuge and a strength and an escape, but stronger than all three stood the Catholic Church' [*M*, p. 199].

Other religious persuasions in McGahern's world

While Ireland is still predominantly a Catholic society, during the time of McGahern it was more of a theocracy. Other religious persuasions soldiered on in the background. In his short story 'The Conversion of William Kirkwood', McGahern refers to those that swapped sides, so to speak, to marry or to prosper:

> Miracles would never cease among the stars of heaven. William Kirkwood, last of the Kirkwoods, was about to renounce the error of their ways and become a Catholic. [*CE*, 'The Conversion of William Kirkwood', p. 289]

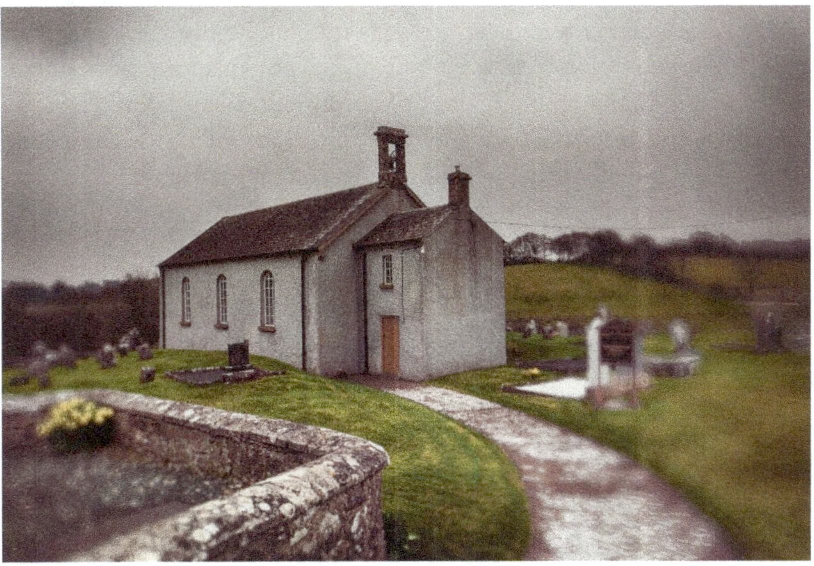

Church of Ireland in the Parish of Drumreilly, County Leitrim – Image: Paul Butler, April 2018.

Photographic Note: In post-production, a layer was added, and an application of High Dynamic Range (HDR) was applied to bring some detail into the sky and to enhance the mood and drama of the scene.

This small Church of Ireland in the parish of Drumreilly stands on a remote peninsula on the north shore of Garadice Lough. It was built in 1737 to replace the church that stood on Church Island.[16] Catholics converting to Protestantism was a fraught though mercenary affair and Protestants converting to Catholicism seemed a last resort: 'Catholics had turned Protestant for money or position, it was an old sore and taunt; but the only reason a Protestant was ever known to turn was in order to marry' [*CE*, p. 288]. McGahern looked on Protestants in a much more favourable light than their Catholic counterparts.

From a photographic perspective, I have always admired the choice of location of the older non-Catholic churches in the Irish countryside. I am unsure whether they were always non-Catholic churches, and from an architectural point of view, they are usually of an appealing aesthetic construction. In my opinion, many of our functional and dour Catholic churches were placed at crossroads or in towns and villages with the sole intention of being the primary landmark within the surrounding countryside. In tandem, the beginning of a village would then sprout around the church, usually led by a public house. It seems that the Catholic church was intent on dominating the landscape instead of complementing it.

Catholic and pagan ritualism

The image 'Offerings at Ogulla Shrine' is another from a location I believe to be a photographic treasure trove. I genuinely feel that this scene contains a touch of the global and the exotic. If one removes the location tag, one could assume that this scene is at a religious site anywhere within the world, be it from Brazil to the Philippines. Ogulla Shrine, in County Roscommon, underlines that tradition of devotion in remote locations, placing the shrine at the centre of its private world. The colourful flowers adorning the figure of Christ really add a splash of colour and lift the ordinary.

16 Oliver Dixon: <https://www.geograph.ie/photo/1310479>.

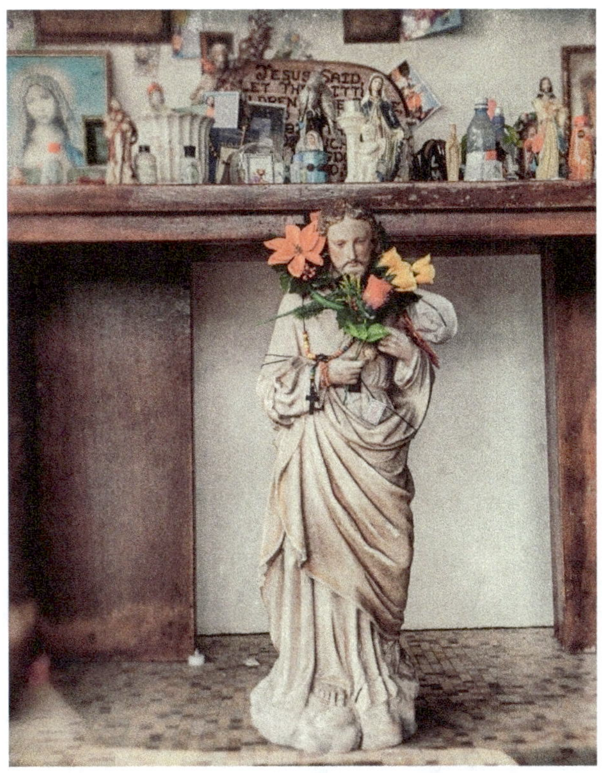

Offerings at Ogulla Shrine, County Roscommon. Image: Paul Butler, July 2016.

Photographic Note: In post-production, I once again used the 'Wet Collodion Process' to adorn this image with a timeless feel. The watermarks and dust scratches within the post-production process enhance its agelessness.

Against this backdrop of religious domination, there were – and still are – strong beliefs in old pre-Christian pagan rituals. In a 2002 interview with Robert McCrum for the *Observer*, McGahern was asked, 'What did you mean by the title: *That They May Face the Rising Sun?*'.

> McGahern replies: 'It goes back to the origin of paganism in Ireland. I belong to the middle class that grew up very influenced by the Catholic Church. The people of the novel are from a more pagan and practical world in which the Christianity is just a veneer.'[17]

17 McCrum, 'The Whole World in a Community'.

This idea of religion as a 'veneer' is very prevalent in McGahern's work. In many instances, he argued that people in rural Ireland were not so concerned with the Church's pronouncements as with getting on with what he referred to once as 'their sensible pagan lives', which is what they had done for centuries. There is an ancient ritual used as a remedy for whooping cough that portrays a respect and understanding of the old ways that really flew in the face of the Church at the time. McGahern describes this remedy which was the mixing of pagan and Christian in this ritual:

> The night was very cold. In a bundle of blankets I was taken out and passed beneath the jennet or donkey three times in the name of the Father and the Son and the Holy Ghost. [*M*, p. 13]

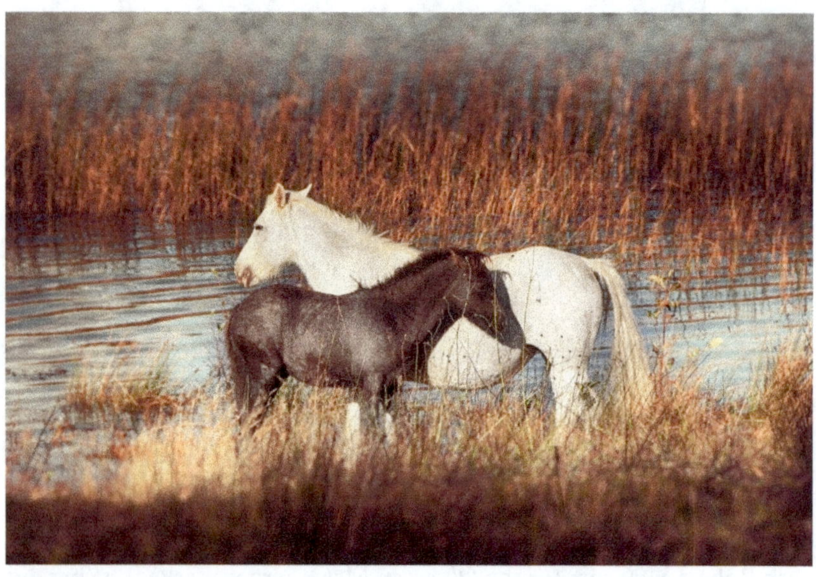

Ponies, Near Dromahair, County Leitrim – Image: Paul Butler, October 2011.

Local beliefs pre-date the Church as Ireland was, and still is, a very deeply superstitious country with strong attachments to nature. There is a grotto within the grounds of St Mary's Church of Ireland in Farnocht. And the next scene 'Secret Grotto' lies within these ruins, which are believed to be the remains of a sixth-century classroom of a monastery dating back to the time of St Manchan. He was an early Christian saint credited with founding many early Christian churches in Ireland. The maintenance of this little grotto and the placing of flowers remained a mystery for many years. I eventually discovered that an elderly couple who own a cottage nearby are responsible for the creation and upkeep of this little shrine. And now, sadly, due to old age and ill health, the couple rarely visit these days. However, the shrine is still maintained. And not far from this little shrine and within old woodland skirting Lough Rinn, you will find swathes of bluebells, the beautiful delicate flowers of April and May. And in McGahern's *The Dark*, we find a mention of the use of rhododendrons branches as decoration, and which complement the scene:

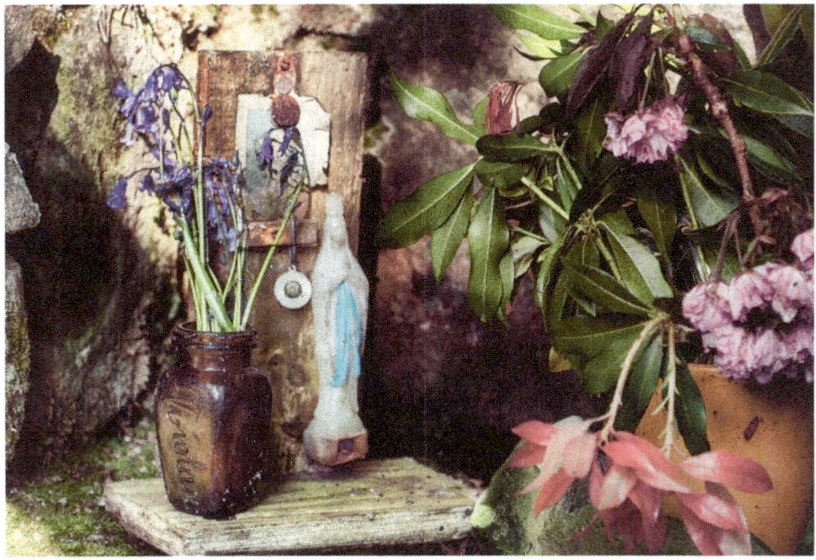

Secret Grotto, Farnocht, County Leitrim – Image: Paul Butler, May 2016.

> The rhododendrons branches were cut out of Oakport same as always to decorate the grass margins of the processional route. [*D*, 58]

Regarding rhododendrons, unfortunately, there is a serious problem with the unchecked growth of this shrub across this area – escapees from the original Lough Rinn estate. This invasive species is a serious threat to our native flora.

While initial observations suggest that this little shrine is religious and a devotion to Mary and looks like so many of the May altars created within schools and churches, I also sense an offering and connection to the pagan ritual of 'Bealtaine', also known as Beltain, Beltainne, Beltaine or Beltany, which is usually held on first day of May. Historically, 'Bealtaine' was a widely observed ritual throughout Ireland. At the beginning of the summer season, bonfires would mark a time of purification and transition, heralding in the season in the hope of a good harvest later in the year, accompanied with rituals to protect the people from any harm by otherworldly spirits.[18]

Throughout this chapter on 'Ritual', as previously mentioned, are a series of images from Ogulla Shrine which is not far from Tulsk in County Roscommon. The village of Tulsk is on the main N5 primary route to Mayo and houses the visitor centre for Rathcroghan. 'Rathcroghan, Cruachan Aí, is known as the Ancient Capital of Connacht, where the festival of Samhain (Halloween) is said to originate. This majestic landscape is the oldest and largest unexcavated Royal Site in Europe.'[19] I chanced upon this shrine one day while out scouting the area for photographic inspiration. This holy well at Ogulla is believed to be the location where St Patrick baptized Ethne and Fidelm, daughters of the O'Connor High King of Ireland, and so began the conversion of Gaelic Connacht.[20] There are so many holy wells across Ireland that are all attributed to St Patrick that I wonder was it practically feasible for a man to have visited every one of these areas?

I found Ogulla Shrine compelling. While it is a sanctuary of religious devotion, it also tilts strongly to old pagan traditions with pieces of ribbon attached to trees and everyday items left as offerings. And in the image 'Offerings for Hope of Divine Intervention', you sense that someone placed great store by their request for divine intervention, putting their precious rosary beads upon the figure. Also noticeable are children's stockings, a baby's bonnet, as all beliefs merge here alongside the hanging of ribbons

18 Newgrange Website, 'Beltane – The Fire Festival': <https://www.newgrange.com/beltane.htm> (2007).

19 Rathcroghan, 'Where History Comes to Life': <https://www.rathcroghan.ie/>.

20 Jim Dempsey, 'Ogulla Holy Well': <http://www.megalithicireland.com/Ogulla%20Holy%20Well%20Tulsk.html> (2011).

from trees and placing of coins in the revered stream. It all works in parallel with a holy water font and the placing of flowers at the altar.

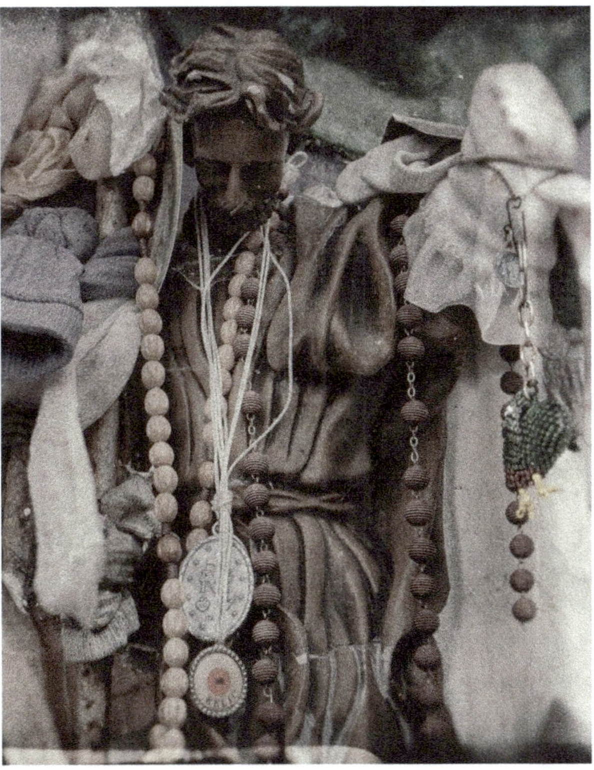

Offerings for Hope of Divine Intervention, Ogulla Shrine, County Roscommon – Image: Paul Butler.

Photographic Note: In post-production, I once again added a treatment of Wet Collodion to create a continuous and timeless feeling to the scene.

I wonder that if within the images of offerings, especially those recorded at Ogulla Shrine, suggest that items left as gifts are in order to gain a relief from a deep 'want'? What I find interesting is that Ogulla Shrine was also a sacred pre-Christian site and still continues to act as a magnet for worship. Therefore, we could assume that the personal pagan offerings adorning many of the religious figures suggest ancient and later belief systems working in tandem. In April 2022, I revisited Ogulla, only to discover that the site of the shrine has been cleared of all religious iconography. All that now remains of the shrine is an enclosed seating area.

McGahern's change of path and the changing Church

As time passed and McGahern ceased the formal practice of Catholicism, the attachment did not wane, as he explained in an interview with Eamon Maher:

> The Church was my first book and I would think it is still my most important book. At that time [the 1930s and 40s], there were very few books in the house. The only pictures we could see were religious pictures, the Stations of the Cross. The only music we would hear was religious hymns; and it's [the Church] all I came to know of ceremony, even of luxury – the tulips that used to come in the flat boxes when I was an altar boy, the candles, the incense. [21]

His mother's death relieved him of a promise he made to be a priest, and as he matured, McGahern's vocation became his writing, his words becoming the sermons he never got to perform for his mother. All his experiences, both light and dark, became the foundation for his words. His detailed memories put to paper became his harbour, sheltering him from the emotional storm that had raged. Eventually a path of estrangement for McGahern from the Church developed, which he details in *Memoir*.

> I would no longer have to die in life in order to circumvent death and the judgement and to keep the promise to her I loved. Instead of being a priest of God, I would be the god of a small, vivid world. [*M*, p. 205]

Instead of opting to become a priest, McGahern chose literature as his vocation. His writing would be the Mass he never got to say for his mother. Reliving and re-enacting the experiences of his past, he seeks solace from the raw suffering of loss which haunted him right throughout his life. Literature is his religion, his comfort. Dana Radler notes: 'Looking at individual and

21 'Catholicism and National Identity in the Works of John McGahern', p. 72.

family memories makes the novelist celebrate and value his decision of embracing writing as a career, a second option turned into reality versus his initial promise to become a man serving the church.'[22] McGahern himself observed: 'Over many days and months, gradually, a fantastical idea formed. Why take on any single life – a priest, a soldier, teacher, doctor, airman – if a writer could create all these people far more vividly?' [*M*, p. 205].

McGahern further elaborates in *A Private World* how he too fell away from the Church, replacing the cross with the pen:

> And a time came when it no longer gave that meaning and I think it happened so gradually and quietly that it was imperceptible. [*PW*]

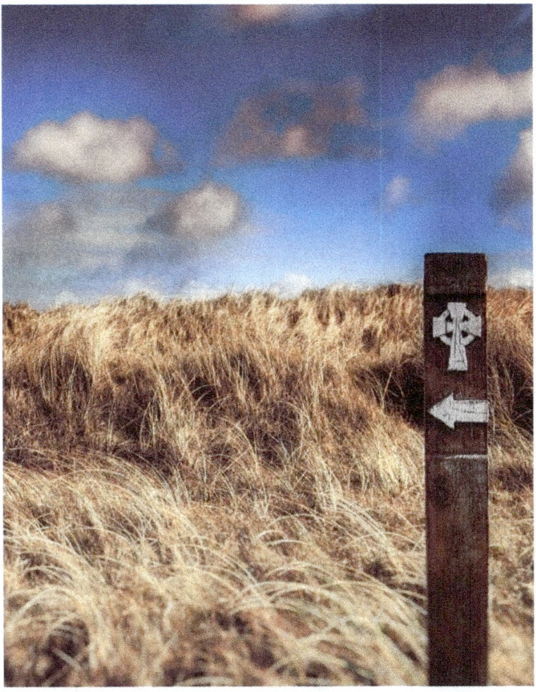

Trail Marker from Strandhill Dunes to the Church at Killaspugbrone, Coolera Peninsula, County Sligo – Image: Paul Butler, March 2015.

22 Radler, 'A Lifetime Memory Quest'.

His yearning for that lost childhood is signified by image of the path marker to Killaspugbrone Church in the dunes at Strandhill, County Sligo. This image adorns the book cover of *Tracing the Cultural Legacy of Irish Catholicism: From Galway to Cloyne and Beyond*.[23]

No matter what way you look at it, McGahern's relationship with the Church was far from simple:

> I would think that if there was one thing injurious about the Church, it would be its attitude to sexuality. I see sexuality as just part of life. Either all of life is sacred or none of it is sacred … And I think that it [The Church] made a difficult enough relationship – which is between people, between men and women – even more difficult by imparting an unhealthy attitude to sexuality.[24]

And McGahern further reflected on the question regarding the Church's attitude to sexuality with Eamon Maher:

> When I was in my 20s it did occur to me that there was something perverted about an attitude that thought killing somebody was a minor offence compared to kissing somebody.[25]

In no small part, the loss of his mother created a void within McGahern that never fully healed, and it flowed throughout his work. In the following passages from his short stories, 'All Sorts of Impossible Things' and 'My Love my Umbrella', McGahern mixes physical intimacy and the mystical with a view to soothing a deep unfathomable emptiness, his 'want'. One wonders if the words mask a latent frustration at the failure of sexual intimacy to rid the soul of his deep trauma:

> As men obsessed with the idea that all knowledge lies within a woman's body, but having entered it to find themselves as ignorant as before, they are driven towards all women again and again: in childish hope that somehow the next time they will

23 Eamon Maher and Eugene O'Brien (eds), *Tracing the Cultural Legacy of Irish Catholicism: From Galway to Cloyne and Beyond* (Manchester University Press, 2017).

24 'Catholicism and National Identity', pp. 73–4.

25 Ibid., p. 74.

> find the treasure, and then the equally childish desire for revenge since it cannot be found, that knife in the unfathomable entrails; and they grow full of hatred. [*CE*, 'All Sorts of Impossible things', p. 104]

And this 'Loss' resurfaces in McGahern's short story 'My Love, My Umbrella', as he writes of love unravelling and, in a way, it runs in parallel with his own loss. The choice of the image of 'Sacred Heart at Ogulla Shrine' peering out through the metal bars is used to represent the idolization of his mother – that intolerable and eternal loss of what was once so close. I use the quote and image to portray lost love and the realization of love having run its course for one party, while the other holds on to a certain hope that it can be revived. In addition, I use it to visualize the pain expressed in McGahern's words that remained a thread linking childhood pain right through to adulthood and middle age. Nothing could fill the emptiness at the loss of his mother's love:

> I would grovel on the earth or anything to keep her then. Little by little my life had fallen into her keeping, it was only in the loss I had come to know it, life without her, the pain of the loss of my own life without the oblivion the dead have, all longing changed to die out of my own life on her lips, in her thighs, since it was only through her it lived. [*CE*, 'My Love, My Umbrella', p. 66]

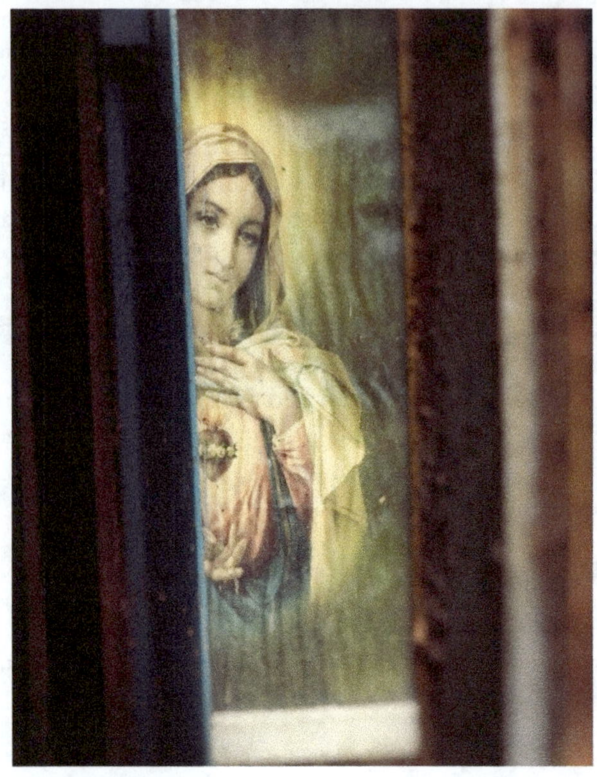

Sacred Heart at Ogulla Shrine, County Roscommon – Image: Paul Butler, July 2016.

The perspective for the scene 'Sacred Heart at Ogulla Shrine' intrigues as the juxtaposition of the image of the Virgin Mary creates the impression of three-hundred-and-sixty-degree vision: it is as though everything is seen. It revives that memory of being a child and the warning that you were not to be bold as God sees everything. Once again, the calm expression on the face of Mary and that unusual shaped heart draws you towards the image.

When asked about his [McGahern's] remark in relation to how such a Catholic country could produce so many lapsed Catholics, McGahern replied:

> I mean I think that's a fact and I think we had a very peculiar type of Catholic Church here in that it was a fortress Church. Very much like an army, it demanded unquestioning allegiance.[26]

Though our attitudes to the Church have changed immeasurably due to the never-ending stream of abuse scandals, we have matured and progressed as a people and nation; however, our countryside is still laden with religious imagery. On a wet Wednesday morning in March 2015 on the N4 about six kilometres from Sligo Town, close to Exit S1 for Strandhill, this sign 'Religious Billboard' caught my attention as I pulled onto the hard shoulder to take a call. A light misty rain was falling, and it clung to the windscreen and through the small droplets, this billboard seemed to have gained an interesting illumination. It made for an intriguing image. This roadside scene generates a quiet emotion, a sadness and a poignancy, as if asking you to give something, which, once given unconditionally, will guide you on a path to home, or redemption. Adding to that poignancy is the location of this sign. This stretch of single carriageway from Castlebaldwin towards the dual carriageway near Collooney had the reputation of being one of the most dangerous stretches of road in Ireland.[27]

26 Ibid., p. 76.

27 Marese McDonagh, '"Most Dangerous" Stretch of N4 to Get €102m Upgrade': <https://www.irishtimes.com/news/environment/most-dangerous-stretch-of-n4-to-get-102m-upgrade-1.2371862?mode=sample&auth-failed=1&pw-origin=https%3A%2F%2Fwww.irishtimes.com%2Fnews%2Fenvironment%2Fmost-dangerous-stretch-of-n4-to-get-102m-upgrade-1.2371862> (2015).

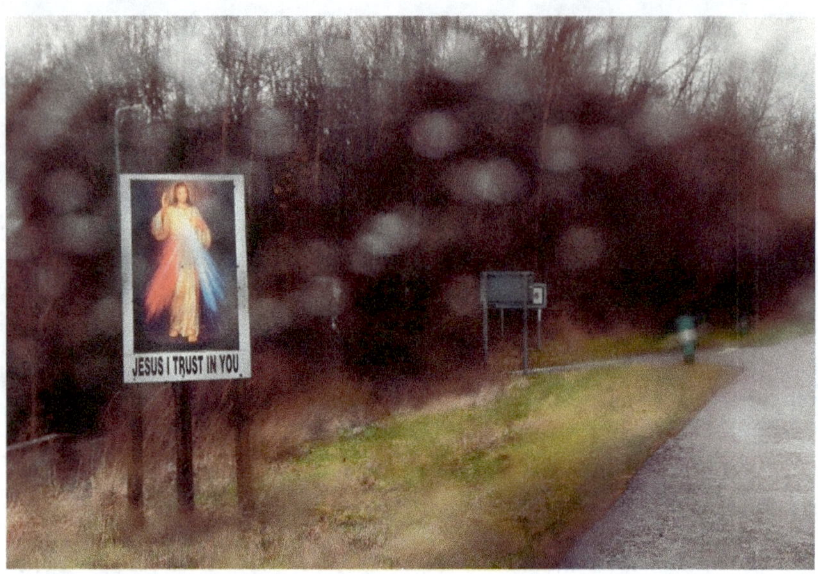

Religious Billboard, Near the S1 Exit on the N4 for Strandhill, County Sligo – Image: Paul Butler.

In September 2021, a replacement dual carriageway from Castlebaldwin to Collooney in County Sligo opened, and what a difference it makes. I did notice, however, while driving on the new stretch of road that some of the formerly hidden little cottages now have a new vista.

In a further extract from an interview with the *Guardian* in 2002, McGahern reflects on the standing of the Church in recent times:

> McG: 'Yes, though I have nothing but gratitude for my upbringing in the Church. I love the description of Gothic churches before the printed word, that they were the bibles of the poor. The Catholic Church was my first book, but I'm delighted that the influence over political and sexual matters has disappeared.'[28]

Mellowing in later years and finding a path back to his faith through his mother, McGahern's memories softened, and when asked why after

28 McCrum, 'The Whole World in a Community'.

all that had happened in connection with the banning of his book, *The Dark*, he retained such a positive attitude towards his relations with the Church, he responded:

> I would think it is neither positive or negative – it's just a fact. *The Dark* was banned and I went on the *The Late Late Show* from, of all places, The King's Hall in Belfast. I was expected to attack the Catholic Church and I said I could no more attack the Catholic Church than I could my own life.[29]

It all comes full circle back to his mother and the days he spent walking those little lanes in childhood wonder with this woman, who, in some ways appeared to a young McGahern as if she was a mythical creature: 'In the beginning was my mother. The only way that life could be continued with her was through prayer' [*M*, p. 203].

For John McGahern, the artistic creation starts from personal memories. As he explains in his manifesto, ''The Image' (1968), art is based on those images that reside in 'that still and private universe which each of us possess but which others cannot see'.'[30]

Religious iconography

In this this section, I look at religious iconography found and recorded within the abandoned homes I have had the opportunity to visit. The importance of 'Sacred Heart' pictures and all the religious icons were so very personal and comforting for their owners. Within the following scenes, you can sense the reverence, solace and comfort obtained from these small confidants. In the scene 'The Font & the Blessing', we have wonderful colour clashes, electricity cabling, light switches and prayers, all offering protection in their own way. Science and the mythology operating in tandem. The scene offers that sense of creeping modernity,

29 'Catholicism and National Identity', p. 73.

30 John McGahern, '"The Image": Prologue to a Reading at the Rockefeller University', *Honest Ulsterman*, Vol. 8 (1968), p. 10.

age-old warmth and messages of peace. All the things that feed the mind, body and soul.

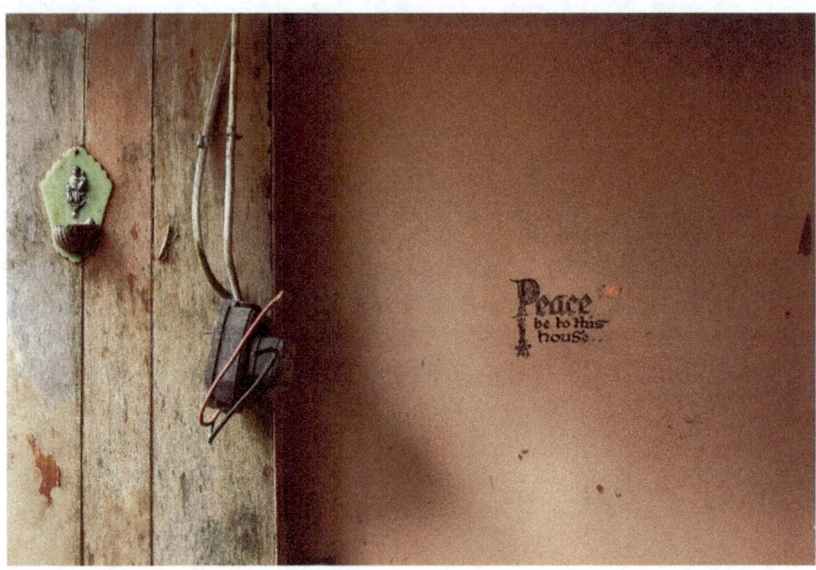

The Font & the Blessing, Roosky, County Leitrim – Image: Paul Butler, February 2014.

Photographic Note: The shadow within this scene creates a degree of depth. Sadly, as previously mentioned in the section on *Place*, this little house no longer exists. It fell to the claws of a bulldozer a few weeks after I recorded some images.

It might be overtly nostalgic, but I will always record these scenes out of respect for what passed before while noting that one day someone may stumble upon my images and see in them the solace they brought me. Both scenes 'The Font & the Blessing' and 'The Pope & the Font' were used for promotional material for my exhibition at the Atrium Gallery, Backstage Theatre, Longford.

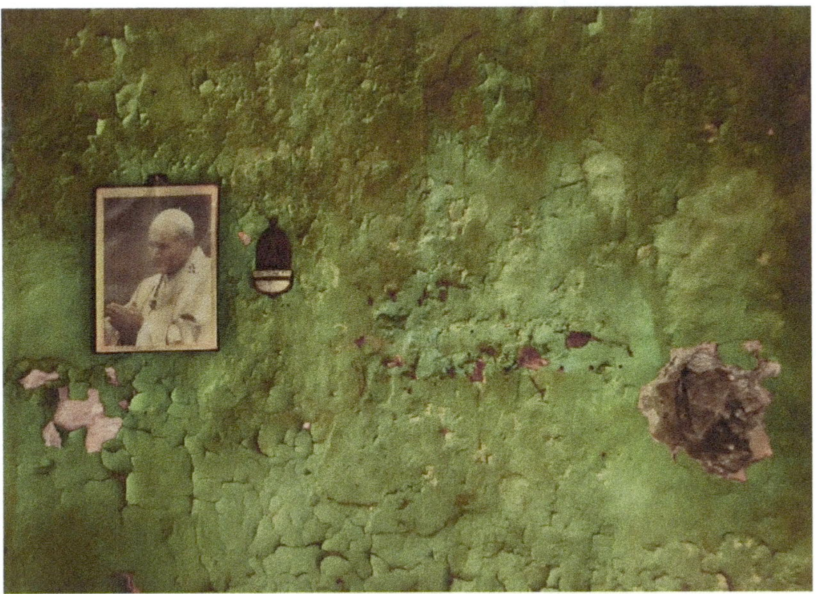

The Pope & the Font, near Ardagh, County Longford – Image: Paul Butler, September 2013.

The flaked green paint really creates an atmosphere and grants a timelessness to this scene. I really like the balance of the image of St John Paul II with the large hole in the masonry. This scene was recorded in a small derelict council house in County Longford, though you could just as easily assume that this image was recorded in a war zone due to the state of the kitchen wall. In some ways, the scene acts as a visual analogy of the damage that the Church has inflicted on the people of Ireland.

The scene 'Padre Pio Over the Door' triggers many memories of the religious imagery at home when we were children. A religious image of the sacred heart hung on our bedroom wall above a little cream-tiled fireplace. The eyes seemed to follow you around the room. In a way, I think we were a bit scared of these images as children as God and the saints were following your every move and watching you carefully.

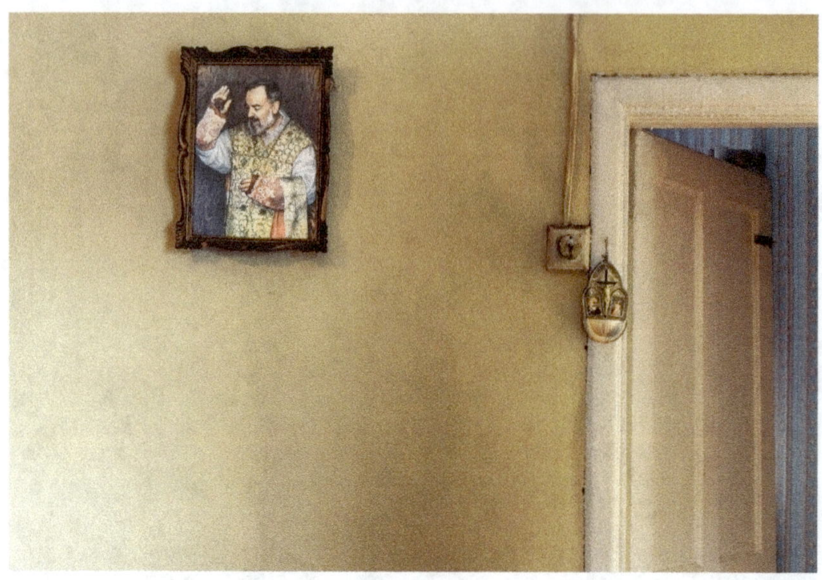

Padre Pio Over the Door, Trish Carrigy's Old Family Home Aughagreagh, Ballinalee, County Longford – Image: Paul Butler, September 2014.

Photographic Note: In post-production, I greatly increased the colour saturation on the small religious picture of Padre Pio to make his figure illuminate from the wall.

I had recorded the image 'Padre Pio' in Trish Carrigy's family home in the townland of Aughagreagh, not far from the village of Ballinalee, County Longford. Their father had recently died, and the house and farmland were to be given to the only son. A strong feeling among Trish and her sisters was that the family house would eventually be sold off or, over time, be allowed to fall into rack and ruin. She asked if I could take images around the homestead as the girls wanted to create an album for posterity. Leading into the kitchen, I was quite taken with the image of 'Padre Pio' wondering whether he was offering a blessing or a slap. The Holy water Font on the door frame creates a nice symmetry.

In another extract from the interview with Eamon Maher, McGahern mentions the fact that religious iconography was to be found everywhere:

> The only pictures we could see were religious pictures, the Stations of the Cross. The only music we would hear was religious hymns; and it's the [the Church] all I came to know of ceremony, even of luxury – the tulips that used to come in the flat boxes when I was an altar boy, the candles, the incense.[31]

There are so many pictorial versions of the Sacred Heart, and who has the original copyright, I wonder? 'Sacred Heart on Green' was recorded within another old and disused family home near Aughnacliffe, County Longford. This scene is visually engaging; I like the Eastern Orthodox vibe of the picture. This sacred heart picture clashes wonderfully with the vibrant green wall and the fact that it hangs slightly crooked adds drama to the scene. I find that there is something quite welcoming about this religious image. And again, though the image was recorded in Aughnacliffe, County Longford, it could easily be a scene from Eastern Europe owing to the iconic style of the religious image.

31 'Catholicism and National Identity', p. 72.

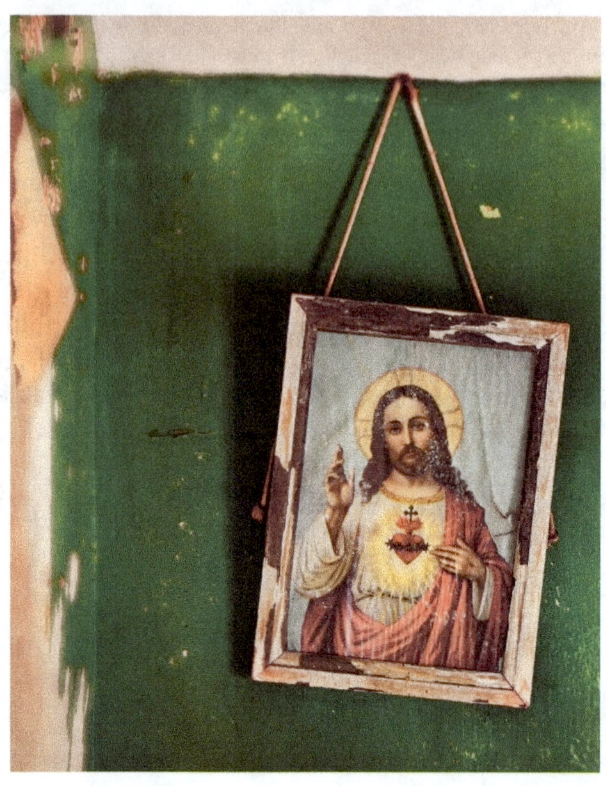

Sacred Heart on Green, Aughnacliffe, County Longford – Image: Paul Butler, May 2017.

I end this chapter on 'Ritual' with a scene of a Marian Shrine which was recorded at the base of Sliabh Bawn, close to Strokestown, County Roscommon. Discovering these hidden, revered places of ritual and worship always brings great reward. There is so little separation between the pagan and the religious within this scene; it is the ancient veneration of the female, of birth and of renewal. The shrines are a personal space for those who may seek solace, comfort, forgiveness or whatever they need, even that other worldliness. To those reaching out, be it towards pagan roots, to mother earth or for something and everything, these places on the soil and surrounded by the natural world, and to which I react strongly and with a very positive connection. As I have always felt about myself: 'Head in the clouds but feet firmly on the ground.'

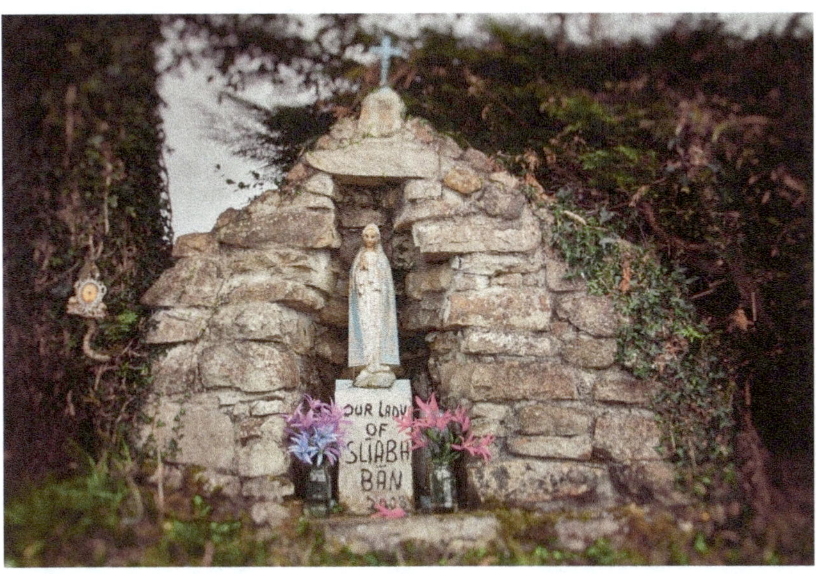

Marian Shrine Close to Sliabh Báwn, County Roscommon – Image: Paul Butler, September 2016.

Photographic Note: I enhanced this image of the Marian Shrine at Sliabh Báwn with a Wet Collodion Process and a slight *Bokeh* to create that feeling of the divine, of mother earth, of heavenliness and pagan devotion.

In a sense the following passage from *Memoir* embellishes that feeling for McGahern:

> I imagined my mother in heaven, close to the throne of God, meeting Mary, walking in the heavenly gardens with the angels and saints. [*M*, p. 203]

And the scene 'Marian Shrine close to Sliabh Báwn' illustrates her presence within McGahern's life, his loss, pain and memory an undying ritual. She was his rock.

At home, I have a copy of a 1972 edition of *The Prophet* by Kalil Gibran (1883–1931), a small book that over the years I always return to. The different passages on so many aspects of life are simply quite beautiful and very powerful. It feels right to insert a small extract from the passage regarding mothers: 'The most beautiful word on the lips of mankind is the word "Mother", and the most beautiful call is the call of "My mother".'[32]

Reading passages from McGahern shines a spotlight on the deeply profound effect of his mother on him during the short time spent together within her safe shelter. Now buried alongside his mother on the grounds of St Patrick's Church, Aughawillan, only a couple of kilometres from their old homestead in Corramahon, one can only hope that they are once again walking those peaceful little country lanes.

I found the section on 'Ritual' developed a personality of its own, and it will be ongoing for me. To make sense of my journey within this project, I realize that the more I dug, the more I can honestly guarantee that McGahern's ongoing adoration of his mother is the complete opposite of my own broken relationship with my mother. I admire and respect the adoration he had for her, but I do not envy nor desire it. Their relationship remains suspended in a particular time, never having had the chance to evolve to a sense of normality, balance and maturity. And at times, reading through his work, there are passages where the line blurs between reality and heavenly devotion. In saying that, I do feel very strongly that while we had very different relationships with our mothers, because of our relationships as children we both succumbed to a powerful artistic drive. And as for McGahern's spiritual mission, it was to find that 'missing' word, while my mission is to find that 'missing' image. No doubt, the creation of imagery will continue as it constantly ebbs and flows. Throughout this book, I really hope that the mix of image and text has opened a door of understanding of McGahern's use of the image as the beginning of an idea and story. Moreover, within this section there remains a hope that this visual portrayal of 'Ritual' intertwined with words from John McGahern can move the reader in some way.

32 Kalil Gibran, 'The Mother': <https://www.alexandrasoveral.co.uk/blog/read_144105/the-mother-by-kahlil-gibran.html> (1923).

CHAPTER 5

Conclusion

This project which began in 2011 has been a long and mostly enjoyable journey. By nature, I like to try and sail forward, but now I am glad I have revisited this project and reworked some parts. A bit like McGahern's writing, I find myself retuning my words and some of the imagery, even replacing them with what I feel may be more appropriate for expression. It was always my intention to create something new or at least something different, a book combining my ability as an image creator to enhance the world of the ordinary with powerful, insightful and at times the hurt words of John McGahern. This has caused me issues as to how you frame this project. It crosses different strands: the written word, a photographic documentation and a melding of the two.

In effect, I occasionally ended up locked in battle as to how my photographic experience and interest could be gainfully applied to McGahern's life and written work. The result was ultimately a rewarding mixture of the visual and the literary, and it brought me into even closer contact with the beautifully unspoilt, global, backward- and forward-looking, religious, pagan and hidden parts of Leitrim. I have constantly tried to match the right words and passages from McGahern to the right scene, thus attempting to undertake a journey using his life and experiences as the backdrop to this canvas while offering a deeper insight into the creation of his words by mapping various reference points in his work. At the same time, I deliberately brought in my own early life experiences to present a co-relation between our paths and our eventual outcomes.

This conclusion is an honest assessment as to what I have learnt and is cognizant of the fact that I will always need to continue learning, as there is no end to this journey. It was never the intention for this book to be just an academic exercise. I really want it to be accessible to all – a journey through words and images that will gladden the heart of the reader. There are two journeys, that of the writer and of myself, that are separated by generations and characterized by how a writer from Leitrim and a photographer from Dublin shared a passion to create something out of the pain and confusion of their lives.

This project has led me down many pathways and at times I really did feel I would never see a conclusion. I became distracted by the vastness of the project, occasionally losing focus (no pun intended) as I headed into too many areas. Yet, during those frustrating times, my absolute passion for the power of the image and its ability to illuminate McGahern's words remained paramount. I am no McGahern expert, but I live in, breathe and really understand his world.

As stated, this book encompasses many strands, as it was a photographic project interwoven with the works of McGahern. It was not just a question of heading to the library and engaging with his works, then researching and writing a thesis. It involved a lot of time and effort travelling the County of Leitrim and the north-west and exploring its deserted past. There were many cold days spent in the field, literally, and many more hours and nights in post-production, filtering and selecting the best imagery suitable for this book. The choice of appropriate texts is in constant flux. There were also photographic exhibitions held in Dublin, Longford and Leitrim as part of this initial project, which required a great deal of coordination. In effect, it is more akin to an ongoing documentary. However, one rule always has remained true throughout: this book project must visualize the words of McGahern and his words must embellish the image. The image or the vision was so important to the writer; his memories created his work and allowed him to express his feelings and experiences through the medium of literature. We both sing from the same sheet in some respects, as I too express myself through photography.

I have already alluded to the belief that I shared a common thread with McGahern in that our childhoods had a profound effect on shaping our future. McGahern continuously strived to perfect the story; his whittling down of words to the bare bones enhanced clarity, and I often wondered if it offered him comfort to recreate all those minute details from his childhood and adult life. These evolving stories could not remain hidden as the drive to put pen to paper gnawed him continuously. This 'want', this feeling of emptiness created by the loss of his mother, drove him on. Likewise, my own past has driven me. I live to photograph, as I see imagery everywhere. It is my escape, and it is my oxygen. Whether the content is in the cloud on Dropbox, or on my laptop, or within an external hard drive, it is among the images I have collected over the years. In addition, a very large selection of these images have found their way into this book. This repository was all part of a visual archive even before the path to a research project, and now a book, even became clear. In this book, certain sections were more natural and comfortable to produce, particularly 'Landscape' and 'Place'. Much discussion focused on why I treated them as separate entities.

Landscape, I argue, is the physical place, the soil, the land, the seasons, the colours. While hands may have shaped the landscape, it never leaves you with a presence, though it does enrich you with a feeling. It creates a sense of the calm, and freezing the image allows one to explore the natural beauty within the frame, be it seasonal, agricultural or natural. The many varied landscapes of Leitrim deserved a chapter of their own because they are unique and can stand alone. McGahern understood his countryside and his descriptions of the weather and the land beautifully frame his initial background. He appreciated the simple things, such as seasonal change. Recording the landscape of Leitrim while reading his stories reinforced the familiarity. If I had merged landscape and place into the one section, it would have reduced the impact of the journey.

During days of filming and exploring, it was a privilege to discover locations immersed in natural beauty. Without a doubt, the stunning scenery of the Glens of Leitrim and Eagle's Rock are a match for the tourist-packed landscapes of our Cork and Kerry cousins. Nevertheless, were it not for a lack of infrastructure, this part of north Leitrim and Sligo would attract a lot more tourists. The landscape in this area has left a lasting impression, and I relish the opportunity to return soon and record it in film. The still image, I feel, does not do this area justice. Likewise, the tiny coastline of Leitrim causes a raised eyebrow when I inform people that the county runs to the sea. A surfing friend of ours from Fuerteventura and his surfing friends travel each September to ride secret waves off the Leitrim coast. It is something I feel quite proud of, even though I am not a native of the county. McGahern may have loved that little nugget of information. It is hard to believe that you are still in the County of Leitrim as you look towards the direction of Sliabh Liag (Slieve League) in Donegal.

A Sense of Place, I believe, is the built presence created by those who have gone before us, a feeling of belonging that you get, a sense that this old house was once alive. The little things I stumble across, an old butcher's calendar left hanging on a faded pink wall, broken windows of a long-abandoned home, the slow waking of Mohill on a winter morning, a forgotten gas cooker sitting in a silent kitchen overgrown with ivy, all reinforce the impression that these places once existed.

Working on the section 'A Sense of Place' was like being an explorer; you never knew what you might find in an old dwelling left exposed to the elements. Each had such a personality and contained many treasures. By freezing these ordinary structures, these everyday items of a life, and locking them into perpetuity, they now become alive again. As I said numerous times, out of obligation comes a commitment to document many of these old homes dotting the landscape of the north-west. I now have a visual record for posterity. McGahern would rummage through his mental filing cabinet and pull out items and locations to create a scene, just as I spot and record little trinkets, the small things that personalize a home.

Another conclusion on the section 'A Sense of Place' is that McGahern's writing was cinematic in its minimalism. Like a script, everything is pared back, with unnecessary words and unnecessary embellishment removed, thereby allowing you to enter his worlds, to feel the colour, simplicity and characters that they evoke. The images of homes and contents I record are deliberately uncluttered – focusing on the smallest thing, allowing for the power of simplicity and symmetry, as was the practice of McGahern. His work is easily transferrable to the big screen, and sometimes I wonder if we could have worked so well together on set. The sections in this book create a strong sense of uniqueness regarding Leitrim, and combined with McGahern's words, they open a door to this world.

As opposed to the imagery on interiors and exteriors within the section 'A Sense of Place', the physical presence left by us and with everything written by McGahern, now all that remains of his childhood home is the rusty gate at Corramahon. And this gate is losing itself within the hedgerow on the little access road. It is a sad sight indeed. And the former schoolhouse at Aughawillan where his mother once taught is now a privately owned home. However, on a positive note, not too far away as you head towards the church, you will find a larger and busier primary school. Times change indeed.

Ritual was a section that I found to be quite a difficult and intriguing produce. Producing imagery of religious iconography was not an issue as it is impossible, even today, to separate the religious from the everyday in this part of the country. As I mentioned in the chapter on 'Ritual', everywhere you find religious imagery, statues and scapulars left in the old homes. I can isolate them on location and within the scene freeze the moment. These images become ever more powerful when combined with passages from *The Barracks*, *Memoir* and some of McGahern's other works; together, they form a very touching and evocative visual statement. I do empathize with his pain as I read his accounts of Susan McGahern's funeral in *Memoir* and the parallel story of Elizabeth Reegan in *The Barracks*. The attention to detail regarding the ceremony of death recalled that of my brother Tony in September 2019, and the humour and difficulty in getting the coffin out the narrow doorway to bring his remains to the nearby church in Clonmel, County Tipperary. The strangest things stay with you. In a brotherly form of solidarity, I too love walking through local graveyards, and during this project, I also came across many a deserted one. There is a beauty and sadness in their isolation, and there are so many intriguing backstories etched on headstones. As mentioned earlier in this work and as a precursor to this project, I provided an exhibition during the McGahern conference held in Dublin City University in 2016 marking the tenth anniversary of McGahern's death. The work combined religious imagery with references from his work centred on the role of ritual and ceremony. It is a fascinating area, though I must step back at times, as I become quite immersed, and it is important to stay connected to the real world.

To be perfectly honest, I have found the past three years very strange and disconnecting. Two of my brothers died suddenly during 2019. Joseph passed away in March 2019 from a short illness and in September, Tony also died from a short illness. Unfortunately, it was by phone that I learnt of both passings. In addition to this, my younger sister, Karen, was diagnosed with breast cancer in May of 2019. Thankfully, after treatment, she was eventually given the 'all clear'. And then Covid struck and what a very peculiar time that was for everyone. To add to this ongoing disconnect, in October 2022, my sister Frances passed away. We were all present for her passing, and I will never forget that day, as the weather was horrendous and the rain torrential. There are scenes locked in my mind from the hours spent in the ICU unit, and they will stay with me forever. After saying my goodbyes to Frances, I went and stood at the back of the room, and I observed a very powerful scene unfold at Frances's bedside. My eldest sister, Mairead, supported by her husband, John, gripped Frances's hand tightly. On the other side of the bed, Frances's husband, Frank, gently stroked his dying wife's hair. It was an incredibly moving scene, painterly in its composition and such a reminder of our mortality. I had a great desire to capture this moment, as it visualized the close friendship they had shared for over forty years. But from a moral perspective, I would not take this image; it is locked in my mind. I did describe this beautiful scene to my family afterwards though. And finally, at three minutes to five on the evening of 19 October 2022, my sister Frances took her last breath. And as she passed, the window behind her bed, still blurred by the incessant rain, became illuminated with a burst of lightning, which was followed immediately by a clap of thunder. We all just looked at each other and between the tears we all laughed nervously, our Frances was not going without a fight. It was such a powerful and spiritual moment, and whether you are religious or not, it hit home hard. Those events over the past few years have really changed my outlook on so many things. Life is made of moments and is so very precious, and those moments, and the powerful feelings they generate, float around me. But when I reach out to touch those feelings, they evade me, it is as if a membrane separates us. It is the best explanation I can give as to how I feel.

It brings life into sharp focus, particularly its fragility and preciousness. What I found strange and a little unnerving was that during Joseph's funeral in March of 2019, I was asked to deliver a reading. Afterwards at the post-funeral reception, my brother Tony came up to me and half-jokingly commented: 'That was great Paul, I hope you do as good a job at my funeral.' He winked and went back to the people he had been chatting with. At the time I understood his dark humour, and I suppose within the Irish psyche is the ability to see the light in the dark. However, that comment has really stayed with me. At Tony's funeral in September 2019, I was asked to write and deliver the eulogy. In a strange way, I felt a bit like McGahern as I prepared the words. I tapped my mental imagery for that piece. While writing, I evoked many memories of being a child on our annual holidays in the counties of Tipperary and Kilkenny. Afterwards, family, relatives and complete strangers came up to me remarking on things I had mentioned – memories, places and everyday events they had long consigned to the far reaches of memory. I was happy to have opened a few 'memory' doors.

Regarding McGahern's mother, Susan, I struggled to find an academic tone while trying to convey McGahern's adoration for this woman, an admiration that bordered on the mythical. It was an interesting visual dilemma: how do you visualize that adoration? I believe the images of the Virgin Mary, particularly from Ogulla Shrine in County Roscommon, are a strong visual reflection of his feelings towards his mother. His love for her froze him at a time, like a hankering for those faint summer days of first love. As I stated in 'Ritual', his adoration of his mother was emotionally locked within his ten-year-old frame, and that adoration never allowed or offered him the chance to see and experience his mother as a real person, warts and all. This I feel coloured his relationships with women throughout his life. How do you compete with ultimate adoration? You cannot.

And something really jars as I near the end of this book: the idea of John McGahern being buried alongside his mother in the cemetery in Aughawillan. It makes me a bit uneasy. This resting place, while it contains a beautiful symmetry, also puts his whole life and all his loves into second place. It feels strange: was it not enough to go and contribute so much to the world and to find one's own loves? His commitment to his mother far exceeded any other feelings he seems to have had on this earth. While I understand that it was always his desire to walk the lanes once more with her, in a sense the apron strings were never loosened. I realize this is just my opinion, though after working on this project for so long, it has evolved into quite a strong feeling. As a parent myself, I subscribe very strongly to the fact that your children are not yours: they are only on loan. And so, it brings me back to a small extract by Kalil Gibran in 'On Children':[1]

1 Kalil Gibran, 'On Children': <https://poets.org/poem/children-1> (1923).

> Your children are not your children. They are the sons and daughters of Life's longing for itself.

It is easier to now accept that my young and formative years with my parents, especially my mother, left me quite damaged, broken and somewhat empty. But I also feel that even from a young age I was always destined to be a very independent-minded person. I would have cut those apron strings myself. It is not coldness I feel, because I do possess a quite sensitive and emotional connection with this world. I just have none of those motherly and heavenly feelings, and I do not know if McGahern carried those feelings after childhood, but if he did, I do not wish to pour scorn on his preferences either. And this is where we diverge: I will be cremated, and my ashes will go to the wind. I would not want to be buried with my parents. As I said, I do have strong emotional and spiritual feelings; I really sense this earth. My compassion, empathy and love are emotions that grew from living life, making mistakes and trying not to look back too much. What has gone is gone. I do love this sweet taste of a shared life that is in the now. I love its happiness, its pain, its laughter, its tears. Tomorrow is for future Paul to live, and once again it is time to move along. Maybe, if there is another life after this, I will be walking and photographing country lanes. But as for whom I walk those country lanes with, without a doubt I would wish for it to be with those I have shared so much with. Our damage, our laughter, our tears and our well-worn hearts will make those walks beautiful. It will be a warm sun that engulfs us.

Those feelings aside, John McGahern's words have been a wonderful part of an expansive personal journey and continuing education. While visualizing and communing with McGahern's words, I discovered there are the many people who have forensically analysed his work. That was never my intention. I just hope that my approach in this book, while at times not fitting comfortably into the academic norm, may offer the reader a new, refreshing and enjoyable visual insight of the writer and his place of home. And just like my own feelings towards the image, John McGahern alluded to the beauty of the ordinary: 'And in fact it is the quality of the seeing not the themes or the places that matter' [PW].

And so, we find ourselves in 2023, which is another extraordinary year, Covid and its ever-evolving variants, still lurk on the horizon. They were two years of a global trauma with so many losing loved ones and being sealed off. The loss of personal freedom, particularly for the younger generation, does, I feel, rhyme in some way with the loss that McGahern suffered as a child. And now, as we reawaken to a shared life, an unjustified, vicious and barbaric war is unleashed on the people of Ukraine. Such needless suffering for so many, once again, puts everything into perspective.

I really wish good things for everyone and hope that soon we all get back to that natural safe feeling, that sacred ground. It is over twenty-one years since my family and I moved to Leitrim, and just like McGahern, the time spent wandering is easing somewhat. Many laneways have been walked, and many old homesteads have been recorded. The 'want' will always be there, but like a signal from a far distant planet, as I move forward, its call becomes faint. There are still many new adventures to begin and different areas to explore. But I can honestly say that the deep beauty and serenity of this special place they call Leitrim is a never-ending joy. It is my haven, and I am home.

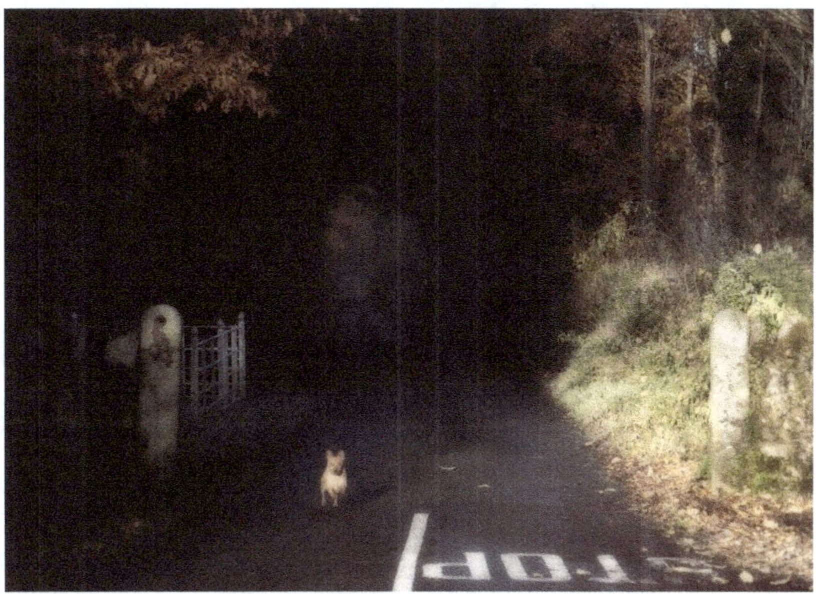

Unconditional Love, Farnocht County Leitrim – Image: Paul Butler, November 2019.

Bibliography

Adams, A. (n.d.). 'The Ansel Adams Gallery': <http://anseladams.com/>

Allsopp, B. (n.d.). 'Photography Quotes': <https://lightiseverything.co.uk/quotes>

Bailey, D. (n.d.). 'Landscape Travel', David Bailey Photography: <http://www.davidbaileyphotography.com/landscapestravel/c6cqzr4v3rtcf06088486vqy1ouvvv>

Baker, N. (2018, 3 April). 'Diocese by Diocese: The State of the Catholic Church on the Island of Ireland Today': <https://www.irishexaminer.com/ireland/special-report--diocese-by-diocese-the-state-of-the-catholic-church-on-the-island-of-ireland-today-469022.html>

Beaufort (1791). 'Sliabh an Iarainn Visitor Centre': <https://www.facebook.com/pages/category/Community/Sliabh-An-Iarainn-Visitor-Centre-1031790276988682/>

Beck, J. (2011). 'The Psychology of Home': Why Where You Live Means So Much': <https://www.theatlantic.com/health/archive/2011/12/the-psychology-of-home-why-where-you-live-means-so-much/249800/>

Black, C. (Director) (1994). *Korea* [Motion Picture]. A Cathal Black Films and Black Stars Films co-production with ZDF/ARTE in association with RTE, NOS, GRECO, Bord Scannán na hÉireann/Irish Film Board and Irish Arts Council. Filmed in Ireland.

Boate, G. (1652). *Ireland's Natural History*. London: John Wright at the Kings Head, Old Bayley.

Bohrer, F. N. (2011). *Photography and Archaelogy*. London: Reaktion Books.

Britannica, T. E. (2021). 'Aaron Siskind', *Encyclopaedia Britannica*: <https://www.britannica.com/biography/Aaron-Siskind>

Buntin, S. B. (n.d.). 'What Is "Sense of Place" and What Does It Have to Do with Ecological Media?': <https://www.terrain.org/ecomedia/q1/definitions.htm>

Butler, E. (2017). 'The Girl from Leitrim Who Became the "Angel" of New Orleans': <https://www.irishtimes.com/life-and-style/abroad/the-girl-from-leitrim-who-became-the-angel-of-new-orleans-1.2964329>

Butler, P. and Maher, E. (2016). 'John McGahern: His Time and His Places', *Canadian Journal of Irish Studies*, vol. 39, no. 2, pp. 27–54.

Butler, P. (Director) (2011). *A Life Over* [Audio Visual]. John McGahern and The Deep Well of Want: portraits of the artist's world. Photographer Paul Butler has captured on film the landscapes and enviroment that inspired the author for an exhibition marking the tenth anniversary of his death.

Butler, P. (2016, 30 March). 'John McGahern and the Deep Well of Want: Portraits of the Artist's World', *Irish Times*: <https://www.irishtimes.com/culture/books/john-mcgahern-and-the-deep-well-of-want-portraits-of-the-artist-s-world-1.2592043>

Butler, P. (2017). 'Under the Irish Skies', Landscape Photography: <https://edgeofhumanity.com/2017/09/23/ireland-3/>

Butler, P. (n.d.). 'Visualising McGahern': <https://www.lensculture.com/paul-butler>

Cartier-Bresson, H. (n.d.). <https://www.henricartierbresson.org/en/hcb/>

Coillte. 'Sliabh Bawn', <https://www.coillte.ie/site/sliabh-bawn-windfarm/>

Conliffe, M. (2014). 'Just A Memory – My Mother's High Nelly', Ireland's Own: <https://www.irelandsown.ie/just-a-memory-my-mothers-high-nelly/>

Counties of Ireland – 'Leitrim': <https://www.ireland101.com/page/leitrim>

Cranfield, U. T. 'Irish Soil Information System', Environmental Protection Agency: <http://gis.teagasc.ie/soils/index.php>

CSO (2011). 'Area Profile for County Leitrim', Central Statistics Office: <http://census.cso.ie/areaprofiles/PDF/CTY/leitrim.pdf>

CSO (2016). 'Census of Population 2016 – Profile 1 Housing in Ireland', Central Statistics Office: <https://www.cso.ie/en/releasesandpublications/ep/p-cp1hii/cp1hii/vac/>

CSO (2016). 'Census of Population 2016 – Profile 8 Irish Travellers, Ethnicity and Religion', Central Statistics Office: <https://www.cso.ie/en/releasesandpublications/ep/p-cp8iter/p8iter/p8rrc/>

CSO (n.d.). 'Life in 1916 Ireland: Stories from Statistics', Central Statistics Office: <https://www.cso.ie/en/releasesandpublications/ep/p-1916/1916irl/economy/tp/>

Dempsey, J. 'Ogulla Holy Well', Megalith Ireland: <http://www.megalithicireland.com/Ogulla%20Holy%20Well%20Tulsk.html>

Dixon, O. (2009). 'Drumreilly Church of Ireland', Geograph: <https://www.geograph.ie/photo/1310479>

Dorrell, P. (1994). 'Photography in Archaeology and Conservation', Pastperfect: <http://www.pastperfect.org.uk/archaeology/photography.html>

Durden M. and Tormey, T. (2020). *The Routledge Companion to Photographic Theory*. London: Routledge.

Edwards, R. (2017). 'Sixty Years since Border Rail Transport Ran Out of Steam', *Irish Times*: <https://www.irishtimes.com/news/ireland/irish-news/sixty-years-since-border-rail-transport-ran-out-of-steam-1.3232191>

Encyclopedia.com. (2019). <https://www.encyclopedia.com/women/encyclopedias-almanacs-transcripts-and-maps/langtry-lillie-1853-1929>

Fáilte Ireland (2014). 'Minister Ring Officially Launches Wild Atlantic Way': <http://www.failteireland.ie/Footer/Media-Centre/Minister-Ring-officially-launches-Wild-Atlantic-Wa.aspx>

Farnworth, R. (2019). 'The Cavan and Leitrim Railway – A Short History, and a Look at Dromod Station': <https://rogerfarnworth.com/2019/05/09/the-cavan-and-leitrim-railway-a-short-history-and-a-look-at-dromod-station/>

Fitzsimons, F. (2020). 'Churching', History Ireland: <https://www.historyireland.com/churching/>

Flanagan, P. J. (1972). *The Cavan & Leitrim Railway*. London: Pan Books.

Fox, C. (2018). 'Leitrim and the Gigantic Forest Debate', Farming Independent: <https://www.independent.ie/business/farming/forestry-enviro/forestry/leitrim-and-the-gigantic-forest-debate-37545279.html>

Gibran, K. (1923). 'On Children', Poets.Org: <https://poets.org/poem/children-1>

Gibran, K. (n.d.). 'The Mother', Soveral: <https://www.alexandrasoveral.co.uk/blog/read_144105/the-mother-by-kahlil-gibran.html>

Goarzin, A. (2019). ''The Sky Above Us': John McGahern, 'The Image' and Paul Butler's Photographs of County Leitrim'. In Hand, D. and E. Maher (eds), *Essays on John McGahern: Assessing a Literary Legacy* (Cork: Cork University Press), 123–134.

Guy, P. D. (n.d.). 'The Art of Memory in the Work of John McGahern', Academia: <https://www.academia.edu/11620656/The_Art_of_Memory_in_the_Work_of_John_McGahern>

Hand, D. and Maher, E. (eds), *Essays on John McGahern: Assessing a Literary Legacy*. Cork: Cork University Press.

Harding, M. (2017). 'Closing the Door One Final Time on the World Where I Was Born', *Irish Times*: <https://www.irishtimes.com/life-and-style/people/closing-the-door-one-final-time-on-the-world-where-i-was-born-1.2969785>

Heaney, S. (1980). 'A Sense of Place (1977)'. In *Preoccupations: Selected Prose*. London: Faber & Faber.

Hermans, J. 'How to Use Gaussian Blur in Photoshop', Expert Photography: <https://expertphotography.com/gaussian-blur-photoshop/>

Hosford, P. (2015). 'Why Did Roscommon-South Leitrim Vote No?' The Journal.ie: <https://jrnl.ie/2121899>

Hull, C. (2019). 'Susan Sontag on Photography Quotes', Expert Photography: <https://expertphotography.com/susan-sontag-on-photography-quotes/>

Hull, C. 'Step by Step Guide to Beautiful Bokeh', Expert Photography: <https://expertphotography.com/beautiful-bokeh-effect-photography/>

Hummingbird Productions (2005). *A Private World* [Motion Picture].

Kasdan, L. (1981). *Raiders of the Lost Ark Screenplay*. IMDB: <https://www.imdb.com/name/nm0001410/?ref_=tt_ov_wr>

Kasten, P. (2015). 'Why Women Stayed Away from Church after a Birth', The Compass: <https://www.thecompassnews.org/2015/02/women-stayed-away-church-birth/>

Keavney, M. (2018). *The Rainy Day*. Castlebar: Mayo Books.

Kehler, K. 'Eulogizing a Home: How to Say Goodbye to a Place with Memories', Design Sponge: <https://www.designsponge.com/2015/02/eulogizing-a-home-how-to-say-goodbye-to-a-place-with-memories.html>

Lamourex, T. (2014). '70 Inspirational Quotes for Photographers', Peta Pixel: <https://petapixel.com/2014/05/29/70-inspirational-quotes-photographers/>

Lee, H. (2004). 'John McGahern': <https://lannan.org/images/lit/john-mcgahern-040407-trans-conv.pdf>

Leitrim Observer. (2018). 'Weather', Leitrim Observer: <https://www.leitrimobserver.ie/news/weather/321546/breaking-status-yellow-high- temperature-warning-in-effect-today-for-leitrim-cavan-and-roscommon.html>

Leitrim Tourism. 'Farnaught Lime Kiln': <http://leitrimtourism.com/products/farnaught-lime-kiln/>

Leitrim Tourism. 'Glenade Lake': <http://leitrimtourism.com/stories/glenadelake/>

Leitrim Tourism. 'Tullaghan': <http://leitrim tourism.com/stories/tullaghan/>

Lewis, S. (1837). 'Leitrim Geology', Library Ireland: <https://www.libraryireland.com/topog/L/Leitrim-Geology.php>

Littlejohn, A. (2019). 'Who Invented Windows and Doors?' Owlcation, Humanities, History: <https://owlcation.com/humanities/Who-Invented-Windows-and-Doors>

Maher, E. (2001). 'Catholicism and National Identity in the Works of John McGahern. Interview between Eamon Maher and John McGahern', *Studies: An Irish Quarterly*, vol. 90, no. 357, pp. 72–83.

Maher, E. (2003). *John McGahern: From the Local to the Universal*. Dublin: Liffey Press.

Maher, E. (2011). *'The Church and its Spire': John McGahern and the Catholic Question*. Dublin: The Columba Press.

McCrum, R. (2002). *The Whole World in a Community. The Guardian*: <https://www.theguardian.com/books/2002/jan/06/fiction.features>

McCullin, D. (n.d.). 'Irreconcilable Truths', Don McCullin: <https://donmccullin.com/>

McCurry, S. (n.d.). 'Steve McCurry', Steve McCurry Blog: <https://stevemccurry.com/>

McDonagh, M. (2015). '"Most Dangerous" Stretch of N4 to Get €102m Upgrade'. *Irish Times*: <https://www.irishtimes.com/news/environment/most-dangerous-stretch-of-n4-to-get-102m-upgrade-1.2371862?mode=sample&auth-failed=1&pw-origin=https%3A%2F%2Fwww.irishtimes.com%2Fnews%2Fenvironment%2Fmost-dangerous-stretch-of-n4-to-get-102m-upgrade-1.2371862>

McDonagh, M. (2018). 'Adapting to Survive: "Mohill Was a Dead Town but It Is Reinventing Itself"', *Irish Times*: <https://www.irishtimes.com/news/ireland/irish-news/adapting-to-survive-mohill-was-a-dead-town-but-it-is-reinventing-itself-1.3671955>

McDonagh, M. (2021). 'Leitrim Rents Driven Up by People Leaving Cities during Pandemic', *Irish Times*: <https://www.irishtimes.com/news/ireland/irish-news/leitrim-rents-driven-up-by-people-leaving-cities-during-pandemic-1.4726167>

McGahern, J. (1963). *The Barracks*. London: Faber & Faber.

McGahern, J. (1965). *The Dark*. London: Faber & Faber.

McGahern, J. (1979). *The Pornographer*. London: Faber & Faber.

McGahern, J. (1984). *The Leavetaking*. 2nd Edition. London: Faber & Faber.

McGahern, J. (1990). *Amongst Women*. London: Faber & Faber.

McGahern, J. (1992). *The Collected Stories*. London: Faber & Faber.

McGahern, J. (2002). *That They May Face the Rising Sun*. London: Faber & Faber.

McGahern, J. (2005). *Memoir*. London: Faber & Faber.

McGahern, J. (2006). 'John McGahern Considers the Role of Religion in His Life', *The Guardian*: <https://www.theguardian.com/books/2006/apr/08/featuresreviews.guardianreview30>

McGahern, J. (2006). 'Saving Grace', *The Guardian*: <https://www.theguardian.com/books/2006/apr/08/featuresreviews.guardianreview30>

McGahern, J. (2009). *Creatures of the Earth: New and Selected Stories*. London: Faber & Faber.

McGahern, J. (2009). *Love of the World: Essays*, edited by Stanley van der Ziel. London: Faber & Faber.

Mining, A. (n.d.). 'Arigna Mining Experience': <https://www.arignaminingexperience.ie/history/>

Nassaney, M. S. (n.d.). *Volume 1 – Social Archaelogy*. Department of Anthropology, Western Michigan University, United States: <https://www.eolss.net/sample-chapters/C04/E6-21-01-12.pdf>

National Inventory of Architectural Heritage. 'St. Marys Church Of Ireland Church, Farnaght, County Leitrim': <https://www.buildingsofireland.ie/buildings-search/building/30936008/st-marys-church-of-ireland-church-farnaght-county-leitrim>

Network, L. T. (2016). 'The History of Leitrim': <https://www.leitrimireland.com/the-history-of-leitrim/>

NUI Galway. (2011). 'Landed Estates Database': <http://landedestates.nuigalway.ie/LandedEstates/jsp/property-show.jsp?id=483>

O'Callaghan, T. (2013). 'Regional Divide in Herd Sizes', Agriland: <https://www.agriland.ie/farming-news/analysing-herd-sizes/>

Office, D. (2022). 'Historical Reference: Merging Together', Ardagh & Clonmacnoise: <https://ardaghdiocese.org/historical-reference-merging-together/>

Osmonds. (n.d.). 'Osmonds Lambing Pack': <https://www.osmonds.co.uk/>

O'Sullivan, K. (2019, 3 September). 'Report on Forestry in Leitrim Confirms Dominant Use of Sitka Spruce', *Irish Times*, Environment Section: <https://www.irishtimes.com/news/environment/report-on-forestry-in-leitrim-confirms-dominant-use-of-sitka-spruce-1.4005658>

Pitts, T. (2013). 'Shadows across the Text: Fiction with Embedded Photographs' (Issue 75). Terry Pitts, Shadows across the Text: Fiction with Embedded Photographs (Source, Issue 75, 2013).

Prasad, J. (2007). '"Derrida: The Father of Deconstruction", As I have Understood Him': <https://newderrida.wordpress.com/2007/11/19/some-key-terms/>

Radler, D. (2015). 'A Lifetime Memory Quest: Identity, Places and Characters in John McGahern's *Memoir*'. *"C Peter McGrath" Research Centre for Cross Cultural Studies.*

Revenue. (2018). 'Section 23 Relief – Rented Residential Relief in a Tax': <https://www.revenue.ie/en/tax-professionals/tdm/income-tax-capital-gains-tax-corporation-tax/part-10/10-11-01.pdf>

Roman Catholic Diocese of Ardagh and Clonmacnoise. (n.d.). Wikipedia: <https://en.wikipedia.org/wiki/Roman_Catholic_Diocese_of_Ardagh_and_Clonmacnoise>

RTE (2012). 'Tubridy 2fm Tracked Down the Calvita Girl, and She's Looking Well': <https://www.facebook.com/2fmofficial/posts/tubridy-2fm-tracked-down-the-calvita-girl-and-shes-looking-well-any-ideas-for-wh/124582471008981/>

Sampson. D. (1991), 'A Conversation with John McGahern', in *Canadian Journal of Irish Studies*, Vol. 17, No. 1, pp. 13–18.

Saunders, F. W. (2018). 'Origins of the Holy Rosary', Catholic Exchange: <https://catholicexchange.com/origins-of-the-holy-rosary>

Schaberg, C. (2009). *Ordinary Effects.* Retrieved from Western American Literature, University of Nebraska: <https://muse.jhu.edu/article/315394/summary>

Stone, L. (2015). 'Does Your House Have a Soul?': <https://www.lauriestonewrites.com/2015/08/13/do-houses-have-souls/>

Thackeray, W. M. (n.d.). 'Full text of *William Makepeace Thackeray; a Biography Including Hitherto Uncollected Letters & Speeches & a Bibliography of 1300*

Items'. Internet Archive: <https://archive.org/stream/williammakepeace01melv/williammakepeace01melv_djvu.txt>

Tiernan, C. (2003). <https://hoganstand.com/county/leitrim/article/index/38808>

Times, T. I. (2015). 'How the Coal Ban Dealt with Dublin's Burning Issue', *Irish Times*: <https://www.irishtimes.com/news/environment/how-the-coal-ban-dealt-with-dublin-s-burning-issue-1.2367021>

Valley, B. (2007). 'Beltane – The Fire Festival': <https://www.newgrange.com/beltane.htm>

What Does It Mean to Experience a Place? (2015). 'Philosophy of Life', Quora: https://www.quora.com/What-does-it-mean-to-experience-a-place

Western Development Commission (2016). 'Leitrim': <https://www.wdc.ie/county-profiles/leitrim/>

Wilde, L. J. (1888). 'Queen Maeve', Library Ireland: <https://www.libraryireland.com/AncientLegendsSuperstitions/Queen-Maeve.php>

Yeshurun, A. (1989). 'Memories Are a House', Poetry Foundation: <https://www.poetryfoundation.org/poetrymagazine/poems/50964/memories-are-a-house>

Image Index

All images are the creation of Paul Butler with the exception of the Map of Leitrim (p41), which is courtesy of the Planning Department at *Leitrim County Council.

Abandoned Boat, 10
After the Rain, a Copper Sunset on Errew, 68
And time is Stilled, 163
Approaching Hailstorm, 50
Arch Masonry CLR Railway Bridge, 129
Autumn Morning Fog on Lough Rinn, 66

Bedroom Interior, 160
Big April Sky at the High Field, 55
Bluebells of May, 43
Bright Moon over Mel Grey's Farm, 63
Burnt Out Car, 21
Butchers Calendar, 87
Buttercup Riot, 47

Calendar at the Kitchen Window, 102
Cattle & Sheep Cures for all ills, 113;
Cattle in May, 51
Child's Lost Wellington Boot, 109
Church of Ireland at Drumreilly, 169
Clock & Calendar, 14;
Cormongan Pier, Lough Allen, 46
Crumbling Frame of Saint Anthony & the Infant, 142;
Crying Child, 161

Dandelion Seed Head, 57
December Sea Mist and Rolling Cloud at Strandhill, 75
Dedication, Ogulla Shrine, 7
Deep Window of Secrets, 117
Derelict Kitchen, 31
Discarded Grave Markers, 11
Dish Scrubber, 93
Disused Commode, 32
Dog Silhouette, 18
Dresser, 114
Drying the First Cut of Silage at the Pheasantry, 60
Dublin GAA Supporters Heading Home, 20

Eagle's Rock, Glenade, 70
Early Morning Fog at Roosky bridge, 69
Evening in Late June, 54

Face Painting at the Dublin Street Carnival, 24
Farmhouse (Now Demolished), 88
Farmhouse Interior, 96
Farnocht Cemetery in Snow, 166
Font & the Blessing, 184;
Forbidding Sky over Blackrock Lighthouse, 77
Forgotten Bedroom, 29
Forgotten Swing, 101
Former Garda Barracks at Cootehall, 9
Frost on McGarry's Field, 83

Gabriel's Cow, 139
Gas Cooker, 108
Glencar Waterfall, 48

Golden Light on Wild Daisies, 59
Golden Sunset at Lough Rinn, 62
Good Suit, 124

Home for Lunch, 136
House of Windows, 125

Ivy-Clad House, 90

Kitchen Interior, Trish Carrigy's, 147

Lakefield House, 97
Lampshade, 115
Lazy Rinn River, 65
Leitrim Coast Road near Tullaghan, 74
Lick of Paint, 35
Little White Statue at Shankill Cemetery, 12
Lonely Chair, 137
Looking from Sliabh Báwn, 58
Looking towards Arroo Mountain, 73

Main Street, Mohill, 134
Maker of the Gate, 100
Map of Leitrim, 41 *(Leitrim County Council)
March of Modernity, 111
Marian Shrine, Sliabh Báwn, 189
Marian Year Cross, Sliabh Báwn, 145
Meadowsweet, 53
Memories of a Home, 30
Misty Birch on the Bogland, 45
MJ Henry's Bar, Cootehall, 133
Mother & child, 148;

Nature's Diffuser, 40
Need to Fly and Create, 1
Net Curtains, 119
November Sun at Farnocht Cemetery, 167

October Fog in the Wood, 81
October Sunrise at Cloone River, 38
Off Season, 78
Offerings at Ogulla Shrine, 171
Offerings for Hope of Divine Intervention, 175
Old Railbus from the CLR, 132
Once a Home, 92
Orange Globe Hangs over Tooman, 61
Original Waiting Room at the CLR, 131

Paddy McManus, 135
Padre Pio over the Door, 186
Pink Cross, 165
Pink Door, 91
Placed in the Wood, 164
Ponies, Near Dromahair, 172
Pope &
the Font, 185;
Powers &
Jameson Whiskey Bottles, 104;

Rainclouds over a Commercial Forest Plantation, 82
Religious Billboard, 182
Ritual of the Razor &
Religion, 155;
Rosary Beads at the Dublin/Sligo Rail Crossing, 153
Rusted key of Many Memories, 106
Rusting Old Citroen DS, 99

Sacred heart at Ogulla Shrine, 180
Sacred Heart Lamp and Bourbon, 4
Sacred Heart on Green, 188
Secret Grotto, 173
Serenity, Ogulla Shrine, 158
Setting Sun over the Cemetery, 84
Snow on the High Field, 6
Statue of Mary in the Dining Room, 150

Summer Light Filtering through Oak Leaves, 56
Sunset at Glenade Lough, 67
Sunset on Great Keppel Island, 26

Towers at Poolbeg Power Station, 23
Trail Marker from Strandhill Dunes, 177
Travel & Tales, 122;
Turf Drying on the Bog, 17

Unconditional Love, 199

Vicious Collie, 127
View towards Glenade Lough, 72

Watching the Surfers, 79
Winter Moon at Morning, 64
Within Reach, 121

Young Boy in Shadow, 27

Index

35mm Negative, 18, 21, 23
'All Sorts of Impossible Things' (McGahern), 83, 178, 179;
Adams, Ansel Easton, 76
Amongst Women (McGahern), 13, 37
Aperture, 64, 104, 147
Archer, Frederick Scott, 158
Arigna Mines, 130
Arroo Mountain, 72, 73
Art of Memory, 141
Aughawillan, 5, 7, 8, 12, 126, 129, 150, 168, 190, 195, 197
Aughris Head, 75, 79
Australia, 25, 26, 27
Auto-Ethnographic, 22, 103

Bailey, David, 22
Ballweg, Julie, 42
Barracks, The (McGahern), 10, 37, 58, 67, 120, 126, 141, 146, 147, 152, 154, 155, 156, 160, 162, 195
Bealtaine, 174
Beautiful Bokeh (Holtzer), 56
Berger, John, viii
Big Skies, 51
Black, Cathal, 67
Bohrer, N. Frederick, 94, 110
Butler, Eoin, 98
Buttercup Binds, 47

Callows, 65
Camera Metring, 47
Carrick-on-Shannon, 10, 34, 41, 43, 45, 112
Cartier-Bresson, Henri, 103
Catholicism and National Identity (Maher), 57, 146, 176, 178, 183, 187
Ceilidh, 108
'Christmas' (McGahern), 81;
Church Control (Maher), 141
(McGahern), 145
Churching, 150, 151
Coillte, 82
Collins, Pat, 9
Conliffe, Mary, 128
'Conversion of William Kirkwood, The' (McGahern), 169;
Corramahon, 7, 8, 129, 190, 194
'Country Funeral, The' (McGahern), 59, 123, 124, 162 ;

Dark, The (McGahern), 11, 167, 173, 183
Dartry Mountains, 70
Deep Red Filter, 18
Deep Well of Want (Exhibition), 33
Dempsey, Jim, 174
Derrida, Jacques, 120
Destruction of Memory, 92
Devlin, Zoe, 53
Dixon, Oliver, 170
Dramatic Format, 55
Drumkeeran, 39
Drumlish to Mohill, 45
Drumshanbo, 39, 45
Durden, Mark, 2

Eagle's Rock, 70, 71, 193
Edwards, Rodney, 131

Farnocht, 30
Farnworth, Roger, 130
Fenagh, 11
Film Graininess, 64
Fitzsimons, Fiona, 151
Ford, Harrison, 94
Fox, Claire, 80
Fox's Pub, 45
Foxfield, 49
Freeman, Paul, 94
From the Local to the Universal (Maher), 14–15, 52

Garadice Halt, 128
Garcia, Serge, 42
Garda Barracks, Cootehall, 8, 9, 10, 67
Gibran, Kilal, 197
Gladwin, Derek, ix
Glencar Waterfall, 48
Glens of Leitrim, 70
Glotfelty, Cheryll, ix
Guy, Declan Peter, 141, 166

Harding, Michael, 107
Heaney, Seamus, 89
High Dynamic Resolution (HDR), 93
'High Ground' (McGahern), 62, 159

Image Noise, 119
Indiana Jones, 94
ISO, 64, 119

Kakadu National Park, 26
Kasdan, Lawrence, 94
Keavney, Martin, 127
Kehler, Kelli, 109
Kodachrome (Movie), 25
Kodak Ektachrome, 25, 28
Kodakchrome 64 25
'Korea' (McGahern), 66, 67

Lakefield House, 96, 97
Langtry, Lillie, 151
Leavetaking, The (McGahern), 161–162, 164
Lee, Hermoine, 138
Leitrim and Cattle, 136
Leitrim and Diocese, 143
Leitrim and the Economic Crash, 138
Leitrim and the Famine, 87
Leitrim History, 39
Leitrim Landmass, 89
Leitrim Population, 89
Leitrim Soil types, 50
Leitrim, Wild Rose County, 47
Lewis, Samuel, 71
Liath Druim, 41
Lifford, 44
Lime Kiln, 84
Littlejohn, Amanda, 117
Long Exposure, 26
Lough Allen, 40, 41
Lough Erne, 46
Lough Gill, 41–42, 47
Lough Melvin, 42
Lough Rinn, 41
Love of the World, (McGahern), 67, 102, 143–144

Magenta Filter, 26
'Manifesto', (McGahern), 183
Manorhamilton, 44, 45
Margaret of New Orleans, 98
McCrum, Robert, 106, 171
McCullin, Don, 30
McCurry, Steve, 27–28
McDonagh, Marese, 133, 139, 181
McGahern and a Fortress Church, (Maher), 178
McGahern and Catholicism, (Maher), 172

McGahern and Religious Iconography, (Maher), 183
McGahern and Sexuality, (Maher), 178
McGahern and the Rosary (Maher), 146
McGahern, Frank, 8
McGahern in Conservation (Sampson), 16
McGahern, Madeline, 49
McGahern on Censorship (Maher), 178
McGahern on Church Ceremonies, (Maher), 149
McGahern on Loss, 179–180
McGahern, Susan, 8, 149, 157, 159, 161
'McGahern: His Time and His Places' (Butler, Maher), 15;
McManus, Paddy, 135
Meadowsweet, 53
Memento Mori, 19
Memoir (McGahern), 6, 49, 51, 56, 76, 122, 126, 128, 133, 142, 145–146, 148, 150, 155-157, 162, 164, 167, 176, 189
Memory and Imagination, 159
Memory Quest, 141
Mohill, 133
Murari, Aishwaya, 89
'My Love, My Umbrella' (McGahern), 179

N4, 43
N15, 44
N16, 44
NCAD, 24
Ní Dhubháin, Áine, 42 ;
Nostalgia Definition, 35

O'Callaghan, Tom, 136
O'Sullivan, Kevin, 80
Ogulla Shrine, 170
'Oldfashioned' (McGahern), 97
Ordinary Affects, (Stewart), 16
Ornithology, 25

Pagan Ritualism, 170
Parkes Castle, 48
Photographic Archaeology, 32
Photographic Feeling, 30
Pornographer, The (McGahern), 167–168
Portraits of the Artist's World (Butler), 13
Private World, A, (Collins) 9
Prophet, The (Gibran), 190
Protestantism, 170

Queen Maedbh's Cairn, 77

R280, 45
Radler, Dana, 141
Rathcroghan, 174
RAW file, 38
Rising Sun, The (McGahern), 17, 130, 134
River Drowses, 44
River Duff, 44
River Shannon, 46
Roosky, 68
Rosary Beads, 152
Roscommon, 42, 45

Samhain, 174
Sampson, Denis, 16
Saunders, William, 152
'Saving Grace' (McGahern), 146
Scramoge, 110
Sensation of Emptiness, 95
Sense of Place, 194
Shannon- Erne Waterway, 46
Simmons, Buntin, 88
Siskind, Aaron, 93
Sliabh Báwn, 58, 188
Sligo, 42

'Slip Up, A' (McGahern), 111
Sontag on Photography, 19, 36
St Anne's Park, Raheny, 18
Stegner, Wallace, vii
Still (Exhibition), 33
Stoettner, Evelyn, 42
Stones, Laurie, 95
Strandhill, 73
'Strandhill, The Sea' (McGahern), 75, 77
Strokestown, 58
'Swallows' (McGahern), 104

Technical Photography, 28
Thackery, William, 95
The Cavan & Leitrim Railway (Flanagan), 46
'The Rose of Inishfree' (W. B. Yeats), 47
'The Sky Above Us' (Goarzin), 31, 34, 36
'The Stolen Child' (W. B. Yeats), 48
Tiernan, Christy, 126
Tooman Bridge, 59
Tormeny, Jane, 2
'Tracing John McGahern's Steps through *Memoir's* Pages and Paul Butler's Images' (Maher), 33
Tullaghan, 44, 73
Turf Ban 2010, 17

Unfulfilled Parents, 19–21

Vinduaga, 117
Violence against McGahern, 19

Wet Collodion Process, 158
'Wheels' (McGahern), 90, 108
Wide-Angle Lens, 21
Wild Atlantic Way, 73
Wilde, Lady Jane Francesca, 78
Windows, 116
'Wine Breath, The' (McGahern), 118, 164–168
World in a Community, 106, 171
Wratten Filter, 38

Yeshurun, Avot, 110

Reimagining Ireland

Series Editor: Dr Eamon Maher, Technological University Dublin

The concepts of Ireland and 'Irishness' are in constant flux in the wake of an ever-increasing reappraisal of the notion of cultural and national specificity in a world assailed from all angles by the forces of globalisation and uniformity. Reimagining Ireland interrogates Ireland's past and present and suggests possibilities for the future by looking at Ireland's literature, culture and history and subjecting them to the most up-to-date critical appraisals associated with sociology, literary theory, historiography, political science and theology.

Some of the pertinent issues include, but are not confined to, Irish writing in English and Irish, Nationalism, Unionism, the Northern 'Troubles', the Peace Process, economic development in Ireland, the impact and decline of the Celtic Tiger, Irish spirituality, the rise and fall of organised religion, the visual arts, popular cultures, sport, Irish music and dance, emigration and the Irish diaspora, immigration and multiculturalism, marginalisation, globalisation, modernity/postmodernity and postcolonialism. The series publishes monographs, comparative studies, interdisciplinary projects, conference proceedings and edited books. Proposals should be sent either to Dr Eamon Maher at eamon.maher@ittdublin.ie or to ireland@peterlang.com.

Vol. 1 Eugene O'Brien: 'Kicking Bishop Brennan up the Arse': Negotiating Texts and Contexts in Contemporary Irish Studies
ISBN 978-3-03911-539-6. 219 pages. 2009.

Vol. 2 James P.Byrne, Padraig Kirwan and Michael O'Sullivan (eds): Affecting Irishness: Negotiating Cultural Identity Within and Beyond the Nation
ISBN 978-3-03911-830-4. 334 pages. 2009.

Vol. 3 Irene Lucchitti: The Islandman: The Hidden Life of Tomás O'Crohan
ISBN 978-3-03911-837-3. 232 pages. 2009.

Vol. 4 Paddy Lyons and Alison O'Malley-Younger (eds): No Country for Old Men: Fresh Perspectives on Irish Literature
ISBN 978-3-03911-841-0. 289 pages. 2009.

Vol. 5 Eamon Maher (ed.): Cultural Perspectives on Globalisation and Ireland
ISBN 978-3-03911-851-9. 256 pages. 2009.

Vol. 6 Lynn Brunet: 'A Course of Severe and Arduous Trials': Bacon, Beckett and Spurious Freemasonry in Early Twentieth-Century Ireland
ISBN 978-3-03911-854-0. 218 pages. 2009.

Vol. 7 Claire Lynch: Irish Autobiography: Stories of Self in the Narrative of a Nation
ISBN 978-3-03911-856-4. 234 pages. 2009.

Vol. 8 Victoria O'Brien: A History of Irish Ballet from 1927 to 1963
ISBN 978-3-03911-873-1. 208 pages. 2011.

Vol. 9 Irene Gilsenan Nordin and Elin Holmsten (eds): Liminal Borderlands in Irish Literature and Culture
ISBN 978-3-03911-859-5. 208 pages. 2009.

Vol. 10 Claire Nally: Envisioning Ireland: W. B. Yeats's Occult Nationalism
ISBN 978-3-03911-882-3. 320 pages. 2010.

Vol. 11 Raita Merivirta: The Gun and Irish Politics: Examining National History in Neil Jordan's *Michael Collins*
ISBN 978-3-03911-888-5. 202 pages. 2009.

Vol. 12 John Strachan and Alison O'Malley-Younger (eds): Ireland: Revolution and Evolution
ISBN 978-3-03911-881-6. 248 pages. 2010.

Vol. 13 Barbara Hughes: Between Literature and History: The Diaries and Memoirs of Mary Leadbeater and Dorothea Herbert
ISBN 978-3-03911-889-2. 255 pages. 2010.

Vol. 14 Edwina Keown and Carol Taaffe (eds): Irish Modernism: Origins, Contexts, Publics
ISBN 978-3-03911-894-6. 256 pages. 2010.

Vol. 15 John Walsh: Contests and Contexts: The Irish Language and Ireland's Socio-Economic Development
ISBN 978-3-03911-914-1. 492 pages. 2011.

Vol. 16 Zélie Asava: The Black Irish Onscreen: Representing Black and Mixed-Race Identities on Irish Film and Television
ISBN 978-3-0343-0839-7. 213 pages. 2013.

Vol. 17 Susan Cahill and Eóin Flannery (eds): This Side of Brightness: Essays on the Fiction of Colum McCann
ISBN 978-3-03911-935-6. 189 pages. 2012.

Vol. 18 Brian Arkins: The Thought of W. B. Yeats
ISBN 978-3-03911-939-4. 204 pages. 2010.

Vol. 19 Maureen O'Connor: The Female and the Species: The Animal in Irish Women's Writing
ISBN 978-3-03911-959-2. 203 pages. 2010.

Vol. 20 Rhona Trench: Bloody Living: The Loss of Selfhood in the Plays of Marina Carr
ISBN 978-3-03911-964-6. 327 pages. 2010.

Vol. 21 Jeannine Woods: Visions of Empire and Other Imaginings: Cinema, Ireland and India, 1910–1962
ISBN 978-3-03911-974-5. 230 pages. 2011.

Vol. 22 Neil O'Boyle: New Vocabularies, Old Ideas: Culture, Irishness and the Advertising Industry
ISBN 978-3-03911-978-3. 233 pages. 2011.

Vol. 23 Dermot McCarthy: John McGahern and the Art of Memory
ISBN 978-3-0343-0100-8. 344 pages. 2010.

Vol. 24 Francesca Benatti, Sean Ryder and Justin Tonra (eds): Thomas Moore: Texts, Contexts, Hypertexts
ISBN 978-3-0343-0900-4. 220 pages. 2013.

Vol. 25 Sarah O'Connor: No Man's Land: Irish Women and the Cultural Present
ISBN 978-3-0343-0111-4. 230 pages. 2011.

Vol. 26 Caroline Magennis: Sons of Ulster: Masculinities in the Contemporary Northern Irish Novel
ISBN 978-3-0343-0110-7. 192 pages. 2010.

Vol. 27 Dawn Duncan: Irish Myth, Lore and Legend on Film
ISBN 978-3-0343-0140-4. 181 pages. 2013.

Vol. 28 Eamon Maher and Catherine Maignant (eds): Franco-Irish Connections in Space and Time: Peregrinations and Ruminations
ISBN 978-3-0343-0870-0. 295 pages. 2012.

Vol. 29 Holly Maples: Culture War: Conflict, Commemoration and the Contemporary Abbey Theatre
ISBN 978-3-0343-0137-4. 294 pages. 2011.

Vol. 30 Maureen O'Connor (ed.): Back to the Future of Irish Studies: Festschrift for Tadhg Foley
ISBN 978-3-0343-0141-1. 359 pages. 2010.

Vol. 31 Eva Urban: Community Politics and the Peace Process in Contemporary Northern Irish Drama
ISBN 978-3-0343-0143-5. 303 pages. 2011.

Vol. 32 Mairéad Conneely: Between Two Shores/*Idir Dhá Chladach*: Writing the Aran Islands, 1890–1980
ISBN 978-3-0343-0144-2. 299 pages. 2011.

Vol. 33 Gerald Morgan and Gavin Hughes (eds): Southern Ireland and the Liberation of France: New Perspectives
ISBN 978-3-0343-0190-9. 250 pages. 2011.

Vol. 34 Anne MacCarthy: Definitions of Irishness in the 'Library of Ireland' Literary Anthologies
ISBN 978-3-0343-0194-7. 271 pages. 2012.

Vol. 35 Irene Lucchitti: Peig Sayers: In Her Own Write
ISBN 978-3-0343-0253-1. Forthcoming.

Vol. 36 Eamon Maher and Eugene O'Brien (eds): Breaking the Mould: Literary Representations of Irish Catholicism
ISBN 978-3-0343-0232-6. 249 pages. 2011.

Vol. 37 Mícheál Ó hAodha and John O'Callaghan (eds): Narratives of the Occluded Irish Diaspora: Subversive Voices
ISBN 978-3-0343-0248-7. 227 pages. 2012.

Vol. 38 Willy Maley and Alison O'Malley-Younger (eds): Celtic Connections: Irish–Scottish Relations and the Politics of Culture
ISBN 978-3-0343-0214-2. 247 pages. 2013.

Vol. 39 Sabine Egger and John McDonagh (eds): Polish–Irish Encounters in the Old and New Europe
ISBN 978-3-0343-0253-1. 322 pages. 2011.

Vol. 40 Elke D'hoker, Raphaël Ingelbien and Hedwig Schwall (eds): Irish Women Writers: New Critical Perspectives
ISBN 978-3-0343-0249-4. 318 pages. 2011.

Vol. 41 Peter James Harris: From Stage to Page: Critical Reception of Irish Plays in the London Theatre, 1925–1996
ISBN 978-3-0343-0266-1. 311 pages. 2011.

Vol. 42 Hedda Friberg-Harnesk, Gerald Porter and Joakim Wrethed (eds): Beyond Ireland: Encounters Across Cultures
ISBN 978-3-0343-0270-8. 342 pages. 2011.

Vol. 43 Irene Gilsenan Nordin and Carmen Zamorano Llena (eds): Urban and Rural Landscapes in Modern Ireland: Language, Literature and Culture
ISBN 978-3-0343-0279-1. 238 pages. 2012.

Vol. 44 Kathleen Costello-Sullivan: Mother/Country: Politics of the Personal in the Fiction of Colm Tóibín
ISBN 978-3-0343-0753-6. 247 pages. 2012.

Vol. 45 Lesley Lelourec and Gráinne O'Keeffe-Vigneron (eds): Ireland and Victims: Confronting the Past, Forging the Future
ISBN 978-3-0343-0792-5. 331 pages. 2012.

Vol. 46 Gerald Dawe, Darryl Jones and Nora Pelizzari (eds): Beautiful Strangers: Ireland and the World of the 1950s
ISBN 978-3-0343-0801-4. 207 pages. 2013.

Vol. 47 Yvonne O'Keeffe and Claudia Reese (eds): New Voices, Inherited Lines: Literary and Cultural Representations of the Irish Family
ISBN 978-3-0343-0799-4. 238 pages. 2013.

Vol. 48 Justin Carville (ed.): Visualizing Dublin: Visual Culture, Modernity and the Representation of Urban Space
ISBN 978-3-0343-0802-1. 326 pages. 2014.

Vol. 49 Gerald Power and Ondřej Pilný (eds): Ireland and the Czech Lands: Contacts and Comparisons in History and Culture
ISBN 978-3-0343-1701-6. 243 pages. 2014.

Vol. 50 Eoghan Smith: John Banville: Art and Authenticity
ISBN 978-3-0343-0852-6. 199 pages. 2014.

Vol. 51 María Elena Jaime de Pablos and Mary Pierse (eds): George Moore and the Quirks of Human Nature
ISBN 978-3-0343-1752-8. 283 pages. 2014.

Vol. 52 Aidan O'Malley and Eve Patten (eds): Ireland, West to East: Irish Cultural Connections with Central and Eastern Europe
ISBN 978-3-0343-0913-4. 307 pages. 2014.

Vol. 53 Ruben Moi, Brynhildur Boyce and Charles I. Armstrong (eds): The Crossings of Art in Ireland
ISBN 978-3-0343-0983-7. 319 pages. 2014.

Vol. 54 Sylvie Mikowski (ed.): Ireland and Popular Culture
ISBN 978-3-0343-1717-7. 257 pages. 2014.

Vol. 55 Benjamin Keatinge and Mary Pierse (eds): France and Ireland in the Public Imagination
ISBN 978-3-0343-1747-4. 279 pages. 2014.

Vol. 56 Raymond Mullen, Adam Bargroff and Jennifer Mullen (eds): John McGahern: Critical Essays
ISBN 978-3-0343-1755-9. 253 pages. 2014.

Vol. 57 Máirtín Mac Con Iomaire and Eamon Maher (eds): 'Tickling the Palate': Gastronomy in Irish Literature and Culture
ISBN 978-3-0343-1769-6. 253 pages. 2014.

Vol. 58 Heidi Hansson and James H. Murphy (eds): Fictions of the Irish Land War
ISBN 978-3-0343-0999-8. 237 pages. 2014.

Vol. 59 Fiona McCann: A Poetics of Dissensus: Confronting Violence in Contemporary Prose Writing from the North of Ireland
ISBN 978-3-0343-0979-0. 238 pages. 2014.

Vol. 60 Marguérite Corporaal, Christopher Cusack, Lindsay Janssen and Ruud van den Beuken (eds): Global Legacies of the Great Irish Famine: Transnational and Interdisciplinary Perspectives
ISBN 978-3-0343-0903-5. 357 pages. 2014.

Vol. 61 Katarzyna Ojrzyn'ska: 'Dancing As If Language No Longer Existed': Dance in Contemporary Irish Drama
ISBN 978-3-0343-1813-6. 318 pages. 2015.

Vol. 62 Whitney Standlee: 'Power to Observe': Irish Women Novelists in Britain, 1890–1916
ISBN 978-3-0343-1837-2. 288 pages. 2015.

Vol. 63 Elke D'hoker and Stephanie Eggermont (eds): The Irish Short Story: Traditions and Trends
ISBN 978-3-0343-1753-5. 330 pages. 2015.

Vol. 64 Radvan Markus: Echoes of the Rebellion: The Year 1798 in Twentieth-Century Irish Fiction and Drama
ISBN 978-3-0343-1832-7. 248 pages. 2015.

Vol. 65 B. Mairéad Pratschke: Visions of Ireland: Gael Linn's *Amharc Éireann* Film Series, 1956–1964
ISBN 978-3-0343-1872-3. 301 pages. 2015.

Vol. 66 Una Hunt and Mary Pierse (eds): France and Ireland: Notes and Narratives
ISBN 978-3-0343-1914-0. 272 pages. 2015.

Vol. 67 John Lynch and Katherina Dodou (eds): The Leaving of Ireland: Migration and Belonging in Irish Literature and Film
ISBN 978-3-0343-1896-9. 313 pages. 2015.

Vol. 68 Anne Goarzin (ed.): New Critical Perspectives on Franco-Irish Relations
ISBN 978-3-0343-1781-8. 271 pages. 2015.

Vol. 69 Michel Brunet, Fabienne Gaspari and Mary Pierse (eds): George Moore's Paris and His Ongoing French Connections
ISBN 978-3-0343-1973-7. 279 pages. 2015.

Vol. 70 Carine Berbéri and Martine Pelletier (eds): Ireland: Authority and Crisis
ISBN 978-3-0343-1939-3. 296 pages. 2015.

Vol. 71 David Doolin: Transnational Revolutionaries: The Fenian Invasion of Canada, 1866
ISBN 978-3-0343-1922-5. 348 pages. 2016.

Vol. 72 Terry Phillips: Irish Literature and the First World War: Culture, Identity and Memory
ISBN 978-3-0343-1969-0. 297 pages. 2015.

Vol. 73 Carmen Zamorano Llena and Billy Gray (eds): Authority and Wisdom in the New Ireland: Studies in Literature and Culture
ISBN 978-3-0343-1833-4. 263 pages. 2016.

Vol. 74 Flore Coulouma (ed.): New Perspectives on Irish TV Series: Identity and Nostalgia on the Small Screen
ISBN 978-3-0343-1977-5. 222 pages. 2016.

Vol. 75 Fergal Lenehan: Stereotypes, Ideology and Foreign Correspondents: German Media Representations of Ireland, 1946–2010
ISBN 978-3-0343-2222-5. 306 pages. 2016.

Vol. 76 Jarlath Killeen and Valeria Cavalli (eds): 'Inspiring a Mysterious Terror': 200 Years of Joseph Sheridan Le Fanu
ISBN 978-3-0343-2223-2. 260 pages. 2016.

Vol. 77 Anne Karhio: 'Slight Return': Paul Muldoon's Poetics of Place
ISBN 978-3-0343-1986-7. 272 pages. 2017.

Vol. 78 Margaret Eaton: Frank Confessions: Performance in the Life-Writings of Frank McCourt
ISBN 978-1-906165-61-1. 294 pages. 2017.

Vol. 79 Marguérite Corporaal, Christopher Cusack and Ruud van den Beuken (eds): Irish Studies and the Dynamics of Memory: Transitions andTransformations
ISBN 978-3-0343-2236-2. 360 pages. 2017.

Vol. 80 Conor Caldwell and Eamon Byers (eds): New Crops, Old Fields: Reimagining Irish Folklore
ISBN 978-3-0343-1912-6. 200 pages. 2017.

Vol. 81 Sinéad Wall: Irish Diasporic Narratives in Argentina: A Reconsideration of Home, Identity and Belonging
ISBN 978-1-906165-66-6. 282 pages. 2017.

Vol. 82 Ute Anna Mittermaier: Images of Spain in Irish Literature, 1922–1975
ISBN 978-3-0343-1993-5. 386 pages. 2017.

Vol. 83 Lauren Clark: Consuming Irish Children: Advertising and the Art of Independence, 1860–1921
ISBN 978-3-0343-1989-8. 288 pages. 2017.

Vol. 84 Lisa FitzGerald: Re-Place: Irish Theatre Environments
ISBN 978-1-78707-359-3. 222 pages. 2017.

Vol. 85 Joseph Greenwood: 'Hear My Song': Irish Theatre and Popular Song in the 1950s and 1960s
ISBN 978-3-0343-1915-7. 320 pages. 2017.

Vol. 86 Nils Beese: Writing Slums: Dublin, Dirt and Literature
ISBN 978-1-78707-959-5. 250 pages. 2018.

Vol. 87 Barry Houlihan (ed.): Navigating Ireland's Theatre Archive: Theory, Practice, Performance
ISBN 978-1-78707-372-2. 306 pages. 2019.

Vol. 88 María Elena Jaime de Pablos (ed.): Giving Shape to the Moment: The Art of Mary O'Donnell: Poet, Novelist and Short Story Writer
ISBN 978-1-78874-403-4. 228 pages. 2018.

Vol. 89 Marguérite Corporaal and Peter Gray (eds): The Great Irish Famine and Social Class: Conflicts, Responsibilities, Representations
ISBN 978-1-78874-166-8. 330 pages. 2019.

Vol. 90 Patrick Speight: Irish-Argentine Identity in an Age of Political Challenge and Change, 1875–1983
ISBN 978-1-78874-417-1. 360 pages. 2020.

Vol. 91 Fionna Barber, Heidi Hansson, and Sara Dybris McQuaid (eds): Ireland and the North
ISBN 978-1-78874-289-4. 338 pages. 2019.

Vol. 92 Ruth Sheehy: The Life and Work of Richard King: Religion, Nationalism and Modernism
ISBN 978-1-78707-246-6. 482 pages. 2019.

Vol. 93 Brian Lucey, Eamon Maher and Eugene O'Brien (eds): Recalling the Celtic Tiger
ISBN 978-1-78997-286-3. 386 pages. 2019.

Vol. 94 Melania Terrazas Gallego (ed.): Trauma and Identity in Contemporary Irish Culture
ISBN 978-1-78997-557-4. 302 pages. 2020.

Vol. 95 Patricia Medcalf: Advertising the Black Stuff in Ireland 1959–1999: Increments of Change
ISBN 978-1-78997-345-7. 218 pages. 2020.

Vol. 96 Anne Goarzin and Maria Parsons (eds): New Cartographies, Nomadic Methologies: Contemporary Arts, Culture and Politics in Ireland
ISBN 978-1-78874-651-9. 204 pages. 2020.

Vol. 97 Hiroko Ikeda and Kazuo Yokouchi (eds): Irish Literature in the British Context and Beyond: New Perspectives from Kyoto
ISBN 978-1-78997-566-6. 250 pages. 2020.

Vol. 98 Catherine Nealy Judd: Travel Narratives of the Irish Famine: Politics, Tourism, and Scandal, 1845–1853
ISBN 978-1-80079-084-1. 468 pages. 2020.

Vol. 99 Lesley Lelourec and Gráinne O'Keeffe-Vigneron (eds): Northern Ireland after the Good Friday Agreement: Building a Shared Future from a Troubled Past?
ISBN 978-1-78997-746-2. 262 pages. 2021.

Vol. 100 Eamon Maher and Eugene O'Brien (eds): Reimagining Irish Studies for the Twenty-First Century
ISBN 978-1-80079-191-6. 384 pages. 2021.

Vol. 101 Nathalie Sebbane: Memorialising the Magdalene Laundries: From Story to History
ISBN 978-1-78707-589-4. 334 pages. 2021.

Vol 102 Roz Goldie: A Dangerous Pursuit: The Anti-Sectarian Work of Counteract
ISBN 978-1-80079-187-9. 268 pages. 2021.

Vol. 103 Ann Wilson: The Picture Postcard: A New Window into Edwardian Ireland
ISBN 978-1-78874-079-1. 282 pages. 2021.

Vol. 104 Anna Charczun: Irish Lesbian Writing Across Time: A New Framework for Rethinking Love Between Women
ISBN 978-1-78997-864-3. 320 pages. 2022.

Vol. 105 Olivier Coquelin, Brigitte Bastiat and Frank Healy (eds): Northern Ireland: Challenges of Peace and Reconciliation Since the Good Friday Agreement
ISBN 978-1-78997-817-9. 298 pages. 2022.

Vol. 106 Jo Murphy-Lawless and Laury Oaks (eds): The Salley Gardens: Women, Sex, and Motherhood in Ireland
ISBN 978-1-80079-417-7. 338 pages. 2022.

Vol. 107 Mercedes del Campo: Voices from the Margins: Gender and the Everyday in Women's Pre- and Post-Agreement Troubles Short Fiction
ISBN 978-1-78874-330-3. 324 pages. 2022.

Vol. 108 Sean McGraw and Jonathan Tiernan: The Politics of Irish Primary Education: Reform in an Era of Secularisation
ISBN 978-1-80079-709-3. 532 pages. 2022.

Vol. 109 Gerald Dawe: Northern Windows/Southern Stars: Selected Early Essays 1983–1994
ISBN 978-1-80079-652-2. 180 pages. 2022.

Vol. 110 John Fanning: The Mandarin, the Musician and the Mage: T. K. Whitaker, Seán Ó Riada, Thomas Kinsella and the Lessons of Ireland's Mid-Twentieth-Century Revival
ISBN 978-1-80079-599-0. 296 pages. 2022.

Vol. 111 Gerald Dawe: Dreaming of Home: Seven Irish Writers
ISBN 978-1-80079-655-3. 108 pages. 2022.

Vol. 112 John Walsh: One Hundred Years of Irish Language Policy, 1922–2022
ISBN 978-1-78997-892-6. 394 pages. 2022.

Vol. 113 Bertrand Cardin: Neil Jordan, Author and Screenwriter: The Imagination of Transgression
ISBN 978-1-80079-923-3. 286 pages. 2023.

Vol. 114 David Clark: Dark Green: Irish Crime Fiction 1665–2000
ISBN 978-1-80079-826-7. 450 pages. 2022.

Vol. 115 Aida Rosende-Pérez and Rubén Jarazo-Álvarez (eds): The Cultural Politics of In/Difference: Irish Texts and Contexts
ISBN 978-1-80079-727-7. 274 pages. 2022.

Vol. 116 Tara McConnell: "Honest Claret": The Social Meaning of Georgian Ireland's Favourite Wine
ISBN 978-1-80079-790-1. 346 pages. 2022.

Vol. 117 M. Teresa Caneda-Cabrera (ed.): Telling Truths: Evelyn Conlon and the Task of Writing
ISBN 978-1-80079-481-8. 228 pages. 2023.

Vol. 118 Alexandra Maclennan (ed.): The Irish Catholic Diaspora: Five Centuries of Global Presence
ISBN 978-1-80079-516-7. 264 pages. 2023.

Vol. 119 Brian J. Murphy: Beyond Sustenance: An Exploration of Food and Drink Culture in Ireland
ISBN 978-1-80079-956-1. 328 pages. 2023.

Vol. 120 Fintan Cullen (ed.): Ireland and the British Empire: Essays on Art and Visuality
ISBN 978-1-78874-299-3. 264 pages. 2023.

Vol. 121 Natalie Wynn and Zuleika Rodgers (eds): Reimagining the Jews of Ireland: Historiography, Identity and Representation
ISBN 978-1-80079-083-4. *Forthcoming*. 2023.

Vol. 122 Paul Butler: A Deep Well of Want: Visualising the World of John McGahern
ISBN 978-1-80079-810-6. 244 pages. 2023.

www.ingramcontent.com/pod-product-compliance
Lightning Source LLC
Chambersburg PA
CBHW071519110726
47908CB00003B/896